la Biennale di Venezia
54. Esposizione Internazionale d'Arte
Partecipazioni nazionali

Empty Zones
Andrei Monastyrski and Collective Actions

Edited by Boris Groys

Ministry of Culture
of the Russian Federation

STELLA ART FOUNDATION

black dog publishing
london uk

Contents

Foreword

The history of the Russian Pavilion at the Venice Biennale stretches back nearly 100 years. Works by Russian avant-garde artists were shown here in the 1920s, thereafter—Socialist Realism. From the early 1990s onwards, the Pavilion has exhibited contemporary art, which was officially frowned upon in the Soviet Union. Over the last 20 years, many interesting curatorial projects and artists have demonstrated the most pertinent developments in Russian contemporary art in the Russian Pavilion.

I am delighted that Stella Art Foundation has been offered the chance to make our contribution to the history of the Russian Pavilion this year, and I sincerely hope that the exhibition Empty Zones. Andrei Monastyrski and Collective Actions will command an international audience and contribute to the understanding of Russia's contemporary art as best as possible.

Stella Kesaeva,
Commissioner, Russian Pavilion
President, Stella Art Foundation

Art Clearings

Boris Groys

Andrei Monastyrski is an artist, poet, writer and theoretician of art. But his name is most closely associated with the group Collective Actions that he organised in Moscow in the middle of the 1970s, which still exists today. The group's activities have had a great influence on the Russian art scene throughout this whole historic period. At different times nearly all the important representatives of the Moscow art scene of recent decades were involved in the artistic practices of this group in one form or another, including Ilya Kabakov, Erik Bulatov and Dmitri Prigov. The most interesting members of the current milieu of younger Russian artists began their artistic development under Monastyrski's direction. The theoretical texts that Monastyrski wrote to justify and explain his practices have profoundly influenced the discourse on art in Russia today. The Collective Actions group was a genuine artistic school, not just for many artists but also for many writers and art critics. But the influence of the group, and in particular of Monastyrski himself, is much broader than the circle of those who worked with him directly. The explosion of performance art in Russia in the 1990s would have been inconceivable without the performance practice of Collective Actions. Today Monastyrski is considered a guru of the new Russian art in Moscow, and his decisive influence on its origins and development is indisputable.

The title of this group "Collective Actions" is, however, somewhat misleading because the goal of the group was—and still is—not so much action but, rather, contemplation. Or, better to say: action in the name of contemplation. In the context of our current civilisation to contemplate is not an easy task. It was not an easy task especially in the Soviet Union, in which the whole population was involved in the all-encompassing project of building the communist future. In such a society, to take a position of contemplation seems to be equivalent to abandoning the front-line during the war—ignoring social responsibilities and duties that are shared by everybody else. But, of course, a capitalist society of the Western type also thinks in terms of progress and change. All modern societies prefer the *vita activa* to the *vita contemplativa*. Contemplation is mostly associated with the passive acceptance of the *status quo*, whereas social and political activism is seen as a struggle to overcome the *status quo* —for a change.

However, under the conditions of modernity it is precisely progress and change that constitute the *status quo*. Every member of modern society is immersed since his or her birth in the process of economic progress, growth and change. Our eyes are permanently directed toward the future—and so we tend to overlook the present. The artistic avant-garde deplored the traditionalist, "passeist" love of the glorious past that generated blindness toward contemporary life. But the fixation on the radiant future leads ultimately to the same kind of blindness. Soviet culture and art constitute an especially good example of this futurist, constructivist blindness towards contemporaneity. An attempt to overcome this blindness and to look more attentively to the present was undertaken by artists more or less everywhere across the globe during the 1960s and 1970s. This attempt actually constituted the phenomenon that we call "contemporary art". In this respect the activities of the Collective Actions group can be seen as a part of the global art practice of the 1970s. But under Soviet conditions one needed to undertake a lot of actions to become able to contemplate. To an even greater extent than elsewhere, the contemplative attitude was marked there by the stigma of privilege: contemplation was associated with the lifestyle of privileged classes that allegedly could only be achieved by exploitation of the non-privileged majority of population. Thus, to live in the classless society meant to work—and not to contemplate.

It is a hidden polemic against this criticism of contemplation as social privilege that ultimately generated the artistic strategy of the Collective Actions group and especially that of Monastyrski himself. Contemplation that was practiced by the group was explicitly non-privileged contemplation—poor contemplation in every sense of the word. First of all it was a minimalist contemplation. The objects of such contemplation, like the sky, a wood, a snow-covered field, were obviously accessible to everybody. And, secondly, the state of contemplation had to be achieved not through some esoteric practice but by "trips out of town"—using public transport. Monastyrski himself describes this strategy extensively in his commentary to *Trips out of Town*.[1] At the same time contemplation was understood here not as an individual but as a collective practice. "Collective Actions were a project of collective *vita contemplativa* in the middle of modern *vita activa*.

During the 1970s and 1980s the activities of the group consisted primarily of the organisation of performances, which, as a rule, took place outside Moscow. The audience, which was usually composed of artists, writers and theorists, was invited to travel to a place a couple of hours away from Moscow to watch the performance. Most of the performances took place in winter. The road was long; it was cold. There was a sense of making a sacrifice for art. The site of the performances was often a snow-covered field. Beyond the field a forest could be seen —as a straight, dark grey line between the white field and the pallid sky. The whole landscape was rendered in an ascetic, reductionistic black-and-white aesthetic evoking the aesthetics of Minimalism and Conceptual Art. The reference to the white background of Malevich's Suprematist paintings was impossible to ignore. The audience stood, froze and stared at the white field. Then something happened. Usually it lasted only a short time, and took place at a considerable distance from the viewers, so that they could not see clearly what it was. Somebody came out of the forest, moved through the field, left several traces behind and went back into the forest. On the long road back to Moscow the viewers had lots of time to discuss what it was and, if it was what they had thought they had seen, what it could possibly mean.

Monastyrski speaks in this respect of the "empty action". Such an action does not use an already existing institutional or private space as its stage. It also does not have a certain, clearly defined, time and space or communicate a certain, fixed meaning. Rather, such an "empty action" creates an open, empty, zero space that can be used as a space of exposure, as a space in which the public can constitute itself and be exposed to itself. Of course, one can argue that the empty, void, zero space always precedes its private or institutional occupation. But in our everyday life we tend to overlook, ignore or forget the ontological emptiness of the space in which we move. This erasure of emptiness was especially obvious in a Soviet Union that was thought of as the total space of the communist project. But the Western urban individual moving through contemporary urban spaces and occupied by his or her own individual, private interests and goals also overlooks the emptiness that makes this movement possible. The crowd in the streets and the urban traffic are experienced by this individual only—or at least primarily—in a negative way: as obstacles preventing this individual's fast and smooth movement through the city. The crowd in the streets is a lonely crowd —a crowd that does not constitute a public. Somewhat paradoxically, the urban space cannot become public because it is overcrowded.

Now, in his essay "The Origin of the Work of Art", Martin Heidegger states that the goal of the artist is precisely to create a void, emptiness, a *Riss* (rift) in the texture of the world, tear this world apart, open a *Lichtung* (clearing) in the middle of it.[2] Only through and in this clearing, inside this rift, the moment of "unconcealment", as Heidegger calls it, becomes possible—the concealment of the world being produced by the routine of everyday life. Heidegger cites as an example the ancient Greek temple with its freely accessible space delineated by columns—space in which the public, the *Versammlung*, or, rather, the people, the *Volk*, could be constituted. Of course, Monastyrski and the Collective Actions did not expect to create an empty space that would become a temple in which the "coming together" (*Versammlung*) of the whole Russian *Volk* could take place. Their goal was much more modest.

Through their "empty actions", they created "empty zones" in which the small *Volk* of Moscow artists and intellectuals could be constituted —by literally finding a clearance (*Lichtung*) in the wood, to redeploy the central notion of Heidegger's late philosophy. Nevertheless, this modest project still retains a vast utopian potential. The *U-Topia* is, actually, a no-place, an empty place, a zero-place. An "empty action", as it is understood by Monastyrski, is a utopian action. But it is not an action that relegates Utopia to the future. Rather, an "empty action" creates a utopian, empty, non-space here and now. And by creating the moment of utopian 'unconcealment' for a close circle of friends this "empty action" does not manifest itself as 'elitist' or 'selective'. It is an action for 'everybody and nobody', creating an open space that can remain void but can also be entered by anyone at will.

In general, art can be defined as the shaping of the relationship between image and public. Usually artists are concerned with creating images for the public. Monastyrski, by contrast, reversed this relationship: he was not only an organiser but also a primary spectator of his own artistic activities and the activities of the group. Admittedly, the shift of interest from the shaping of art objects to the shaping of a public and, in particular, an art public was characteristic of all international, conceptually-oriented art in the 1960s and 1970s. Monastyrski himself views his own artistic practice in the context of international Conceptual Art, which already had a parallel in Russia as well, by the late 1960s and 1970s —above all in the work of Ilya Kabakov. But work with the public differed in East and West because the structure of the public was different. Western, as well as contemporary Russian art, is heavily involved in, and actually dominated by, the art market. The relationship to the art market and the criteria that it imposes on art production, distribution and reception was the main point of concern for many artists in the West—and still is. In the Soviet Union the art market did not exist. The art world was defined in ideological terms—and its relationship to the public was also ideologically determined. Thus, the goal of alternative artistic practices of individual artists and groups, like Collective Actions was to create alternative social communities and milieus in a time in which such an ideologically independent social activity was not only suspiciously watched by the authorities but even strictly forbidden. Interestingly however, several aspects of the artistic practice of Collective Actions have become particularly relevant for our own time. The growing commercialisation of art we are experiencing today on a global scale—particularly in Russia —is leading to a loss of public for all those art practices that cannot be easily commercialised or that actively resist commercialisation. Artists are increasingly compensating for this loss of a public by collaborating with one another and with representatives of the sciences or of various political movements, in order to produce another, alternative public. These kinds of collaborative communal practices which create 'another' public beyond the global art and media market are characteristic of art all over the world today. In this respect Monastyrski also remains today an important father figure for the young Russian artists who try to cope with the contemporary political situation in their country.

But now the question arises whether and (if yes) to what extent, the utopian moments of unconcealment that were created by Monastyrski's "empty actions" can be recreated through their representation in an art exhibition space. Of course, it is a question that haunts all the attempts to document and represent different kinds of performance practices outside of their original context. In recent decades one could witness an increasing presence of art documentation inside art exhibition spaces—the documentation of actions, happenings, art events, political interventions, social projects and so on. This phenomenon raises anew the question of the extent to which art documentation presented to us is art. The artwork is traditionally understood as something that embodies art, making it immediately present and visible. When we go into an art exhibition, we normally assume that what we see there—whether paintings, sculptures, drawings, photographs, videos, ready-mades or installations—is art. The works of art can, of course, refer in one way or another to something they are not—say, real objects or events—but they do not refer to art; they are art.

However, this traditional precondition of an exhibition or museum visit turns out, more and more, to be misleading. Art documentation is perceived, as a rule, not as art; it seems to merely refer to art and thereby makes clear that art is no longer present and immediately visible here. Thus, it seems that to show documentation of art events means to betray their character as art. If performance art has as its goal the creation of a feeling of presence, its documentation only stresses the absence of this feeling. Notwithstanding their growing popularity and public presence the exhibitions of art documentation function, thus, more as rituals of the mourning of past events than their representations or recreations.

However, the performances by Collective Actions happily relieve the curator of their documentation from any work of mourning. Indeed, for Monastyrski the production of art documentation is the true goal of his artistic practice. The action itself is, for him, always only a fleeting moment in time that leaves the participants rather perplexed and confused —they do not quite understand when the actions began, when they ended and what actually happened. Thus, the action emerges as such and becomes visible, truly experienceable only *post-factum*—only through its documentation, through the effort of memory and interpretation. The presence of the action is always constituted as a flashback. And this flashback is always thoroughly planned.

The members of the group informed the viewers in conversations or in writing about what the course of the action actually looked like and what the authors had intended. Neither of these things, however, were considered binding. Quite the contrary, the members of the audience were asked to describe their own experiences and propose their own interpretations. Later all this written material was gathered and edited and supplemented with the photographs of the action and sometimes with the schema for the course of the action and Monastyrski's subsequent commentaries on it. This publication, circulated amongst those involved, represented, in effect, the self-contained artwork. Later these publications were collected in volumes titled *Poezdki za gorod* (Trips out of Town).[3] Five such volumes were published between 1976 and 1989, and in 1998 they were published as a book under that title. Today this book functions like an encyclopaedia of advanced art in Moscow of this period.

Only the long process of clarification by reconstruction and documentation let the action emerge as a certain event in space and time. In fact, the production of documentation was—and still is—for Monastyrski the actual field of artistic practice. However, this practice remains open and structurally unfinished—and unfinishable—in time and space. Every further presentation of documentation and every further documentation of this presentation inscribes itself in a potentially infinite process of clarification and interpretation of the 'original' "empty action"—actually, in the process of the creation of this action, as such, through a procession of flashbacks. Here the originality of an action becomes secondary in relationship to its documentation—every documentation being not merely a re-presentation of this action but a further contribution to its creation.

1 see: Monastyrski, Andrei, "Collective Actions and Trips out of Town, The Aesthetics of Collective Actions", in this publication.

2 Heidegger, Martin, "The Origin of the Work of Art, 1935-1936", (first published as "Der Ursprung des Kunstwerkes in Holzwege", Frankfurt: 1950) in David Farrell Krel ed., *Heidegger: Basic Writings*, London: Routledge and Kegan Paul, 1993.

3 Kollektivnye deistviya, *Poezdki za gorod*, Moscow: Ad Marginem, 1998.

Zones of Indistinguishability: The Collective Actions Group and Participatory Art

Claire Bishop

The rise of participatory art since the 1990s invites us to constitute a history for this practice, and ideally one that reflects the global spread of this work today.[1] In charting this history, important variants appear that challenge the dominant way of thinking about participatory art in Western Europe and North America, where this work tends to be positioned as a political, constructive and oppositional response to spectacle's atomisation of social relations. By contrast, the participatory art of Eastern Europe and Russia from the mid-1960s to late 1980s is frequently marked by the desire for an increasingly subjective and privatised aesthetic experience. At first glance, this seems to be an inversion of the Western model (despite Guy Debord's observation that bureaucratic communism is no less spectacular than its capitalist variant; it is simply "concentrated" as opposed to "diffused").[2] However, and crucially, the individual experiences that were the target of participatory art under existing socialism continue to be framed as *shared* privatised experiences: the construction of a collective artistic space amongst mutually trusting colleagues. Rather than frame this work as 'implicitly political', as is the habit with current Western approaches to Eastern bloc art history, this essay will argue that work produced under state socialism during these decades should be viewed in more complex terms. Given the saturation of everyday life with ideology, artists did not regard their work to be political but rather as existential and apolitical, committed to ideas of freedom and the individual imagination. At the same time, they sought an expanded—one might say democratised—horizon of artistic production, in contrast to the highly regulated and hierarchised system of the official Union of Soviet Artists.

In the present essay, I want to focus on the Collective Actions group, active in Moscow from the mid-1970s onwards, from the perspective of Western participatory art. Unlike many recent socially-engaged artists, for whom social participation in art denotes the inclusion of the working class, marginalised communities, or at least everyday nonprofessionals (rather than the artists' friends and colleagues), the political context of the Collective Actions group rendered such distinctions redundant. The impulse to collaborate with disenfranchised communities that we see so frequently today was a somewhat alien concept in the 1970s: under Cold War socialism, every citizen was (nominally at least) equal, a coproducer of the communist state. Class difference did not exist.[3] Finding participants for one's art was therefore a question of selecting reliable colleagues who would not inform on one's activities. In an atmosphere of near constant surveillance and insecurity, participation was an artistic and social strategy to be deployed only amongst the most trusted groups of friends. The restrictions of life under Cold War communism do more than simply affect the question of who participates in art, they also govern the appearance of these works: materially frugal and temporally brief, many of these actions and events were located in the countryside, far away from networks of surveillance. The fact that many of these actions do not look like art is less an indication of the artists' commitment to blurring 'art and life' than a deliberate strategy of self-protection, as well as a reaction to the state's own military displays and socialist festivals as a visual reference point; these events dissuaded artists from contrived displays of collective participation even if they had had the resources to emulate them.[4]

It is useful to remind ourselves that unofficial art had begun in Moscow in 1962, after Khrushchev visited the thirtieth anniversary show of the Moscow Union of Artists at the Manezh Gallery, which had included a display of non-figurative, abstract paintings; Khrushchev declared these to be (among other things) "private psycho-pathological distortions of the public conscience".[5] The extent of his reaction led to the ever increasing domestic isolation of independent artists and their being denied the right to show their works to the public in any place and form. And yet, despite being severely criticised and censured, unofficial art continued into the mid-1970s, when the first legalised exhibitions took place or a shadow union for unofficial artists was set up (the Graphics Moscow City Committee). After the controversial 'Bulldozer' exhibition of September 1974 (in which an exhibition of unofficial art was destroyed by bulldozer), cultural authorities decided to regulate and legalise their relationships with 'underground' art via the State Committee for Security (KGB). Most unofficial art was exhibited inside private apartments, forcing a convergence of art and life that surpassed what the majority of twentieth century avant-gardists had ever intended by this term. The phenomenon of 'AptArt' (apartment art), an initiative by Nikita Alekseev, referred to exhibitions and performances taking place in private homes, for small networks of trusted friends, and flourished in the early 1980s.

It was in this context that the most celebrated of Moscow Conceptualists, Ilya Kabakov (b 1933), developed his personal work alongside his official job as a children's book illustrator. Kabakov's *Albums*, 1972–1975, are illustrated narratives, each revolving around one fictional character, most of whom are isolated, lonely, idiosyncratic figures on the margins of society, cocooned in a private dream world. The first, *Sitting-in-the -Closet Primakov*, is typical in that it describes the life of a boy who sits in a dark closet and refuses to come out; when he does, he sees the world in terms of modernist abstract paintings. Each *Album* contained drawings, and general comments on the character spoken by different fictional commentators. Crucially, these *Albums* were not read as books but were performed by the artist for small groups of friends. Boris Groys recalls that one would make an appointment with Kabakov (rather like organising a studio visit) and go to his home, where the artist would place the book on a music stand and read the entire text in a neutral and unexpressive tone of voice. The experience was extremely monotonous, but had a ritualistic quality in which the turning of the pages became central. Most readings took an hour, although Groys recalls once undergoing a five hour performance.[6] One of the key points to emerge here is the use of a neutral, descriptive, analytical language, focusing on the inconspicuous, the banal and the marginal; another is that the stories are geared more towards invented forms of survival and endurance than of criticism; and another is the repeated motif of isolated individuals negotiating the endless and uncomfortable scrutiny of the communal apartment.[7] All of these points provide an important contextual precursor for the work discussed in the remainder of this chapter.

It is in this literary context, with a strong reverence for textual expression, that the Collective Actions group (Kollektivnye Deistvia, or K/D) was formed in 1976; at its inception there were four members; by 1979 there were seven; and in 2005 there were six.[8] The group took its lead from the first generation of Moscow Conceptualists, especially Kabakov, whose installations implied characters and viewing subjects caught between "a communal body" and "an existential individualist".[9] The central theorist of Collective Actions group, Andrei Monastyrski (b 1949), has recalled that their earliest pieces were perceived as a form of poetry reading. The group continue to produce around eight performances a year, although the character of this work has changed considerably since 1989: the actions are more complex, with more references to Eastern mysticism, and frequently make use of documentation (especially tape recordings) from earlier actions. Since the focus here is on participatory art under socialism, the following discussion will concern a selection of actions produced in the first decade of the group's existence. Most of these actions typically followed a standard format: a group of 15 to 20 participants were invited by telephone (at a time when, of course, phone lines could be tapped) to take a train to a designated station outside Moscow; they would walk from the station to a remote field; the group would wait around (not knowing what would happen), before witnessing a minimal, perhaps mysterious, and often visually unremarkable event. On returning to Moscow, participants would write an account of the experience and offer interpretations of its meaning; these subsequently became the focus of discussion and debate amongst the artists and their circle.[10]

It should immediately be apparent that the intellectualism of this structure is a considerable step away from the 1960s model in both Europe and North America, in which it was regarded as sufficient simply for things to 'happen', and through which the participating subject would attain a more vivid, authentic level of reality (as seen for example in the work of Knížák and Kaprow). Monastyrski complicates this paradigm by aiming to produce situations in which participants had no idea what was going to happen, to the point where they sometimes found it difficult to know whether or not they had in fact experienced an action; when participants' engagement finally occurred, it was never in the place where they were expecting it.[11] Collective Actions group stretched the temporality of event-based art away from pure presence and into a relationship of distance between 'then' (I thought I experienced...) and 'now' (I understand it to be otherwise...). It is also of central importance that this production of distance was not only temporal but social, prising open a space for modes of communicational practice otherwise absent in the rigid and monolithic ideology of Soviet collectivism. The event itself is effectively an "empty action", designed to preclude interpretation from taking place during the performance, and thereby serving to prompt a wide range of descriptions and analyses, which were undertaken individually but shared within the group.

The first key action that crystallised this form of working was *Appearance*, 13 March 1976. Devised by Monastyrski, Lev Rubinstein, Nikita Alekseev and Georgy Kizevalter, it involved around thirty audience members as participants. On arriving in the remote field at Izmaylovskoe, the group was asked to wait and watch for something to appear in the distance. Eventually a couple of the organisers became visible on the horizon, in what Monastyrski refers to as the "zone of indistinguishability": the moment when one can tell that something is happening but the figures are too far away for one to clarify who they are and what exactly is taking place. The figures approached the group and gave them certification of having attended the event (Collective Actions group refer to this as "factography"). Monastyrski later explained that what had happened in the field was not that they (the organisers) had appeared for the participants, but rather, that the participants had appeared *for them*. This inversion of what one might expect to experience with an artistic action—an unfurling of events for the *organisers* rather than for an audience—was matched by the group's preference for the banality of waiting rather than the production of a vivid and visually memorable event: Monastyrski described the participants' eventual appearance in the work as a "pause", thereby reconceptualising the waiting not as a prelude to some more specific action, but as the main event.[12] Typically, the Collective Actions group's primary focus is never on the ostensible action taking place in the snowy landscape, but the deferral and displacement of this action both physically (events happen where one was not prepared to see them) and semantically. The phenomenological level of immediate events was subordinated to the conceptual and linguistic activity that subsequently took place in the participants' consciousness: in Monastyrski's words, the mythological or symbolic content of the action is 'used only as an instrument to create that "inner" level of perception' in the viewer.[13]

This technique can be seen in other early works such as *Pictures*, 11 February 1979, which divided the participants into two groups, one of whom undertook an action in the snow, watched by the other group. 12 sets of 12 coloured envelopes (in gradually larger sizes) were distributed to 12 of the 30 participants. Inside each envelope was a description of the key components of the event: from schedule, setting and weather to audience reaction, meaning and interpretation. After they had read the instructions, the participants were instructed to fold and paste each set of envelopes on top of each other, with the largest on the bottom, to form a concentric pattern of colour; these were later signed as certification of the participants' attendance. While all this was going on, three of the participants (the organisers) crossed the field and wandered into the woods on the other side. Once again, the "zone of indistinguishability" was put into play: the participants' preoccupation with making the pictures was a distraction from the action on the margin, namely the organisers' disappearance into the woods. The participatory activity (finding and assembling the coloured envelopes) was undermined as a central focus by the sly subtraction of the organisers' presence, indicating that—contra the US model of the Happening—in Collective Actions group's works there is no authentic shared experience underlying the event.

In his article "Seven Photographs", 1980, Monastyrski presents seven near identical photographs of a snowy field, each of which relate to a different action by Collective Actions group, including *Appearance* and *Pictures*. The bleak similarity of the images is amusing, but drives home his point that secondary material such as photographs, instructions, descriptions and participant recollections have a completely separate aesthetic reality to the action itself. (At best, he writes, "a familiarity with the photographs and texts can bring about a sensation of positive indeterminacy.")[14] Influenced by semiotics and making frequent reference to Heidegger, Monastyrski argues that the group's actions result for the participants in a real experience, but not in an image of that experience. The event's existential presence takes place in the viewer's consciousness (as a state of "completed anticipation") and thus cannot be represented: "The only thing that can be represented is the thing that accompanies this internal process, the thing that takes place on the field of action at the time."[15] The exquisite precision of this idea, in which documentation is conceived as a representation of what accompanied an artistic experience, explains the repetitive quality of Collective Actions group's photographs of (apparently) nothing taking place, since they record only what seems to be a withdrawal of action. Each photograph is to be considered, Monastyrski writes, as "a sign of a higher order, a sign of an 'unarbitrary emptiness' with the following meaning: 'nothing is represented on it not because nothing happened at that given moment, but because the thing that happened is essentially unrepresentable.'"[16] The highly theorised, quasi-mystical flavour of this position gives Collective Actions group a unique status within a history of performance documentation, while also being highly suggestive of an approach to documentary ripe for re-exploration today.

Monastyrski's article was written before *Ten Appearances*, 1981, and seems to pave the way for the centrality of photography in this work. The participants were notified that everyone attending would have to be a participant in the work; those who were not so willing should not come.[17] The action took place in a snowy field, and was organised around a flat board with dozens of nails with bobbins, each wound with 200 to 300 metres of white thread. The assignment was for the ten participants to walk away from the board in different directions towards the forest that surrounded the field, while holding onto the end of the thread that had been given to each of them. Kabakov describes the minutiae of his volatile emotions as he underwent this process: from anxiety (about how long he would be standing in the cold) to fear (suspecting the organisers of sadism) to sheer joy and "mystic melancholy" on finally reaching the end of the thread, to which was affixed a piece of paper bearing the "factographic text" (the name of the organisers, time, date and place of the action).[18] At this point it was up to the participants to decide what happened next. Eight of them walked back out of the forest to rejoin the group; two did not return and got a train back to Moscow. Those who returned were given a photograph of themselves emerging from the forest in the "zone of indistinguishability", with each image captioned "The appearance of [name] on the first of February, 1981." This simulated photographic documentation had been taken a few weeks earlier but was not differentiable from the actual appearance of the participants as they emerged from the forest. Monastyrski refers to these photographs as an "empty act": a mere sign of the elapsed time between the end of the first phase of the action for the participants (receiving the "factographic text") and their reappearance in the field ("the signified and culminating event in the structure of the action").[19] Both the act and the image are empty signifiers; the meaning is formulated subsequently by reflection on the totality of the events experienced.

Of course, the poignant fact that two participants, Nekrasov and Zhigalov, did not return to the group did not mean that the work was a failure. Rather, Monastyrski asserted, it showed that the participants had emerged from a "non-artistic, non-artificially-constructed space"—in other words, an everyday reality in which they were capable of acting of their own free will.[20] This, Monastyrski reasoned, was why the same people kept coming back to their events over the course of 15 years: the pre-textual nature of the experiences that the group constructed ensured that participants were continually intrigued, as well as continually motivated to write descriptions and analyses. Since it was near impossible to scrutinise the events as they were happening, these hermeneutical narratives had a compensatory aspect, endlessly chasing a meaning that remained elusive, precisely because the generation of different interpretative positions *was* the meaning.[21] The surfeit of texts that resulted from these actions were collected into books every three to five years, and are published in Russian and German under the title "Trips out of Town"; the group is currently at work on an eleventh volume.[22] Volume two, from 1983, for example, is typical in its structure: a theoretical preface by Monastyrski; descriptions of the events with photographs; an appendix of documentation, which includes the schema of *Ten Appearances* and a list of slides; texts by participants (including Kabakov on *Ten Appearances*); photographs and descriptions of actions by individual artists that are close to Collective Actions group's actions, such as Monastyrski's *Flat Cap*, 1983; commentaries and photographs. Later volumes also include interviews and a list of videos, produced after the German artist Sabine Hänsgen joined the group.

Boris Groys has observed how Collective Actions group's performances were "meticulously, almost bureaucratically, documented, commented on, and archived".[23] This textual production is one of the dominant characteristics of their practice, and positions it as the inverse of the impulse to make participatory art in Western cultures—which can broadly be summarised as positioned against the atomisation of social relations under consumer spectacle. Groys has argued that Soviet society, by contrast,

> ... was a society of production without consumption. There was no spectator and there was no consumer. Everyone was involved in a productive process. So the role of Collective Actions and some other artists of the time was to create the possibility of consumption, the possibility of an external position from which one could enjoy communism.[24]

What Collective Actions group's works gave rise to, then, was not unified collective presence and immediacy but its opposite: difference, dissensus and debate; a space of privatised experience, liberal democratic indecision, and a plurality of hermeneutical speculation at a time when the dominant discourse and spectatorial regime was marshalled towards a collective and rigidly schematised apparatus of meaning. This is borne out by Monastyrski's observation that

> ... in the Stalin or Brezhnev era, contemplation of an artwork involved a certain compulsion, a kind of tunnel vision. There was nothing peripheral. But when one comes to a field—when one comes there, moreover, with no sense of obligation but for private reasons of one's own—a vast, flexible space is created, in which one can look at whatever one likes. One is under no obligation to look at what is being presented—that freedom, in fact, is the whole idea.[25]

The use of a field as the backdrop to so many of Collective Actions group's works is therefore doubly salient.[26] It did not designate a specific rejection of the city or a conscious embrace of nature; as Sergei Sitar notes, the field is not chosen for its independent aesthetic merits, "but simply as 'the lesser evil'—as a space that is the least occupied, the least appropriated by the dominant cultural discourse".[27] For Monastyrski, it is a space "free from any affiliation": "the countryside, for us, isn't the countryside tilled by peasants but that of the thinking classes' vacation retreats".[28] The fields are less about framing (in the way that Prague's Wenceslas Square frames Jiří Kovanda's contemporaneous actions) than unframing; the countryside's multiple perspectives corresponded to the group's open-ended, neutral actions that were contrived to leave room for the greatest number of hermeneutic possibilities. The result was a privatised liberal space that existed in covert parallel to official social structures. As Kabakov recalls:

> From the moment I got on the train... my goals, the questions and affairs that constantly preoccupied me, my fears of myself and others, were all, as it were, taken away from me. The most remarkable thing, however, was that those who led us had no goals either! And, of course, there is something else: for the first time in my life, I was among 'my own'; we had our own world, parallel to the real one, and this world had been created and compressed by the Collective Actions group until it had achieved complete materiality, or, one might say, tangibility—if this notion is at all applicable to something absolutely ethereal and elusive.[29]

And again, in concluding his account of Ten Appearances:

> This [action] actualised one of the most pleasant and practically unknown sides of the socius, the socius that is so painful in our time. Here the social is not antagonistic to you, but instead good-willed, reliable, and extremely welcoming. This feeling is so unusual, so not experienced before, that it not only recovers you, but also becomes an amazing gift compared to everyday reality.[30]

Between Monastyrski's highly theoretical musings on semiotics and orientalism, and the more accessible narratives of those who participated in the works, it was this emphasis on freedom—the self-selecting construction of a self-determining social group—that formed the social core of Collective Actions group's practice. Participation here denoted the possibility of producing individual affect and singular experience, relayed through a meditative relationship to language that in turn presupposed collective reception and debate.

Participatory art under state socialism in the 1960s and 1970s provides an important counter-model to contemporaneous examples from Europe and North America. Rather than aspiring to create a participatory public sphere as the counterpoint to a privatised world of individual affect and consumption, artists working collaboratively under socialism sought to provide a space for nurturing individualism (of behaviour, actions, interpretations) against an oppressively monolithic cultural sphere in which artistic judgements were reduced to a question of their position within Marxist-Leninist dogma. This led to a situation in which most artists wanted nothing to do with politics—and indeed even rejected the dissident position—by choosing to operate, instead, on an existential plane: making assertions of individual freedom, even in the slightest or most silent of forms. We can also contrast this approach with that taken by artists in South America, where participation was used as a means to provoke art audiences into heightened self-awareness of their social conditions and thereby (it was hoped) to impel them to take action in the social sphere. For artists living under communism, participation had no such agitationary goals. It was, rather, a means of experiencing a more authentic (because individual and self-organised) mode of collective experience than the one prescribed by the state in official parades and mass spectacles; as such it is frequently figured as escapist or celebratory, regardless of whether it took place on a physical or solely cerebral level. Today the escapist and celebratory tend to be weak terms in contemporary art criticism, signifying a wilful refusal of artists to engage in their political reality and to express a critical stance towards it. However, the example of the 1960s and 1970s avant-garde under socialism reminds us that there is an unimaginably large gap between managing such contextual awareness and heroic acts of dissidence (the latter being, for the most part, a Western fantasy). The reality of daily life under these regimes necessitates a more sober understanding of the artistic gestures achieved there, and appreciation of the consummate subtlety with which so many of them were undertaken.

1 This essay forms part of a chapter in my forthcoming book, *Artificial Hells: Participatory Art and the Politics of Spectatorship*, London: Verso, 2011.

2 "The spectacle exists in a concentrated or a diffuse form depending on the necessities of the particular stage of misery which it denies and supports. In both cases, the spectacle is nothing more than an image of happy unification surrounded by desolation and fear at the tranquil center of misery. ...If every Chinese must learn Mao, and thus be Mao, it is because he can be nothing else. Wherever the concentrated spectacle rules, so does the police". Debord, Guy, *The Society of the Spectacle*, New York: Zone Books, 1994, sections 63 and 64.

3 Of course, memories of class difference were not entirely erased. In "The Power of the Powerless", Václav Havel speaks of his social awkwardness at having to work in a brewery in the mid-1970s. See Havel, Václav, *Open Letters*, London: Faber and Faber, 1991, pp. 173–174. The artist Vladimír Boudník (1924–1968) worked in a print factory and declared, a good decade before Joseph Beuys did, that everyone was artist. He viewed his art as having an educative mission: he produced work in the streets (late 1940s–1950s), finding images in peeling paint and stains on walls, occasionally adding to them, and framing them (for example with paper), before encouraging passers-by to converse with him about their meaning. See *Vladimír Boudník*, Prague: Gallery, 2004. Mílan Knížák was aware of Boudník's work, and some of his early actions make reference to everyday workers. For example, *Anonymous*, 1965, involved scattering the following script in the street: "1. A HAPPENING for street-sweepers and janitors. 2. ENVIRONMENT for pedestrians. 3. DELIGHT for the creator, resulting from the action." See Knížák, Milan, *Actions For Which at Least Some Documentation Remains, 1962–1995*, Prague: Gallery, 2000, p. 73.

4 The socialist calendar in Slovakia, for example, included organised mass parades for Victorious February (25 February), International Women's Day (8 March), International Workers' Day (1 May), Liberation Day (9 May) and International Children's Day (1 June), as well as Nationalisation (28 October) and the Great October Socialist Revolution (7 November). See Keratova, Mira, *"Vivez sans temps mort"*, *Transforming 68/89*, Berlin: Zentrum für Zeithistorische Forschung, 2008, pp. 528-537. For the Yugoslav context, see Jakovljevic, Branislav, "Balkan Baroque: Yugoslav Gestural Culture and Performance Art", in Claire Bishop and Marta Dzeiwańska eds., *1968–1989: Political Upheaval and Artistic Change*, Warsaw: Museum of Modern Art, 2010, pp. 31–50.

5 Erofeev, Andrei, "Nonofficial Art: Soviet Artists of the 1960s" (1995), in Pospiszyl and Hoptman eds., *Primary Documents*, p. 42. See also William J Tompson, *Khrushchev: A Political Life*, Basingstoke: MacMillan, 1995, Chapter 10.

6 Groys, conversation with the author, New York, 28 January 2010.

7 "The communal apartment is a place where the social dimension occurs in its most horrifying, most obtrusive, and most radical form, where the individual is laid bare to the gaze of others. Furthermore, this gaze belongs to largely hostile strangers who consistently exploit their advantages of observation in order to gain advantage in the power struggle within the communal apartment." Groys, Boris, "The Theatre of Authorship", in Toni Stoos ed., *Ilya Kabakov: Installations 1983–2000, Catalogue Raisonné, Vol.1*, Kunstmuseum Bern: Richter Verlag, 2003, p. 40.

8 According to an interview with Monastyrski in *Flash Art*, October 2005, p. 114. The initial group were Nikita Alekseev, Georgy Kizevalter, Andrei Monastyrski and Nikolai Panitkov, later joined by Igor Makarevich, Elena Elagina and Sergei Romashko. On the literary aspects of Moscow Conceptualism, Kabakov has noted the central role of the Russian literary tradition of the nineteenth century: "Literature took upon itself all moral, philosophical, pedagogical, and enlightening functions, concentrating them all in itself and not simultaneously in the plastic arts, which did happen in the West." See Kabakov, "On the Subject of the Local Language", in Kabakov, *Das Leben der Fliegen*, p. 237.

9 Misiano, Viktor, "Solidarity: Collective and Collectiveness in Contemporary Russian Art", in WHW, *Collective Creativity*, Kassel: Fridericianum, 2005, p. 185.

10 It should be noted that Collective Actions group also designed actions for individuals or pairs; for example *For N Panitkov (Three Darknesses)*, 1980; *For G Kizevalter (Slogan–1980)*, 1980; *The Encounter*, 1981; *For N Alekseev*, 1981. It was

rarer for actions to take place in private apartments (*Playback*, 1981) or in the city streets (*Exit*, 1983; *The Group*, 1983).

11 Monastyrski refers to this as a psychological state of "pre-expectation", created through the form of the invitation, and through the spatio-temporal peculiarities of the journey to the site of the event. See Monastyrski, Andrei, "Preface to the First Volume of Trips to the Countryside", in Boris Groys ed., *Total Enlightenment: Conceptual Art in Moscow 1960–1990*, Frankfurt: Schirn Kunsthalle/Hatje Cantz, 2008, p. 335.

12 "And yet, if the experience so far was that of pure expectation, this experience now transforms upon the appearance of the object of perception on the real field. *It is interrupted*, and there begins a process of strenuous looking, accompanied by the desire to understand what this object means. In our view, this new stage of perception constitutes a pause. While it is a necessary stage in the process of perception, it is by no means the event for the sake of which all of this was arranged." See Monastyrski, "Preface to the First Volume of Trips to the Countryside", p. 336.

13 Monastyrski, "Preface to the First Volume of Trips to the Countryside", p. 333.

14 Monastyrski, Andrei, 'Seven Photographs', Yelena Kalinsky trans., available at http://conceptualism.letov.ru (last accessed 23 July 2009).

15 Monastyrski, "Seven Photographs".

16 Monastyrski, "Seven Photographs".

17 This, reports Kabakov, was unusual in setting up a particular experience of expectation: "one was going there with the idea of participation, and one was wondering what would happen" See Kabakov, Ilya, "Ten Appearances", in Kollektivnye deistviya, *Poezdki za gorod*, Moscow: Ad marginem, 1998, p. 151. Translated by Anya Pantuyeva.

18 Kabakov, "Ten Appearances", pp. 151–152.

19 Monastyrski, Andrei, "Ten Appearances", 1981, reprinted in Claire Bishop ed., *Participation*, London: Whitechapel and Cambridge, MA: MIT Press, 2006, p. 129.

20 This is what I understand him to mean by the following dense sentence: "The fact that of the ten possible appearances only eight, and not all ten, came to pass, represents in our view not a failing of the action but, on the contrary, underscores the realisation of zones of psychic experience of the action as aesthetically sufficient on the plane of the demonstrational field of the action as a whole" Monastyrski, "Ten Appearances", p. 29. This is corroborated by Kabakov's more amenable narrative: "I had some space of freedom and I had to make up my mind what to do then. But actually, I had no doubt or speculation about what to do—to leave, etc.—not at all. What I wanted to do immediately was to share this joy I experienced with the others, and also thank those people who made it happen for me." See Kabakov, "Ten Appearances", p. 153.

21 Viktor Tupitsyn: "The same happens in combat: while you're in the thick of it, everyone is so busy with the 'physical stuff' that all kinds of hermeneutic activities are foreclosed. Later, though, this void is going to be filled with interpretations, whose excessiveness will compensate for the lack of interpretation at the site of Action." Monastyrski: "Exactly! ... Quite a number of texts about our Actions were composed by both spectators and organisers, who were equally fond of writing down what had really happened —first Kabakov, followed by Leiderman, and then by Bakshtein and others. They were impelled to do so in order to compensate for the impossibility of commenting on and interpreting the Actions as they occurred." From: Tupitsyn and Monastyrski, unpublished interview, 1997, archive of Exit Art, New York.

22 English translations of the works and photo-documentation can be found at http://conceptualism.letov.ru (last accessed 23 July 2009).

23 Groys, Boris, "Communist Conceptual Art", in Boris Groys, *Total Enlightenment: Conceptual Art in Moscow 1960 – 1990*, Frankfurt: Schirn Kunsthalle/Hatje Cantz, 2008, p. 33.

24 Groys, Boris, in Claire Bishop and Boris Groys, "Bring the Noise", *Tate Etc*, Summer 2009, p. 38.

25 Tupitsyn and Monastyrski, unpublished interview, 1997, archive of Exit Art, New York. However, it is worth noting that Monastyrski goes on to assert (contra Groys) that Collective Actions group sought to *erase* the distinction between work of art and spectator and with it the critical distance that might constitute the political:

> Take our 'empty action', in which we purposely directed spectators' attention to what is nonsensical and just plain

unnecessary to look at: the wall of trees, the state of the weather, the clouds drifting by, or the empty time of the spectators, which they're spending idly, privately, before who knows what. The opposition between 'spectator' and 'work of art' was placed under erasure, that rigid opposition which left none of the distance that would have allowed artists to engage seriously in the political sphere.

We can read this two ways. Firstly, the idea of 'political' art for this generation, as with Czech and Slovak artists of the 1970s, is generally not viewed as desirable as a result of their daily experience of a Soviet ideology overdetermining all artistic meaning. (Groys again: "When looking at a painting, normal Soviet viewers quite automatically, without ever having heard of Art and Language, saw this painting inherently replaced by its possible ideological-political-philosophical commentary, and they took only this commentary into account when assessing the painting in question—as Soviet, half-Soviet, non-Soviet, anti-Soviet, and so on." See Groys, "Communist Conceptual Art", p. 31. Secondly, although the participatory event could be argued to foreclose the distance between viewer and work of art, in reality this was complicated by a number of spectatorial models (ten participants watched by 20 others, etc.) and reinstated by the textual analyses that ensued from these experiences in the following weeks.

26 The snowy fields have variously been compared to Malevich's *White Paintings* and the white pages of Kabakov's albums. It is worth noting that Collective Actions group were not the first to use white fields as the site for art: Francisco Infante had also deployed the field as a backdrop for photo-conceptualist works in the late 1960s, such as *Dedication*, 1969, a Malevich-style constructivist composition made of coloured papers on white snow.

27 Sitar, Sergei, "Four Slogans of Collective Actions", *Third Text*, 17 April, 2003, p. 364.

28 Tupitsyn and Monastyrski, unpublished interview, 1997, archive of Exit Art, New York.

29 Cited in "*Serebrianyi Dvorets*", a conversation between Ilya Kabakov and Victor Tupitsyn, *Khudozhestvennyi Zhurnal no.42*, Moscow, 2002, pp. 10–14, cited in Tupitsyn, Viktor, *The Museological Unconscious: Communal (Post-)Modernism in Russia*, Cambridge, MA: MIT Press, 2009, p. 70.

30 Kabakov, "Ten Appearances", p. 154.

31 See for example the interview with Joseph Beuys undertaken by two Russians, V Bakchahyan and A Ur, in the samizdat magazine *A-Ya* at the time of Beuys' Guggenheim retrospective. Their questions make explicit their wariness of art having anything to do with social change, since the work of the avant-garde post-1917 was so flagrantly co-opted by political officials to be a harbinger of communism: "Our Russian experience shows that to flirt with politics is dangerous for an artist. ... Aren't you afraid that the artist who's inside you is being conquered by the politician?" See Backchahyan, V, and A Ur, "Joseph Beuys: Art and Politics", *A-Ya*, 2, 1980, pp. 54–55.

TRIPS OUT OF TOWN

Collective Actions, 1976–2011

The Appearance

Moscow, Izmaylovskoe field,
13 March, 1976.

Collective Actions group:

A Monastyrski, L Rubinstein,
N Alekseev, G Kizevalter.

Viewers and participants:

A Abramov, M Saponov, I Golovinskaya,
V Chinaev, N Panitkov, N Nedbailo,
R and V Gerlovin and 21 others.

The audience was offered invitations for an action titled *The Appearance*. When all the invitees gathered (approximately 30 people) on one side of a field, five minutes later two participants of the action appeared from the forest on another side. They crossed the field, approached the audience and distributed papers ("documentary verification") to certify one's presence at *The Appearance*.

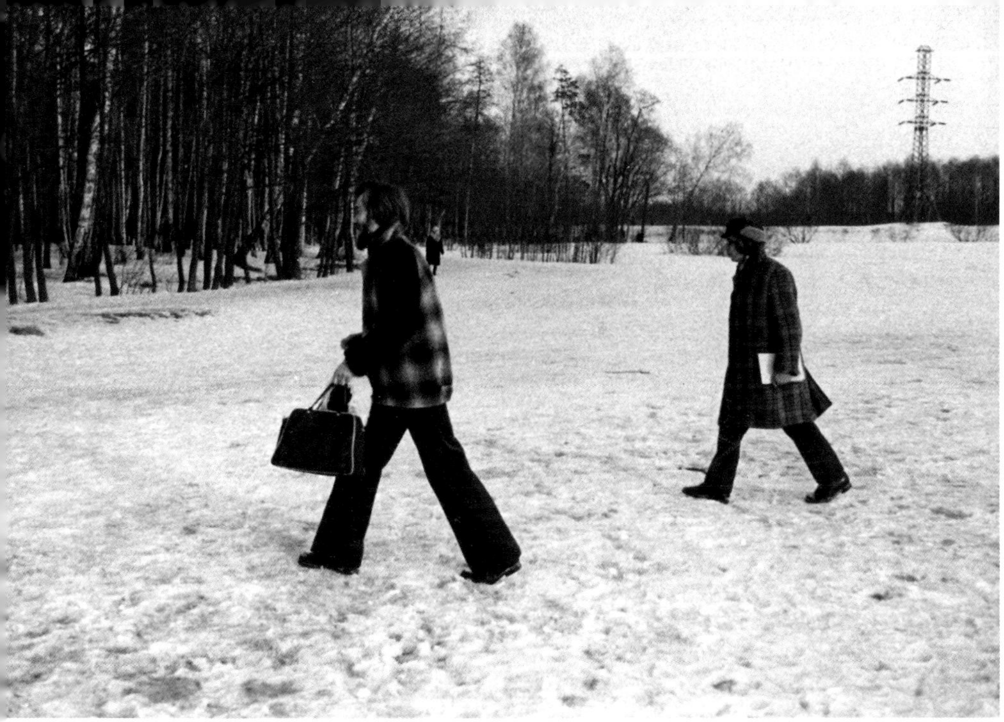

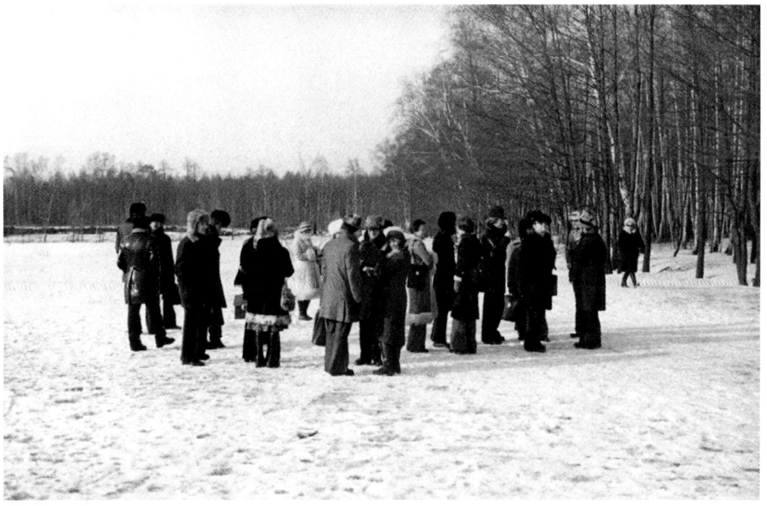

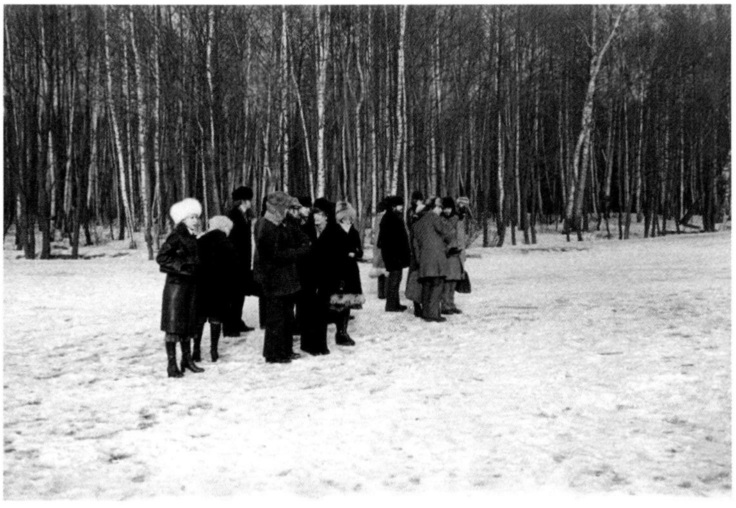

The Tent

Moscow region, Savyolovskaya railway line, Depot station, 2 October, 1976.

Collective Actions group:

N Alekseev, MK, A Monastyrski, G Kizevalter, N Panitkov, V Miturich-Khlebnikova, St Andrae.

12 stylised paintings of size 1 x 1 metre, each created by N Alekseev, were stitched into one cloth and put up like a tent in a forest not far from Moscow.

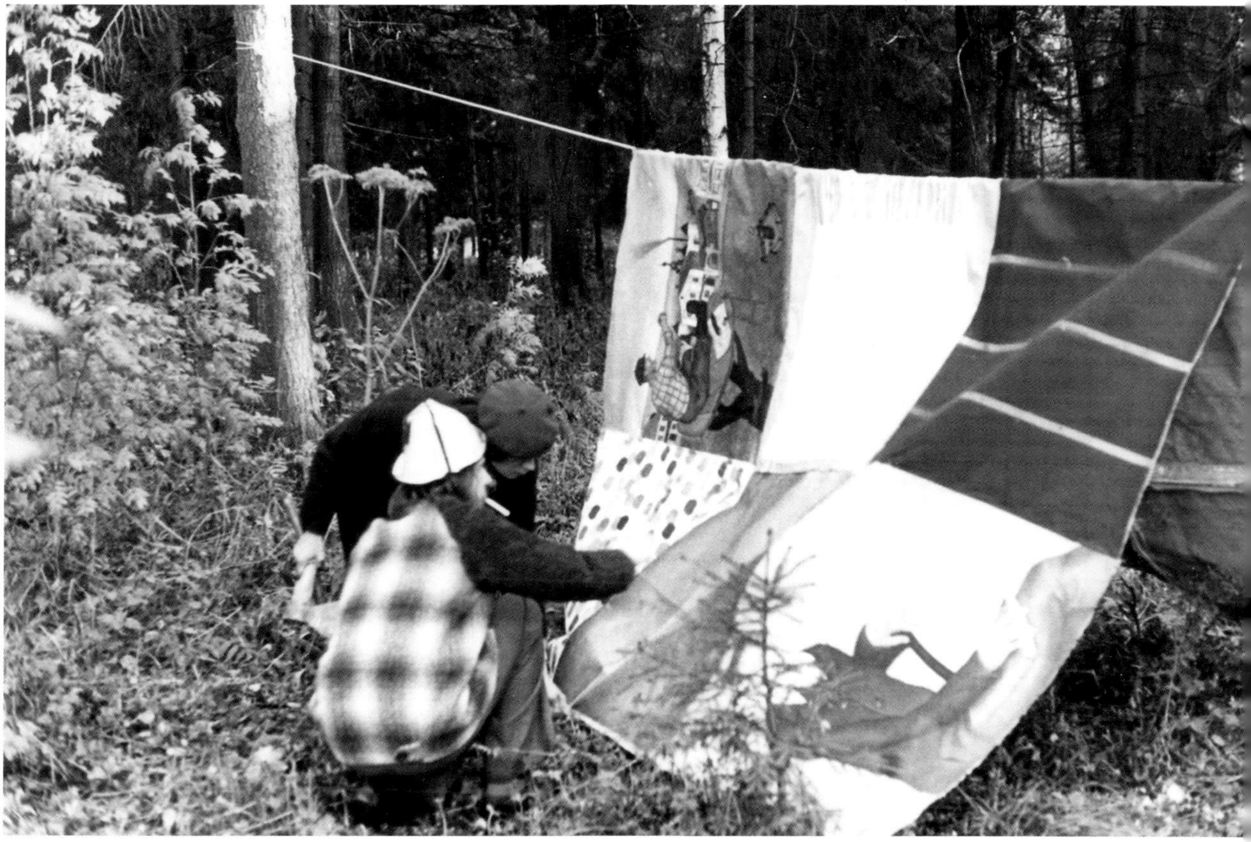

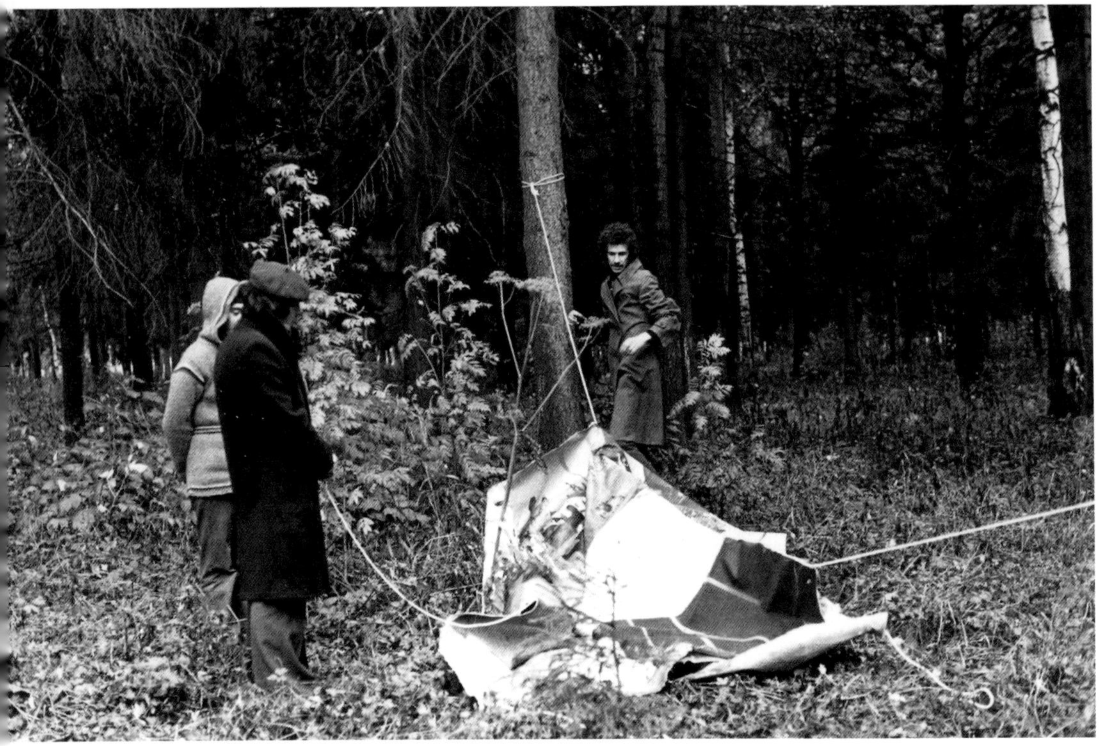

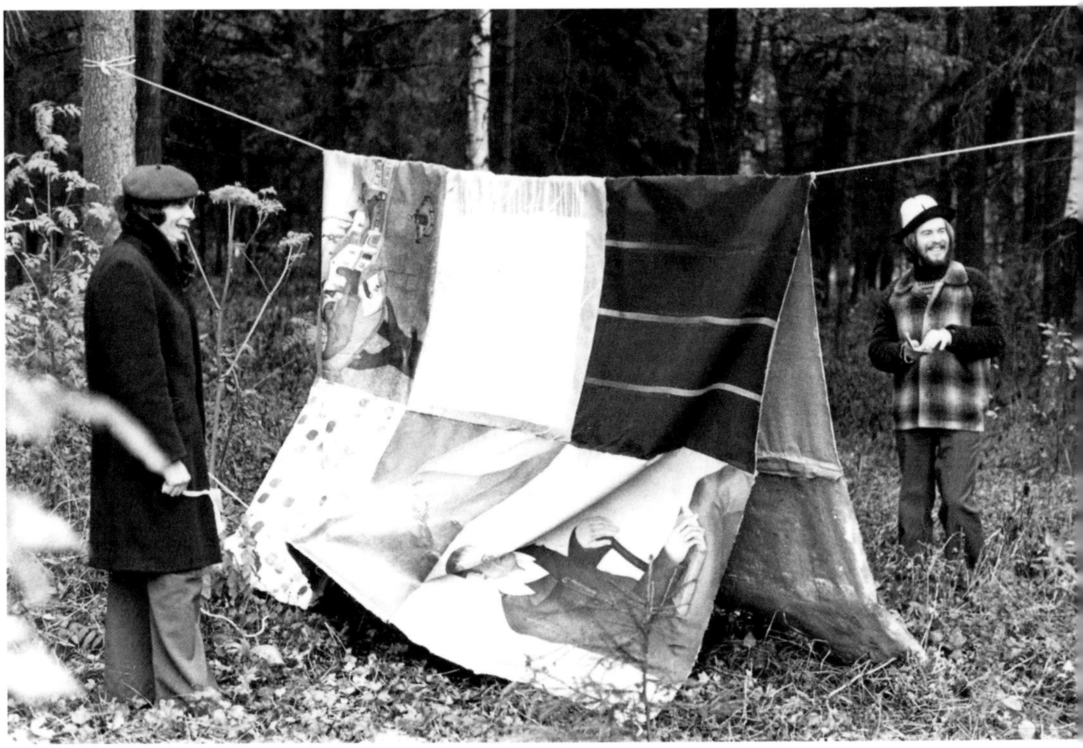

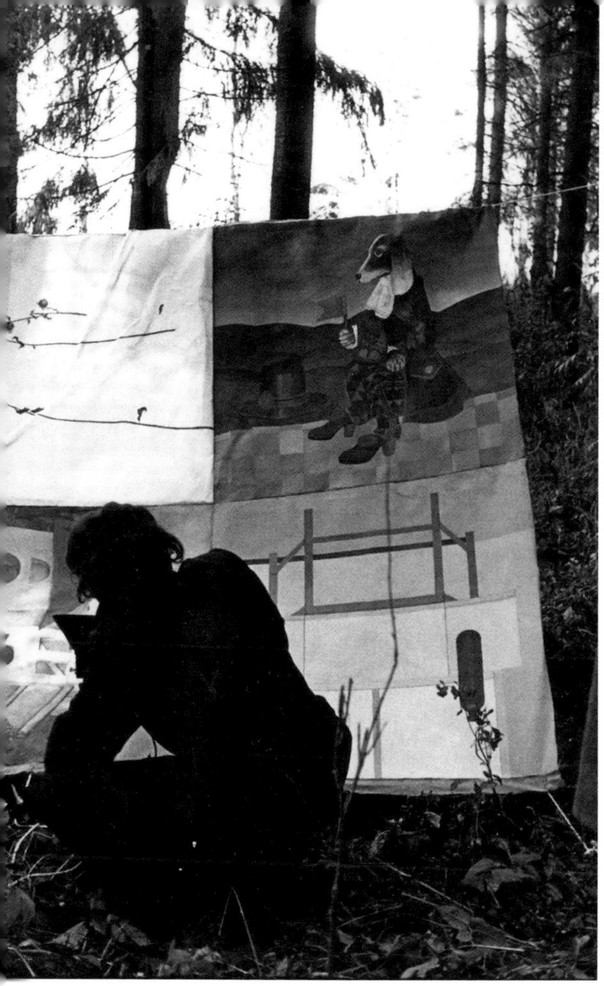

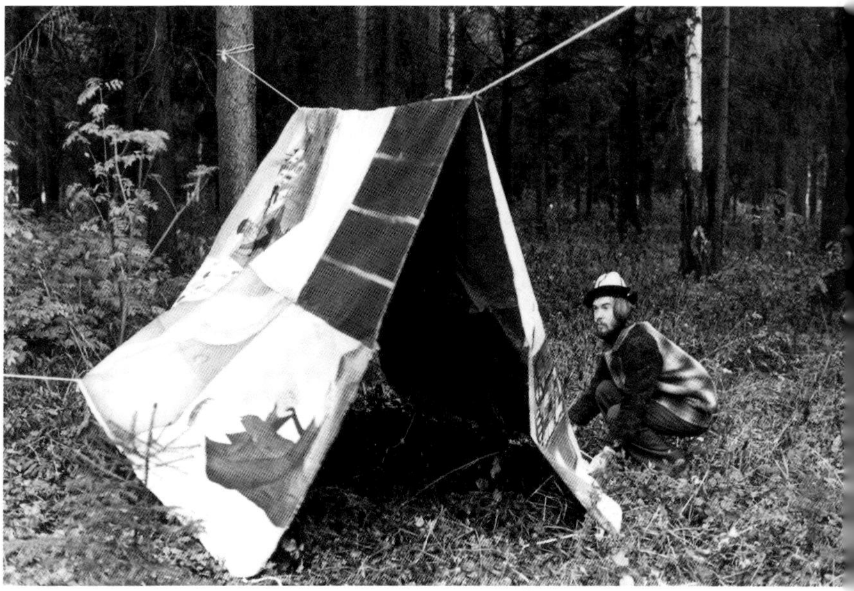

The Slogan-1977

Moscow region,
Leningradskaya railway line,
Firsanovka station,
26 January, 1977.

Collective Actions group:

A Monastyrski, V Miturich-Khlebnikova, N Alekseev, G Kizevalter, N Panitkov, MK, A Abramov.

A piece of red cloth (1 x 10 metres) was hung between two treetops on a hill. An inscription in white stencilled letters said:

> I do not complain about anything and I like it here, although I have never been here before and know nothing about this place.
> *Nothing Happens,* A Monastyrski

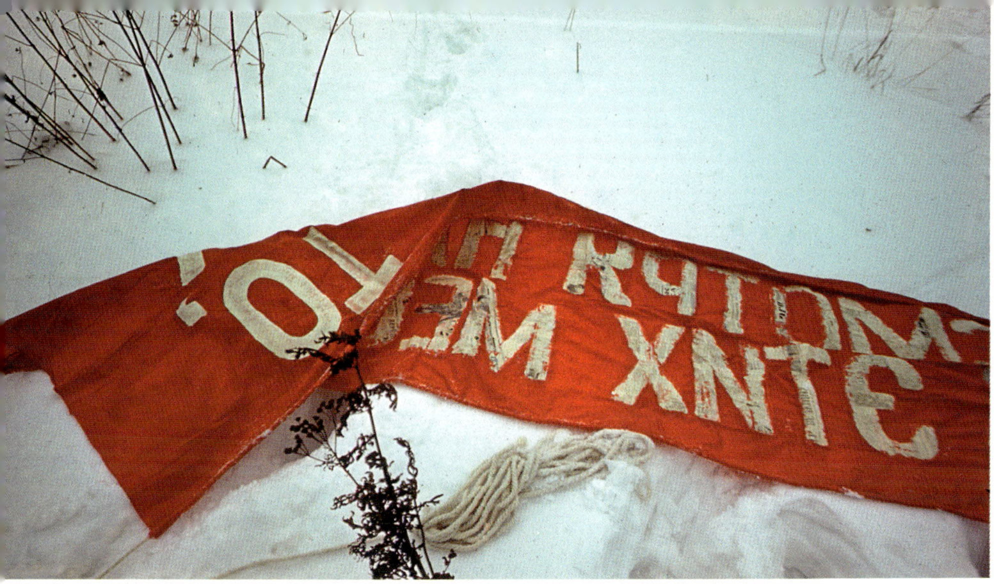

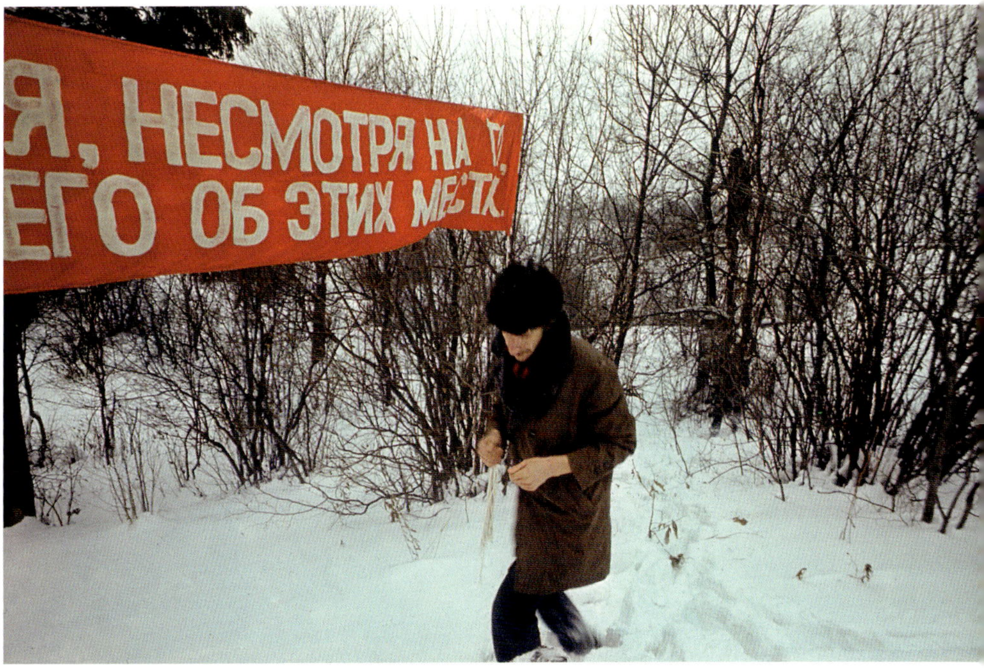
Я, НЕСМОТРЯ НА
ЕГО ОБ ЭТИХ

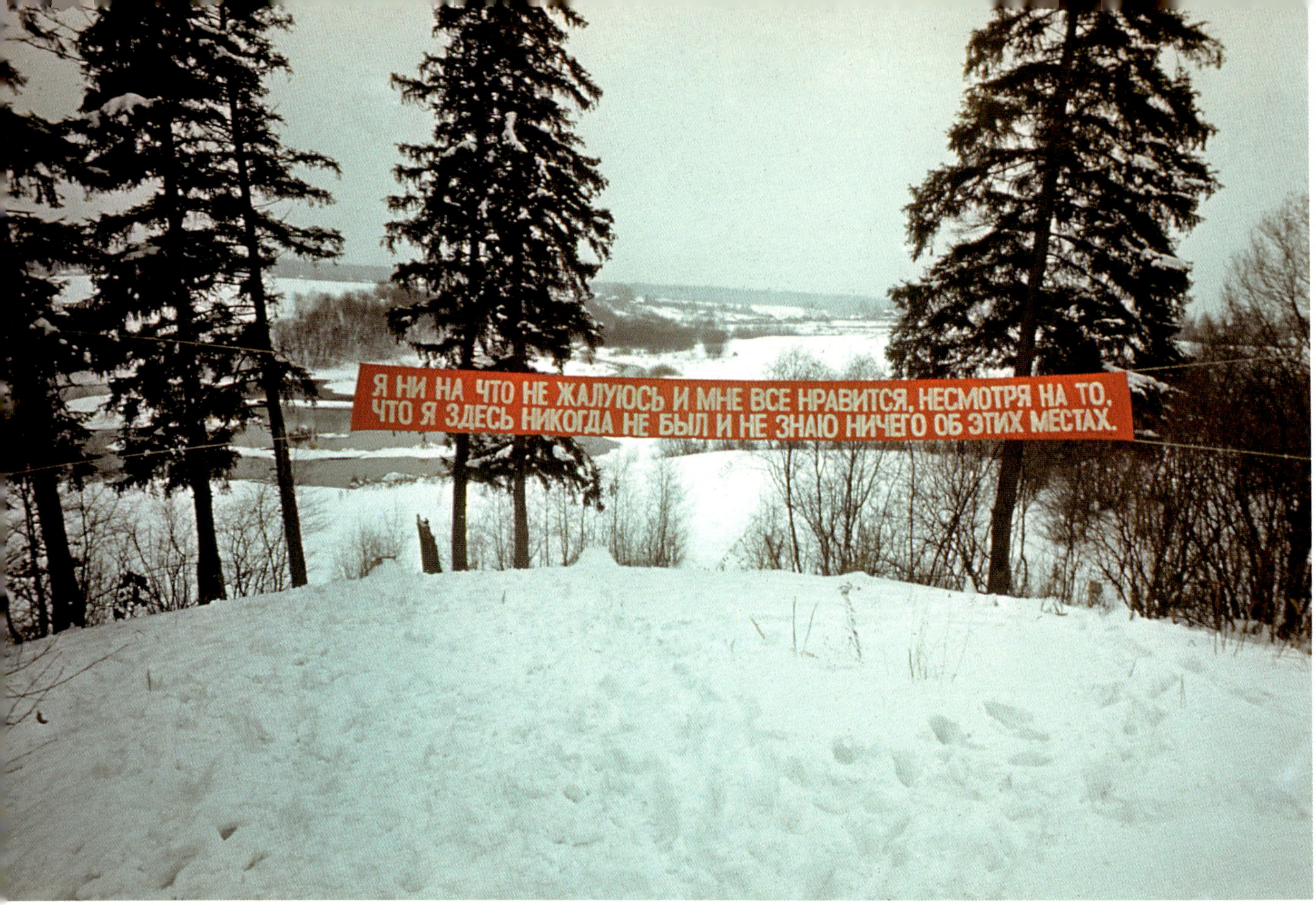
Я НИ НА ЧТО НЕ ЖАЛУЮСЬ И МНЕ ВСЕ НРАВИТСЯ, НЕСМОТРЯ НА ТО,
ЧТО Я ЗДЕСЬ НИКОГДА НЕ БЫЛ И НЕ ЗНАЮ НИЧЕГО ОБ ЭТИХ МЕСТАХ.

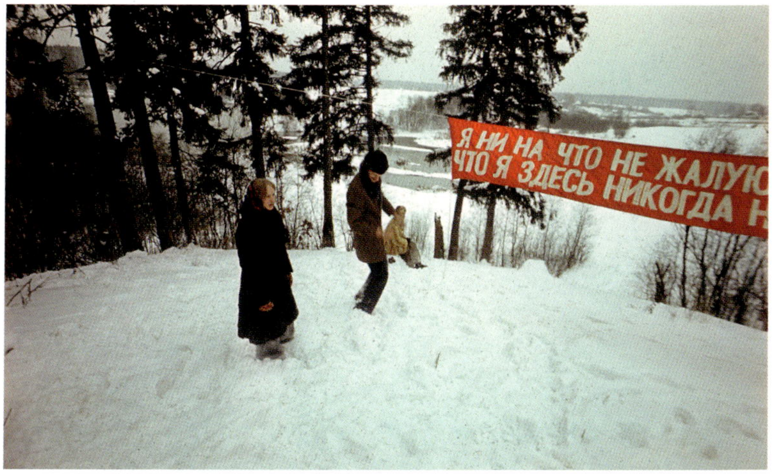
Я НИ НА ЧТО НЕ
ЧТО Я ЗДЕСЬ НИКОГДА

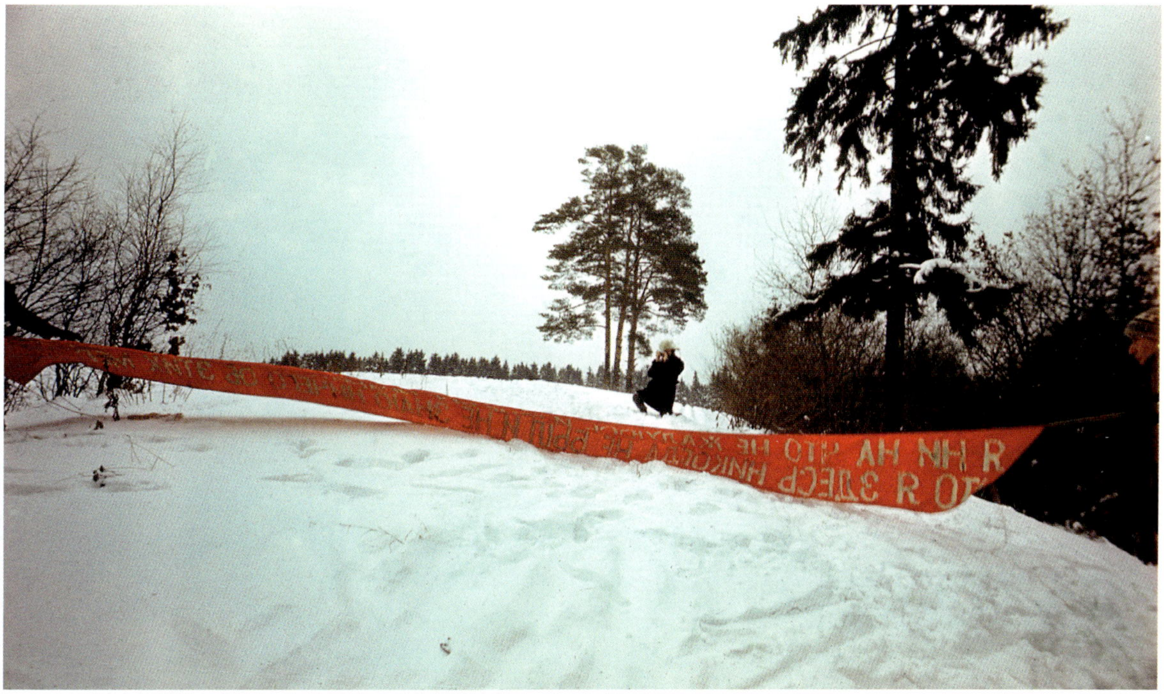

The Balloon

Moscow region, Gorkovskaya railway line, Nazaryevo station, 15 June, 1977.

Collective Actions group:

A Monastyrski, N Alekseev, G Kizevalter, L Veshnevskaya, A Abramov, MK.

Viewers and participants:

Madis Kolk, I Bigniamini and one other.

Pieces of coloured calico were sewn to form an envelope for the balloon (four metres in diameter). Later in the forest, out in the rain, we inflated toy balloons and stuffed the big one with them. The whole process took six hours. After the balloon was finished, we put inside it a ringing alarm clock and let the whole haystack-shaped thing drift down the river Klyazma.

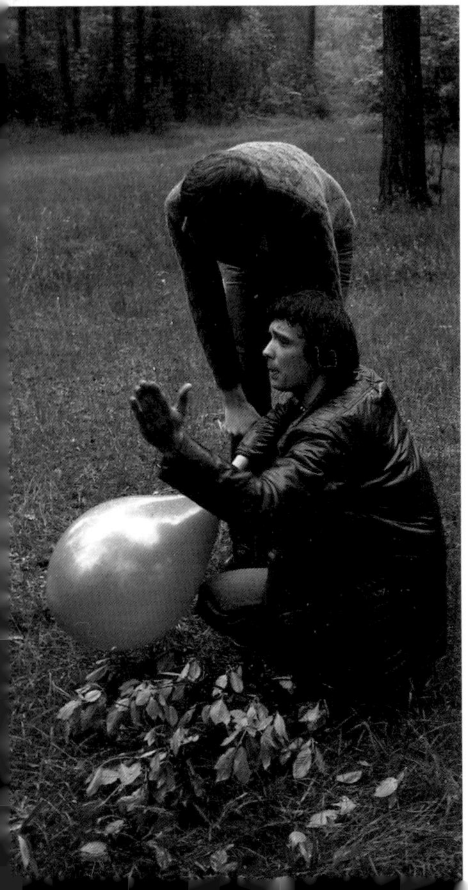

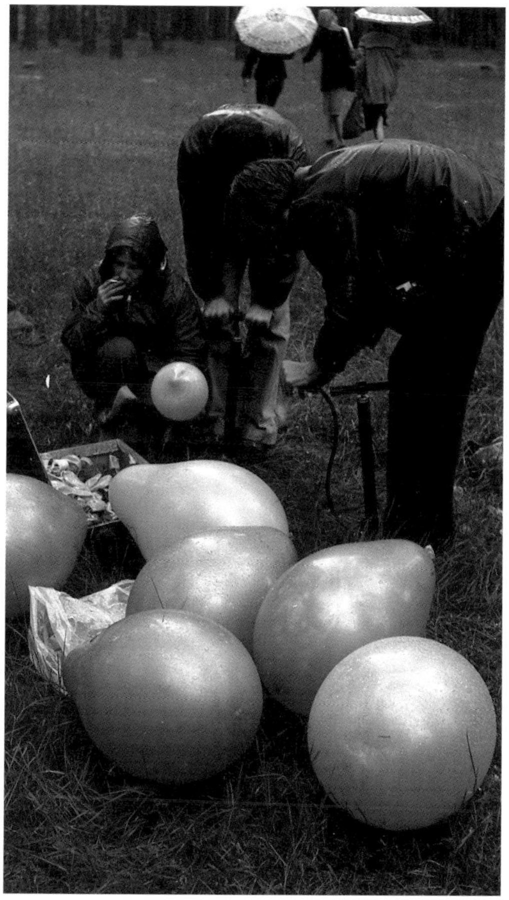

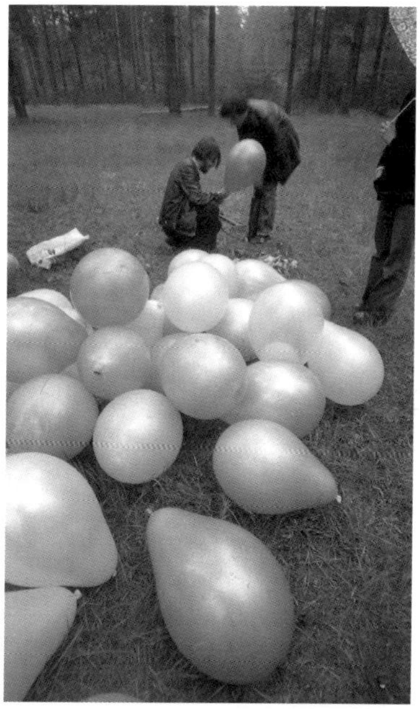

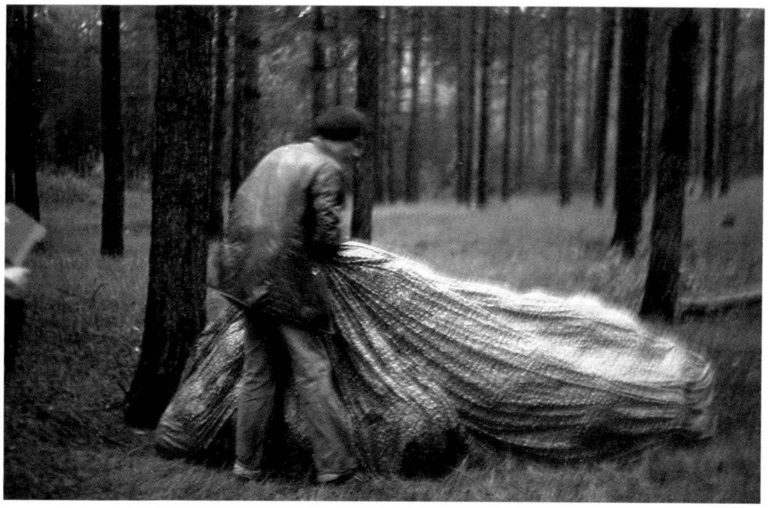

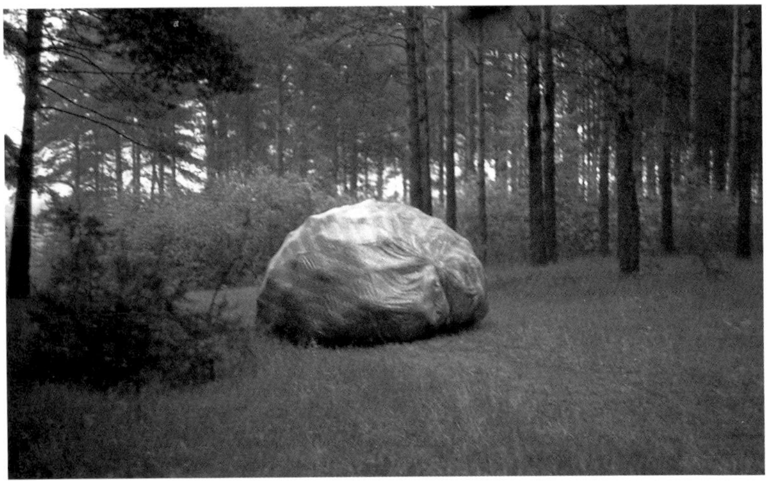
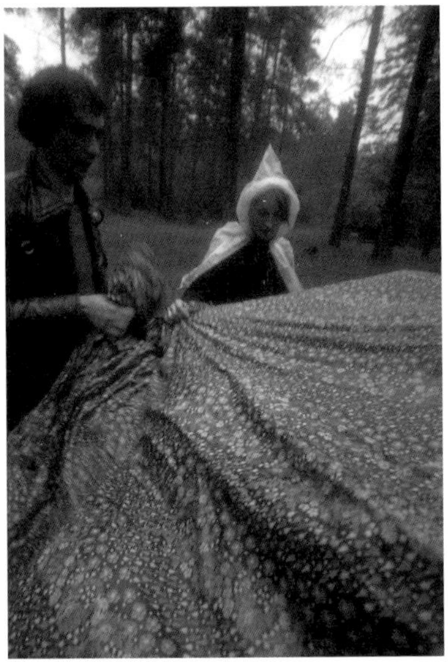
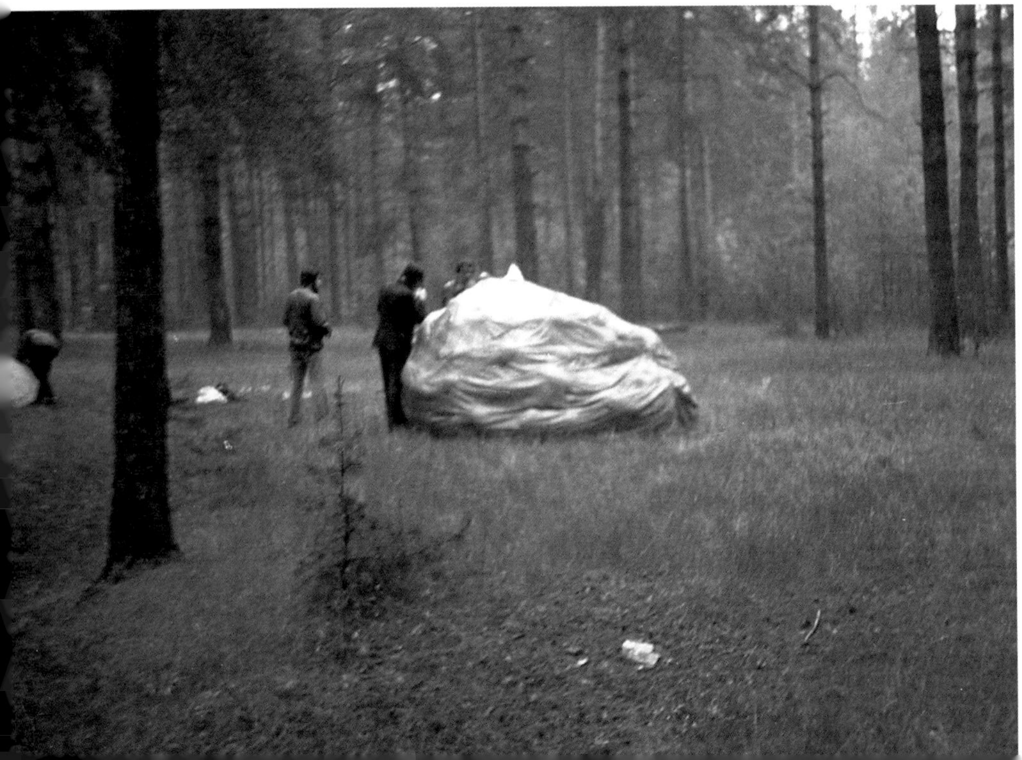

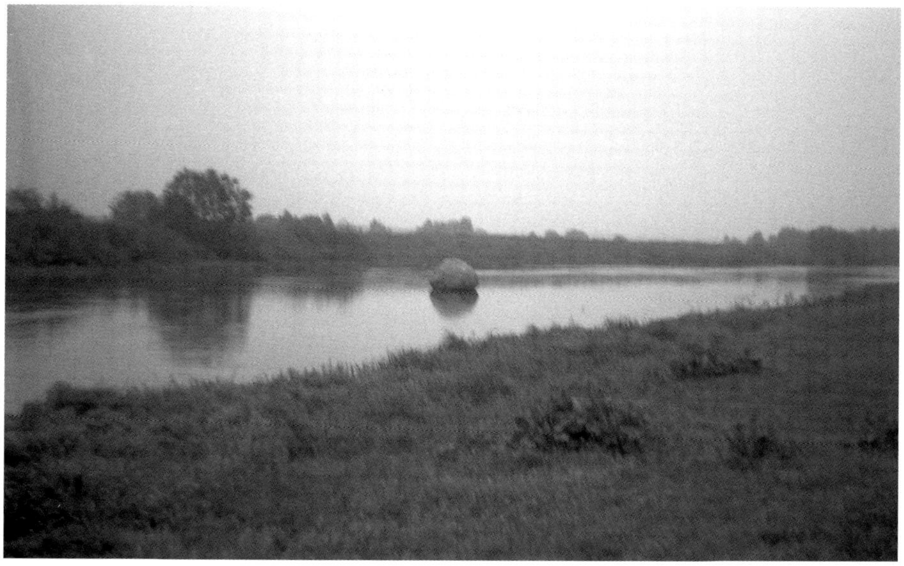

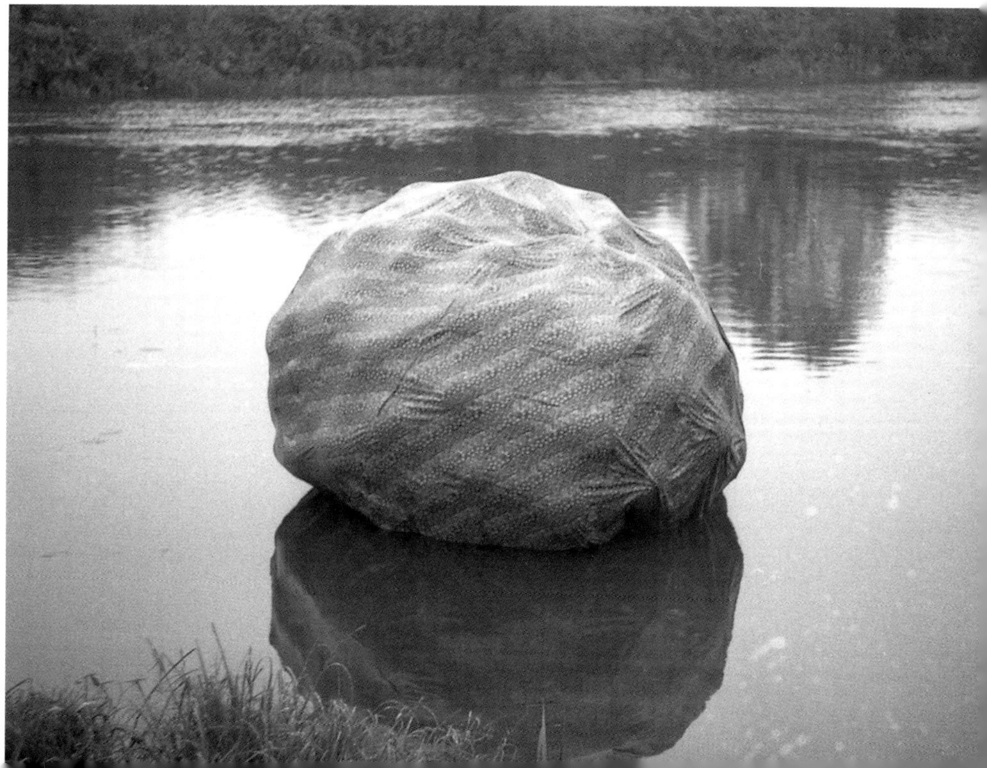

The Comedy

Moscow region, Savyolovskaya railway line, field near Kyevy Gorky village, 2 October 1977.

Collective Actions group:

A Monastyrski, V Miturich-Khlebnikova, N Panitkov, N Alekseev.

Viewers and participants:

I Kabakov, V Mochalova, E Gorokhovsky, S Shablavin and eight others.

The viewers who had received invitations (ten people) gathered on the Lobnya station and were met by one of the participants of the action (estimated time of travel by train—40 minutes). After reaching the village of Kyevy Gorky by shuttle bus (estimated time—20 minutes) and crossing the forest (ten minutes), the audience found itself on one side of a field. Two other participants appeared on its opposite side. One of them, who was noticeably taller, wore a long loose ochre robe. The other participant in casual clothes went behind him, carrying the tails of the robe. When the distance between them and the audience reduced to 80 metres, the man in the robe stopped, facing the audience. The other one in casual clothes crawled under the overalls and in such a way they proceeded towards the audience. When they were 25 metres away from the viewers, the robed participant lifted the robe's tail and it became clear that the second participant had gone. Then the first participant turned right and disappeared in the forest.

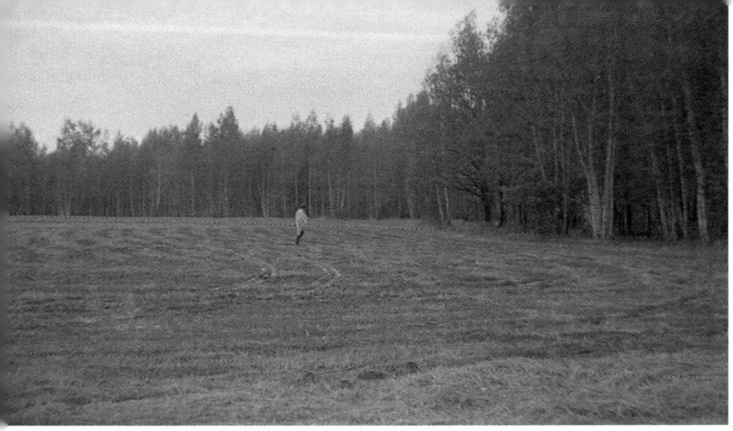
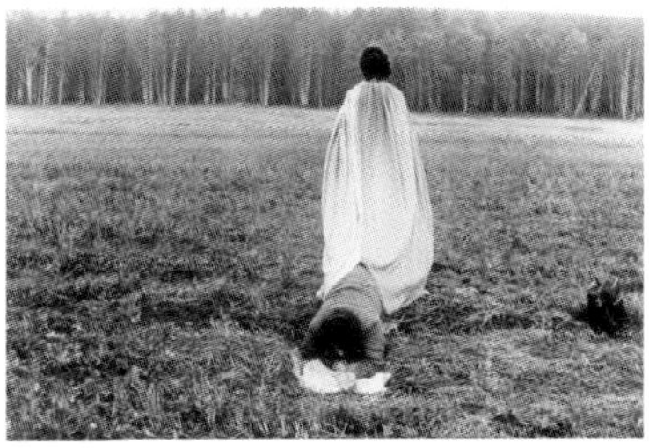
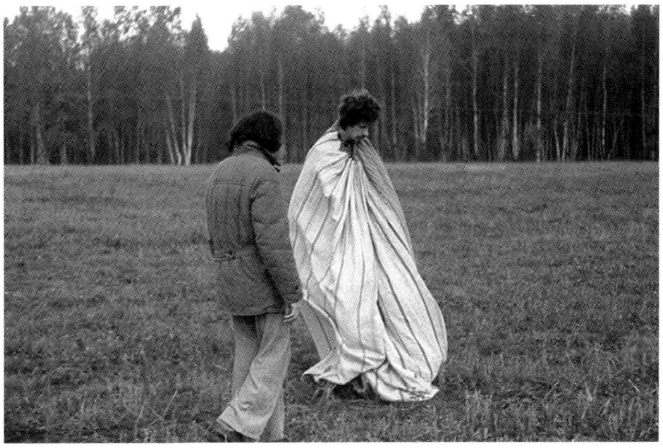
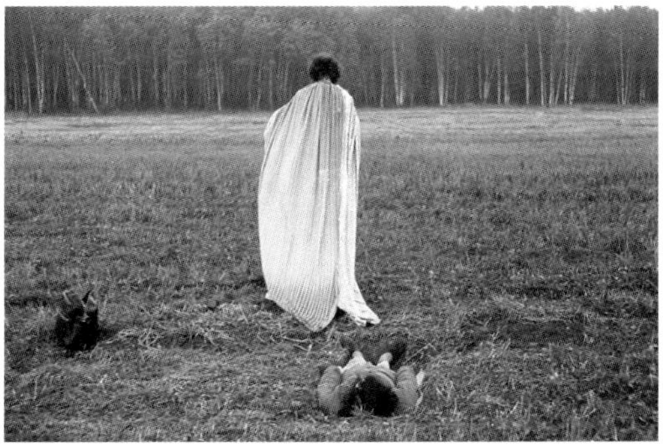
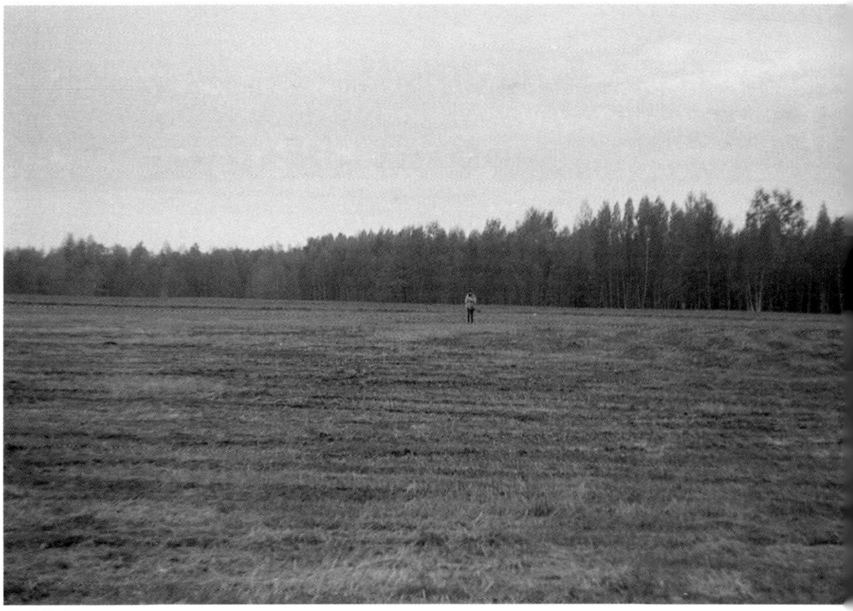

The Slogan–1978

Moscow region, Belorusskaya railway line, near the city of Zvenigorod, 9 April, 1978.

Collective Actions group:

A Monastyrski, N Alekseev, I Yavorsky, V and L Veshnevsky.

A piece of navy blue cloth (1 x 12 metres) with white stencilled letters was hung on the riverbank. The inscription said:

> I wonder why I lied to myself that I had never been here and was totally ignorant of this place—in fact, it's just like anywhere else here, only the feeling is stronger and incomprehension deeper.

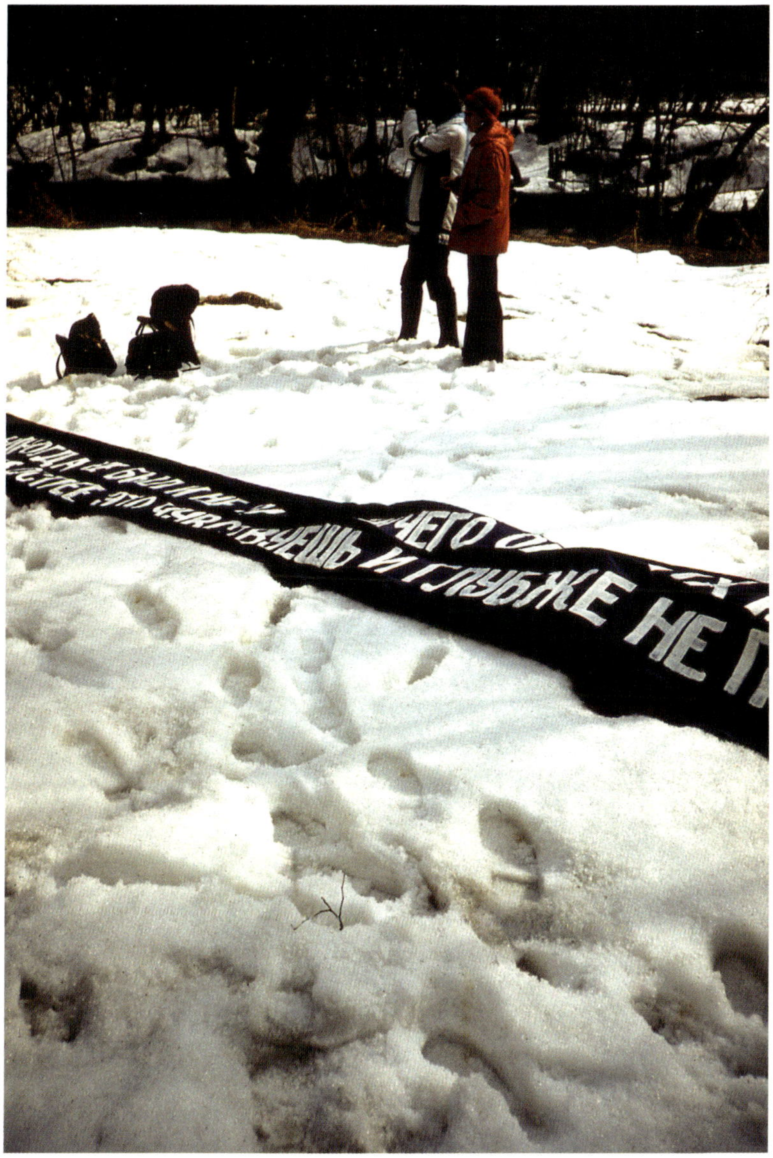

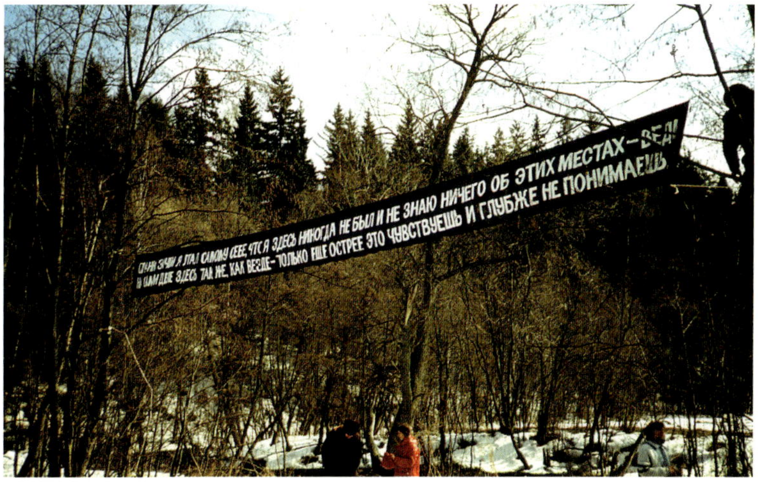
САМОМУ СЕБЕ, ЧТО Я ЗДЕСЬ НИКОГДА НЕ БЫЛ И НЕ ЗНАЮ НИЧЕГО ОБ ЭТИХ МЕСТАХ—
ЗДЕСЬ ТАК ЖЕ, КАК ВЕЗДЕ—ТОЛЬКО ЕЩЕ ОСТРЕЕ ЭТО ЧУВСТВУЕШЬ И ГЛУБЖЕ НЕ ПОНИМАЕШЬ

The Third Varient

Moscow region, Savyolovskaya railway line, near Kyevy Gorky village, 28 May, 1978.

Collective Actions group:

A Monastyrski, V Miturich-Khlebnikova, N Panitkov, N Alekseev, MK.

Viewers and participants:

I Kabakov, V Mochalova, L Talochkin, S Bordachev, V Veshnevsky, A Urusov, A Rokhlis and ten others.

The invited audience (approximately 20 people) gathered on one side of a field. On their right, 50 metres from the viewers, one participant appeared, dressed in a purple robe. He walked along a line parallel to viewers and lied down in a pit, thus disappearing from sight. Three minutes later his figure appeared from another pit, 30 metres to the left of the first one. He wore the same purple robe, but with a red balloon instead of his head. He then pierced the balloon with a stick, and it burst into a cloud of white dust. The now headless man lied back in the pit from which he had appeared moments before. At the same time he rose from the first pit (30 metres to the right), this time in casual clothes, and left for the woods in the same direction from which he had emerged at the beginning of the action.

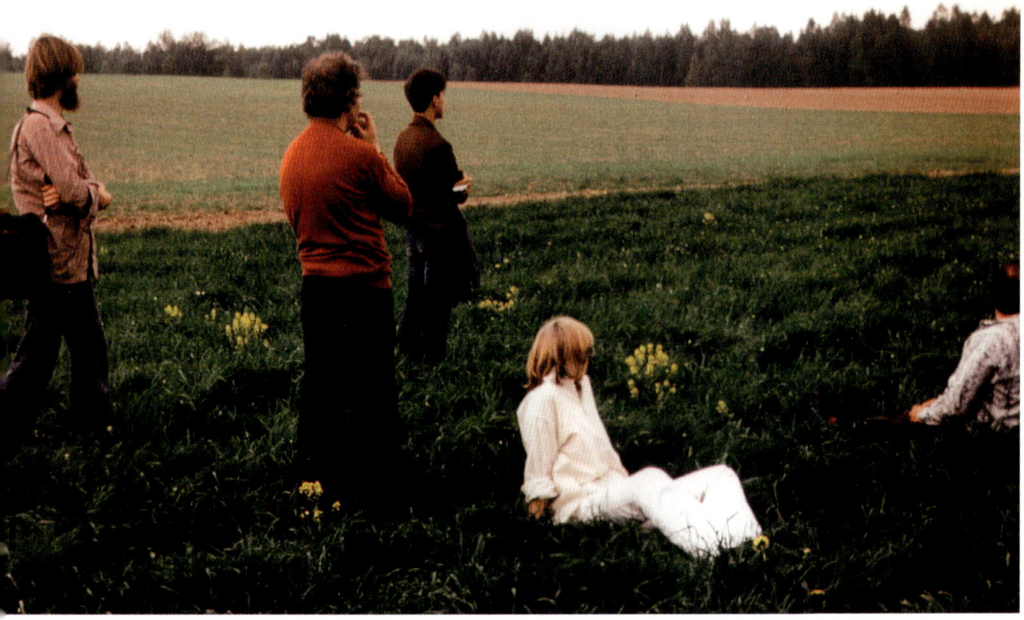

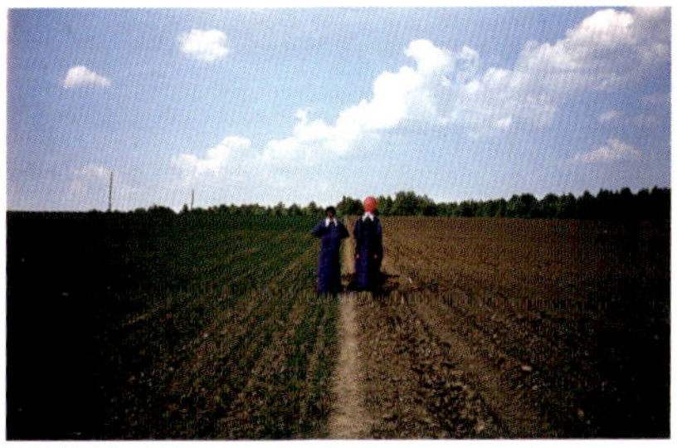

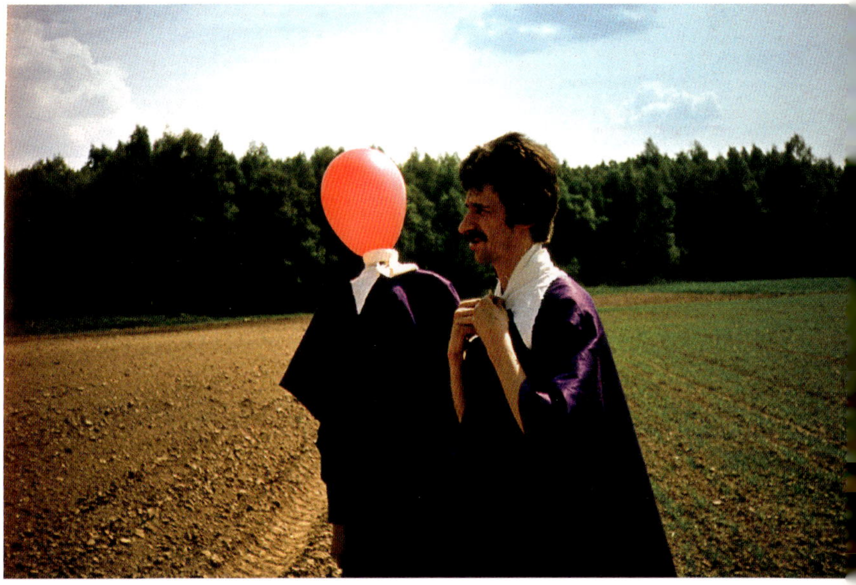

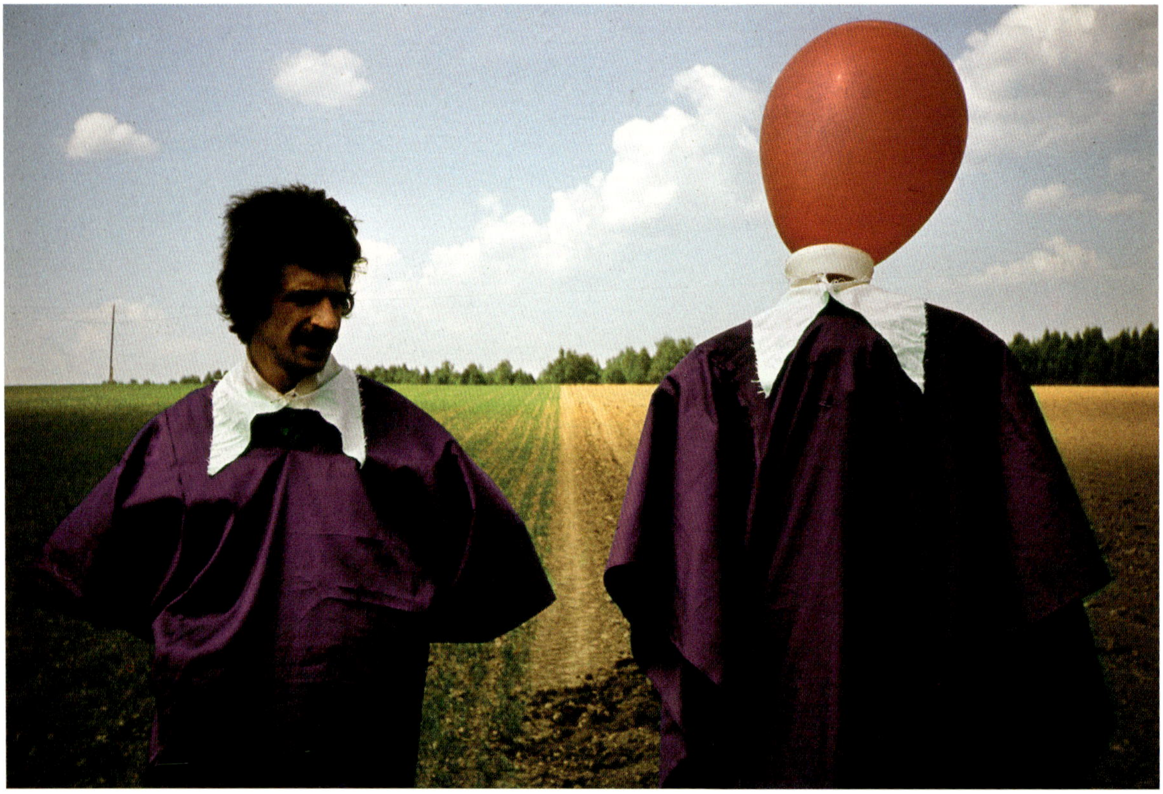

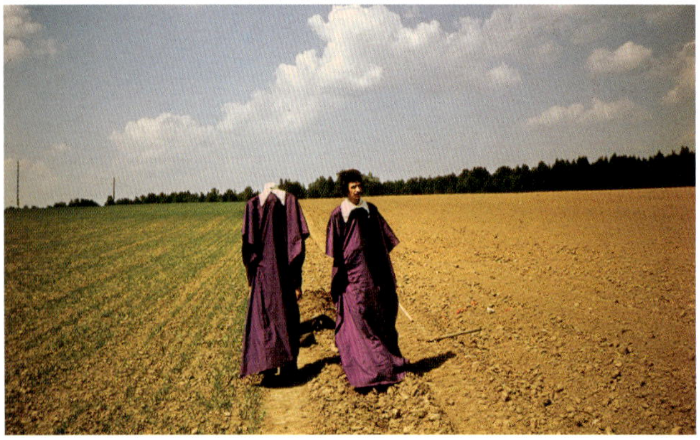

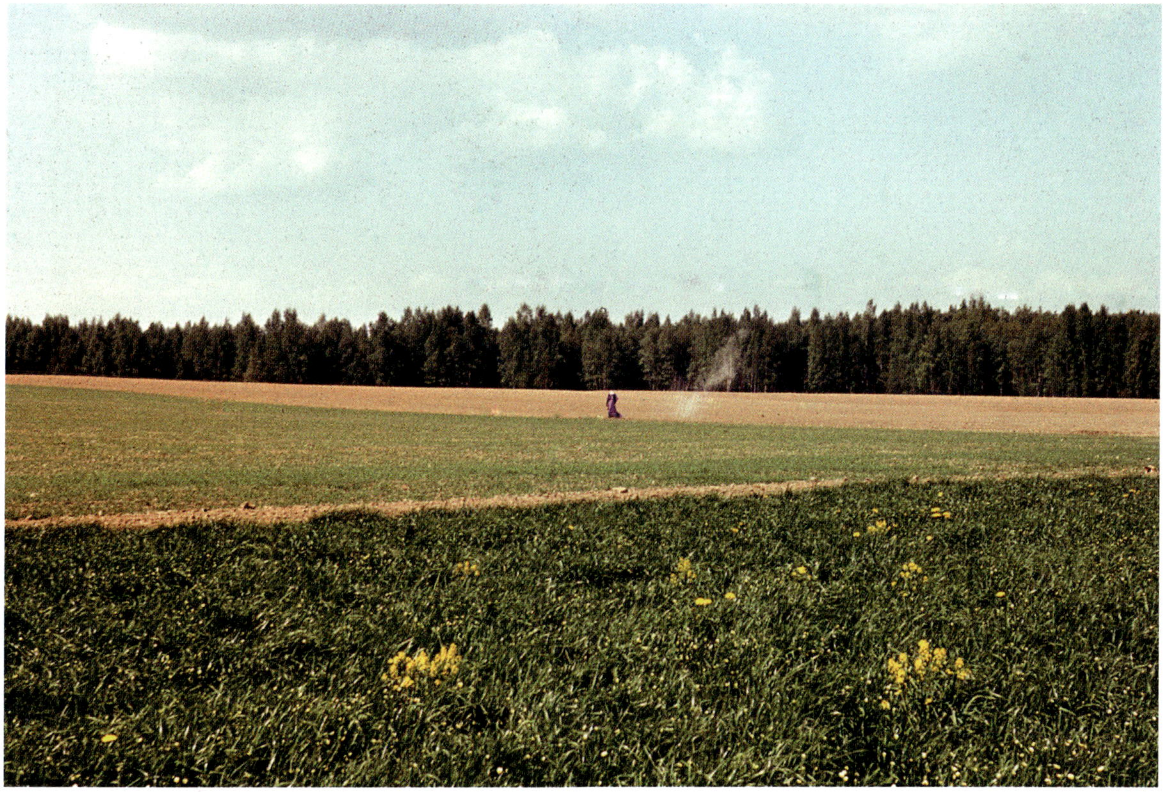

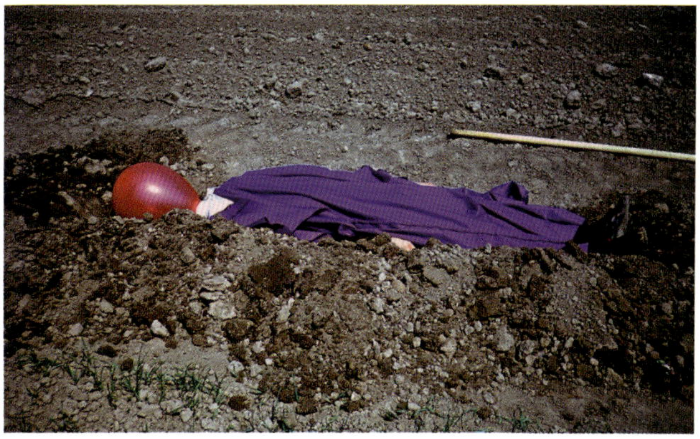

Time of Action

Moscow region, Savyolovskaya railway line, near Kyevy Gorky village, 15 October, 1978.

Collective Actions group:

A Monastyrski, N Alekseev, N Panitkov, A Abramov.

Viewers and participants:

L Sokov, L Bazhanov, F Infante, I Zatulovskaya, L Talochkin, I Chuikov, I Pivovarova, P Pepperstein, V Mochalova and five or six others.

In a forest not far from the field's edge a reel with seven kilometres of white rope was hung between two trees. The reel was hung in such a way that it could not be seen from the opposite side of the field where at a distance of 200 metres through broken ground, one end of the rope was drawn, and where the audience (approximately 15 people) and two participants of the action were waiting (the third participant stood by the reel in the woods).

From 13.30 to 15.00 (an hour and a half) the participants and some of the audience were hauling upon the rope in turns. As its other end had not been attached to the reel, the rope was completely extracted in the process.

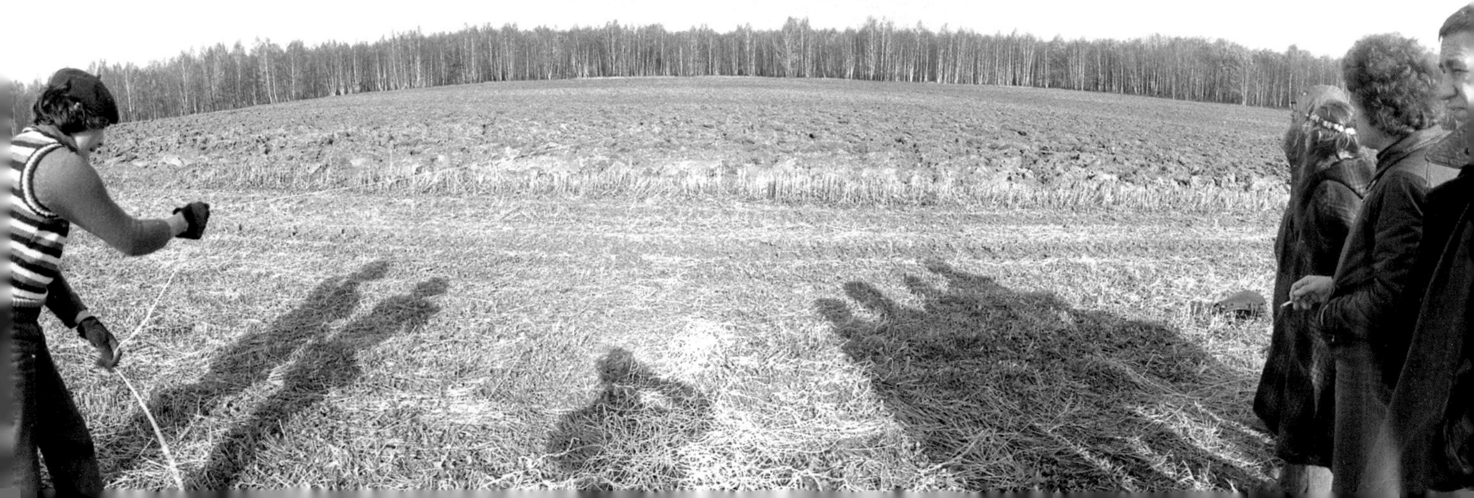

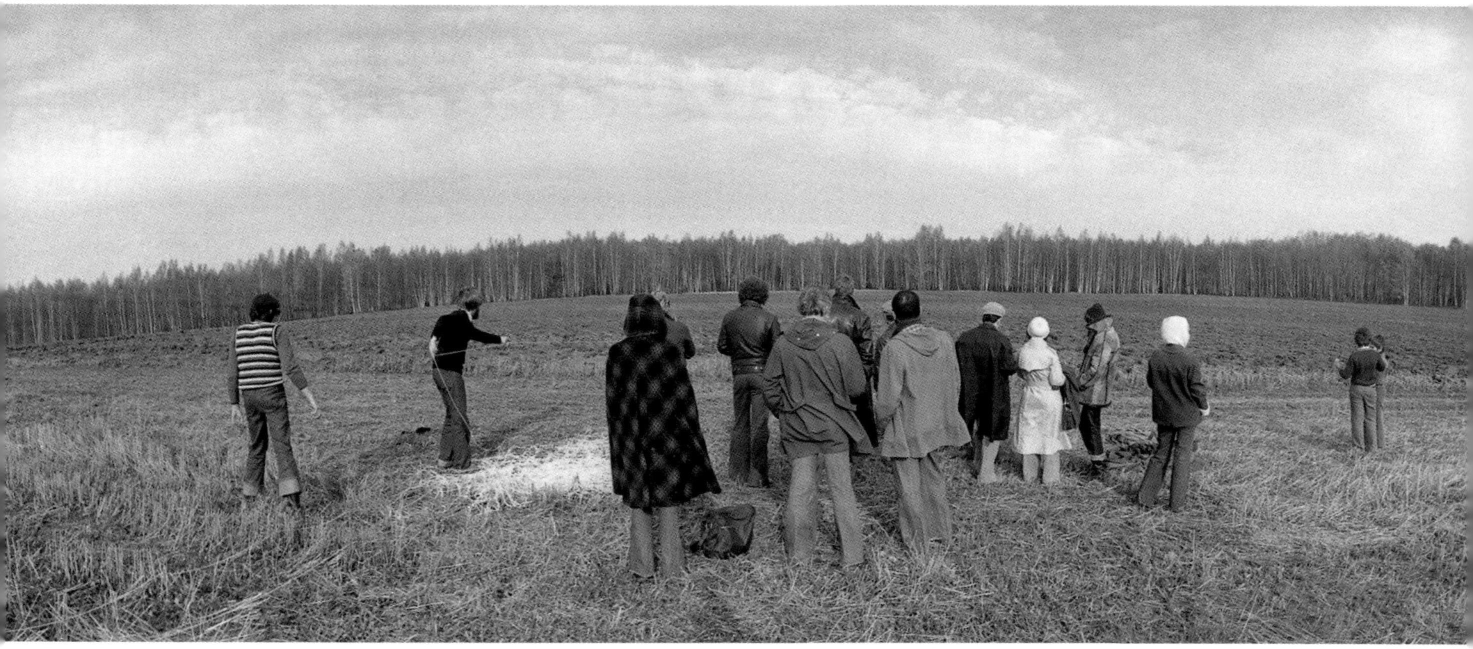

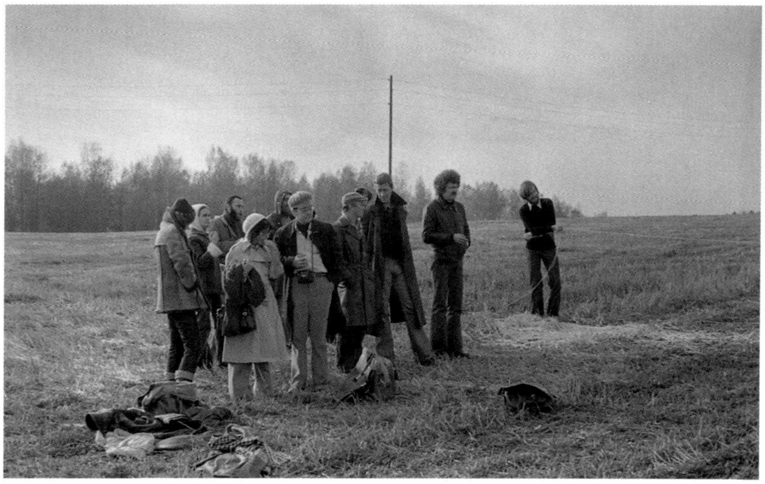

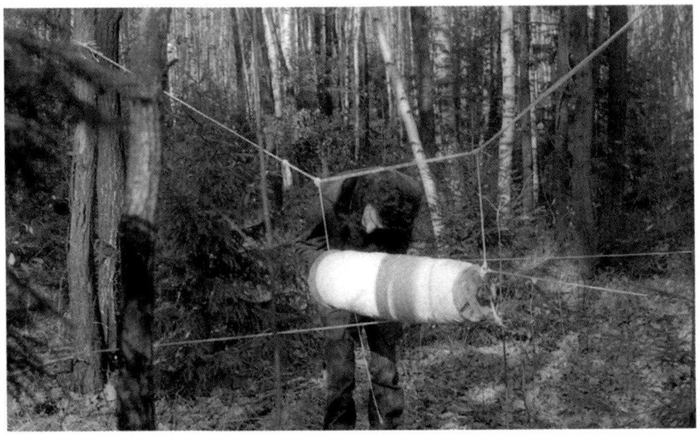

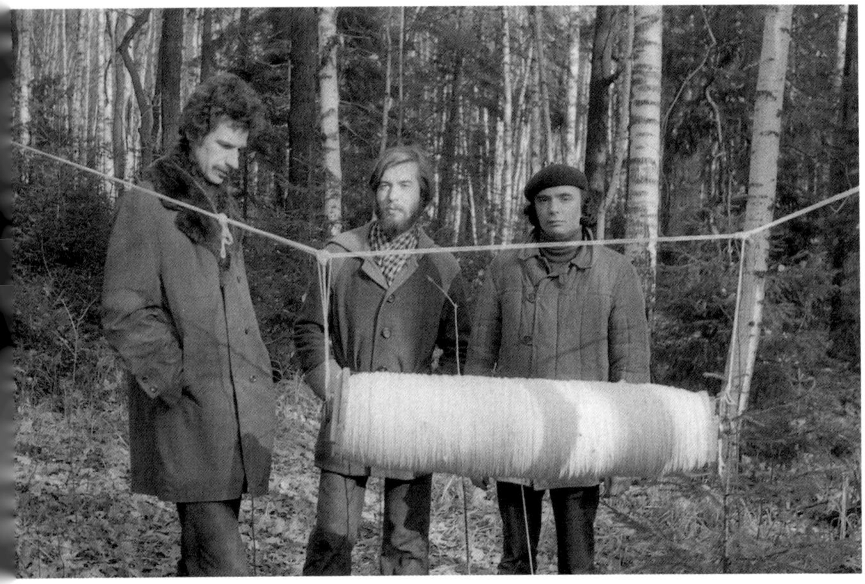

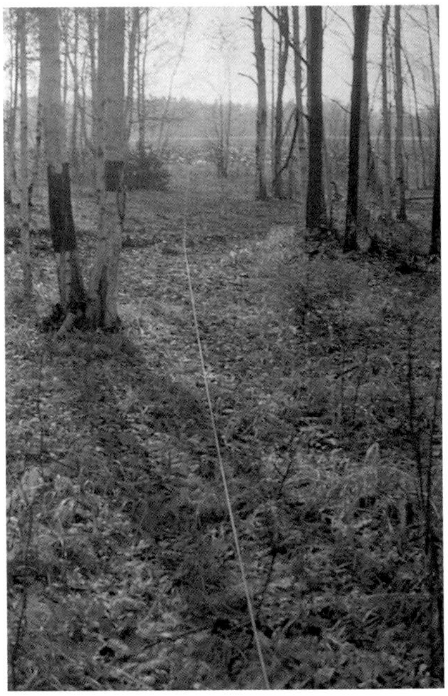

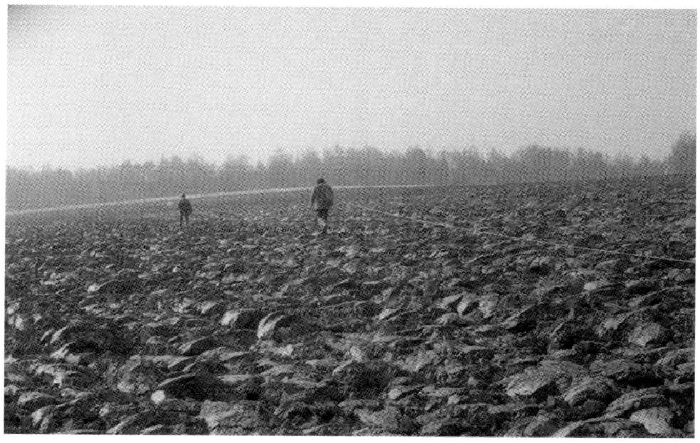

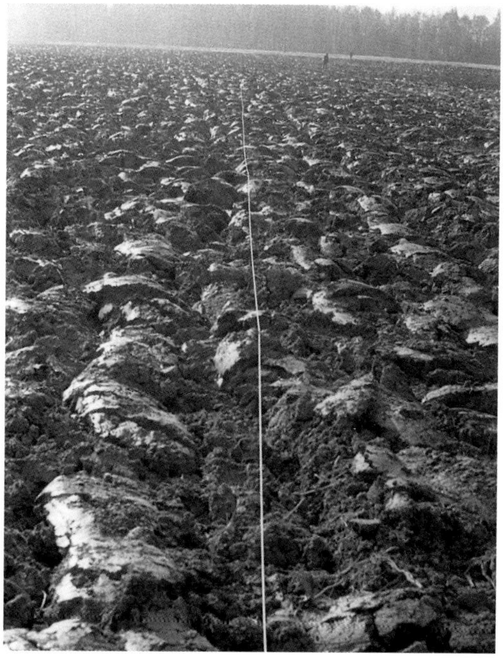

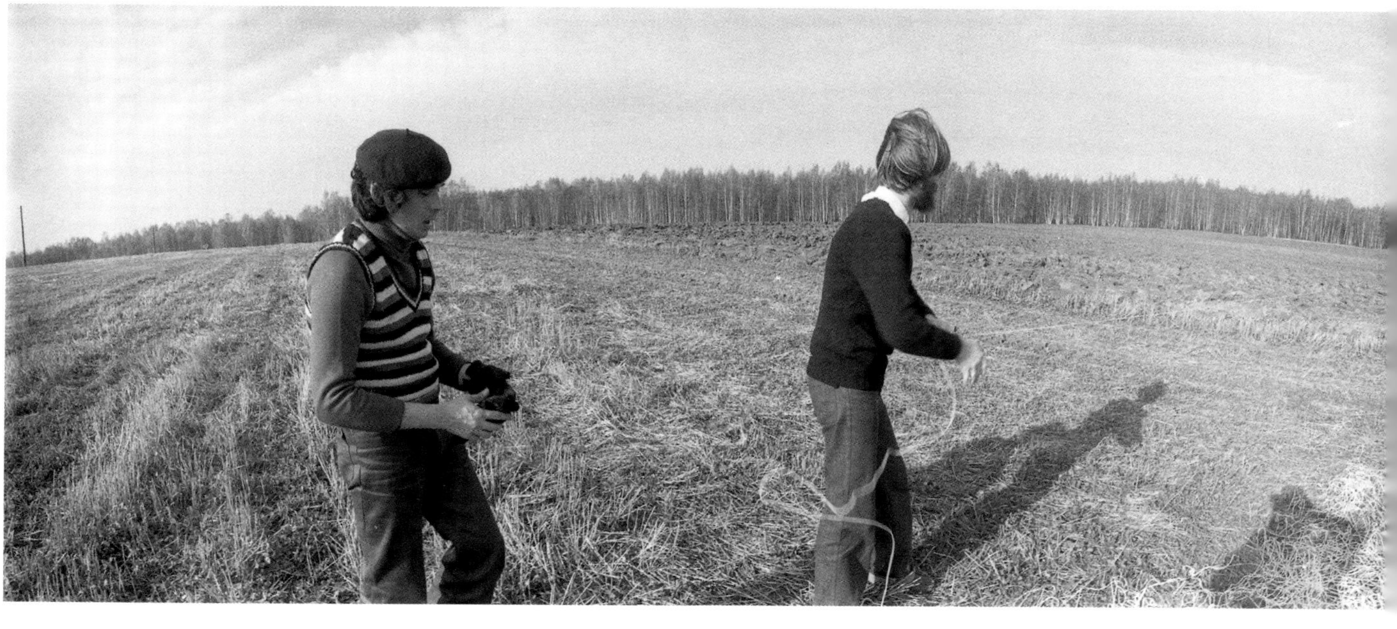

Pictures

Moscow region, Paveletskaya railway line, Rastorguyevo station, Sukhanovo park.

Collective Actions group:

A Monastyrski, N Alekseev, N Panitkov, I Yavorsky.

Viewers:

I Kabakov, M Miturich-Khlebnikov, R Arutyunian, R Gerlovina, V Sokhransky, V Nekrasov, E Gorokhovsky, I Pivovarova, V Dobroselsky, V Mochalova, I Bakstein, B Groys, N Nikitina, L Sokov, I Chuikov, I Golovinskaya, and 12 or 15 others.

144 envelopes crafted from white and coloured paper were interleaved and compiled into 12 sets of 12 envelopes each (the largest one 42 x 40 centimetres, the smallest 13 x 8 centimetres). Each envelope contained a description of the shape-generating points of the happening, according to the following paradigm: 1—guidelines for the audience, 2—timeline of the whole action, 3—setting, 4—weather, 5—colour of the envelopes, 6—sound, 7—phenomenon, 8—end time of a gesture (action), 9—the audience's reaction, 10—meaning of a gesture (action), 11—interpretation, directive, 12—factography. These sets were distributed among invited guests who had gathered on the field (30 people, 12 of them received sets). While the viewers were unsealing the envelopes and arranging them in a line on the snow (approximately 50 metres long), three participants crossed the field and disappeared in woods on the opposite side. After reading inscriptions on the envelopes the viewers folded and pasted each set of envelopes to form 12 coloured framework pictures: the largest envelope on the bottom, a smaller one on it and so on. All of the inscriptions, except for factographic text (i.e. place and time of action, list of participants, etc.), became hidden under envelopes. Later these pictures were distributed among the audience as factual certificates of the action.

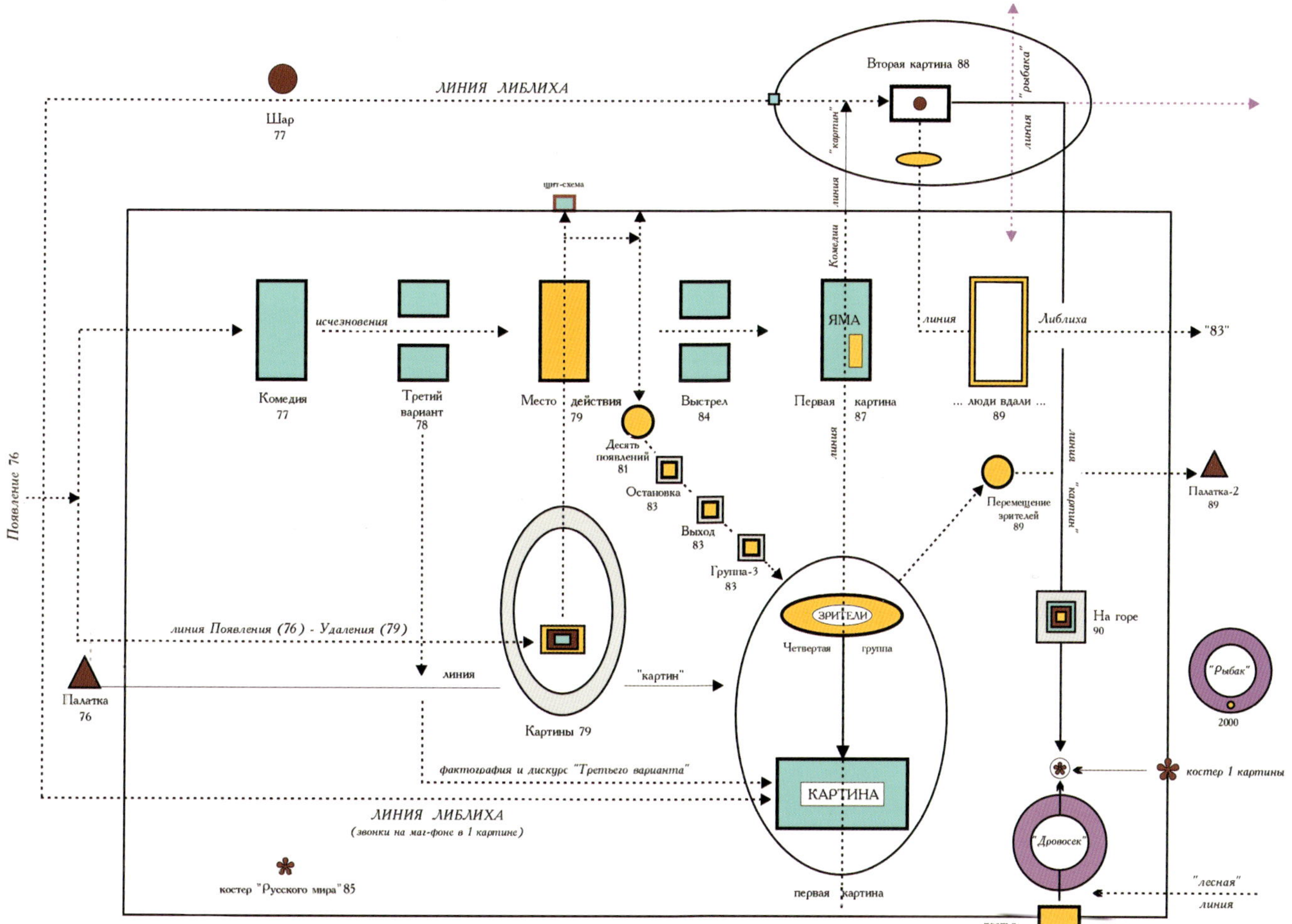

А.М. СХЕМА "ПОЛЕ КОМЕДИИ И ЛИНИЯ КАРТИН В АКЦИЯХ КД". 2002.
(зрители обозначены желтым цветом)

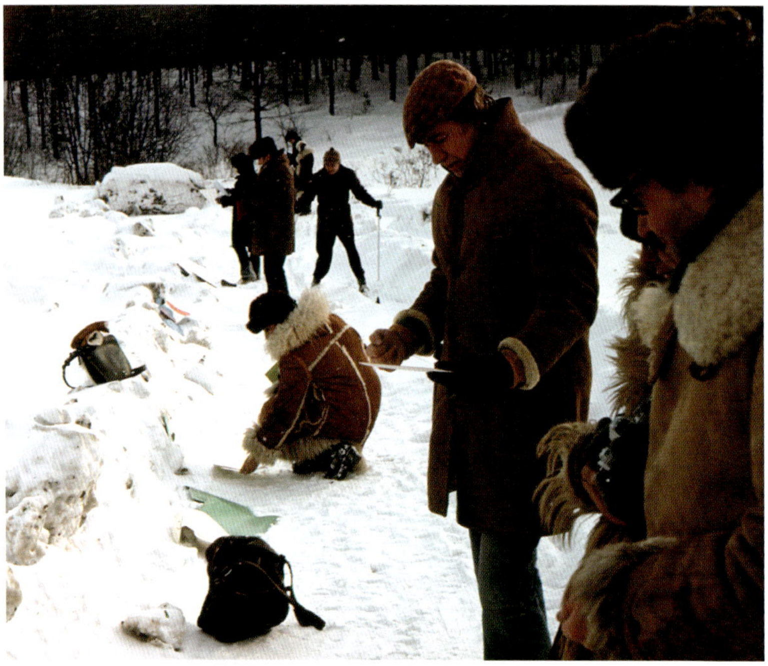
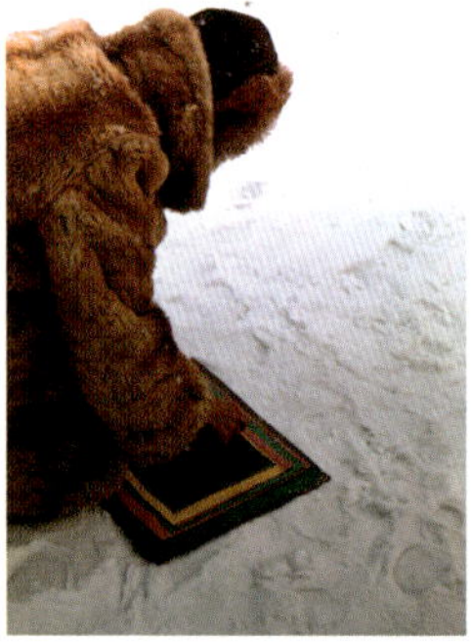
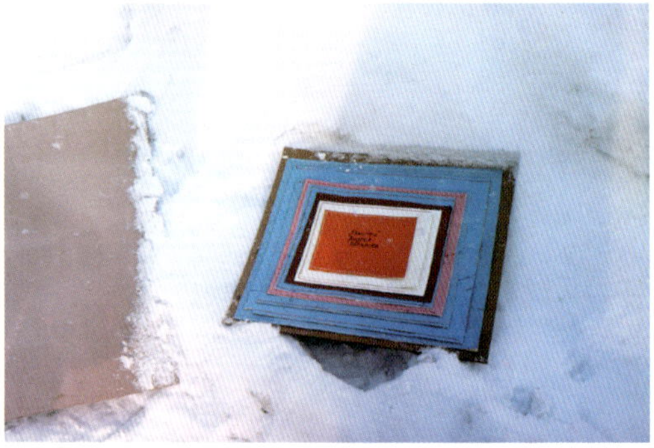
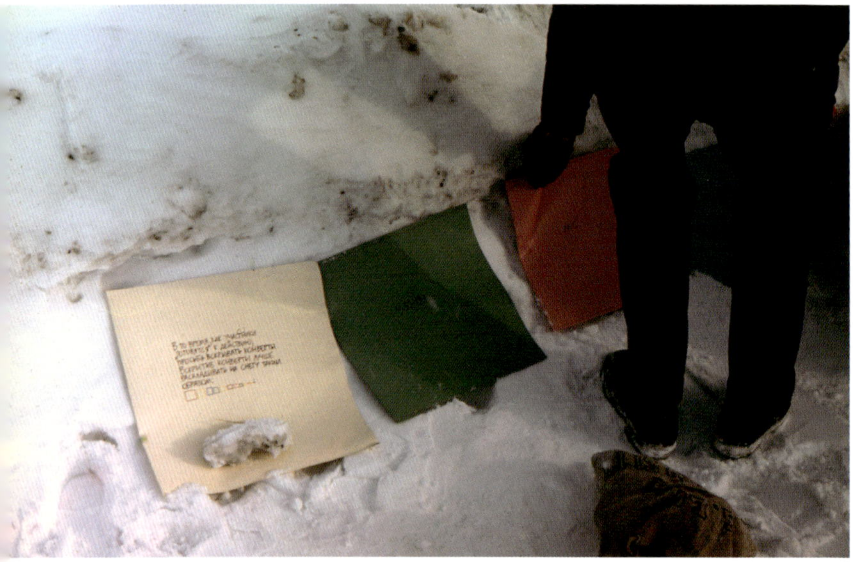

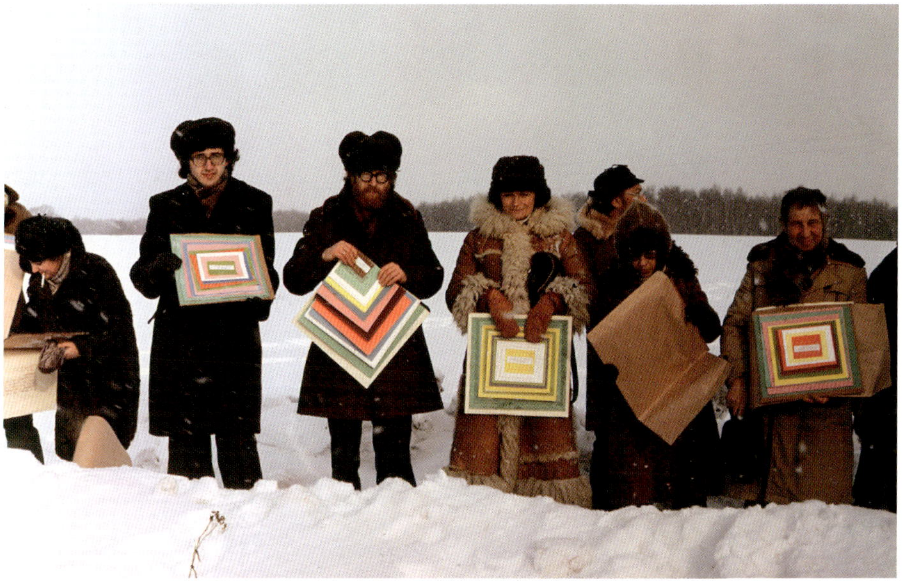

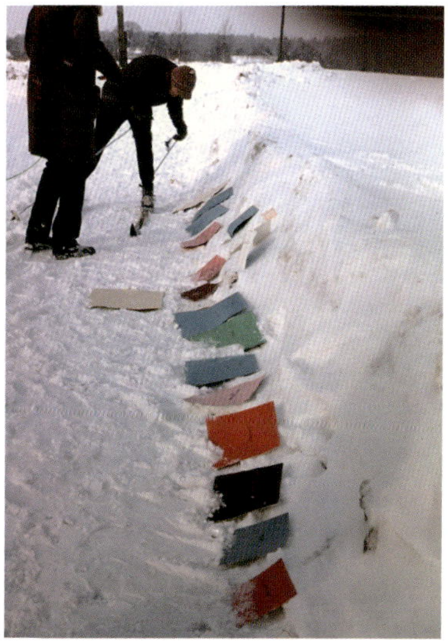

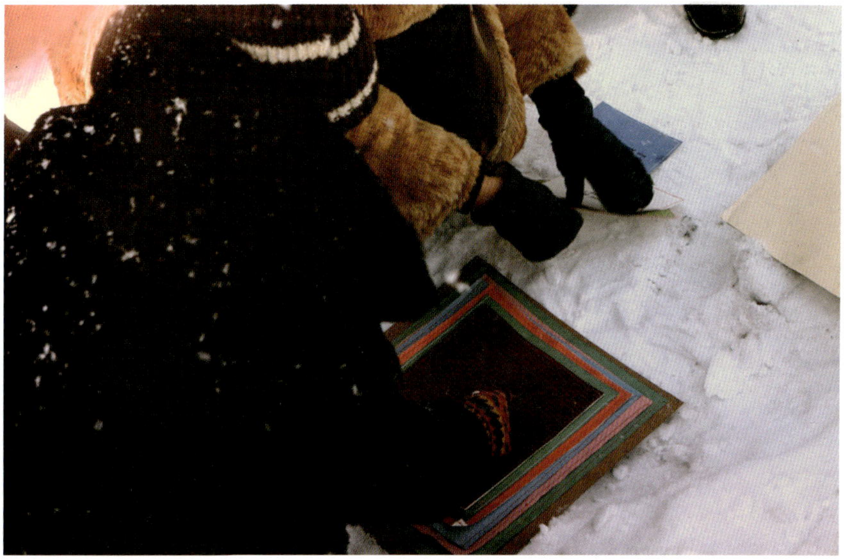

The Exit

Moscow, Pushkinskaya Street,
20 March, 1983.

Collective Actions group:

A Monastyrski, G Kizevalter,
S Romashko, N Alekseev, N Panitkov,
E Elagina.

Viewers and participants:

I Kabakov, I Bakstein, I Nakhova,
S Hänsgen, V Mironenko, A Zhigalov,
N Abalakova, V Nekrasov,
E Gorokhovsky, A Anikeev, Yu Albert,
A Filippov, V Zakharov, N Kozlov,
L Talochkin, S Gundlakh and 14 others.

A group of viewers was met by the action's organisers at a trolley bus stop Pushkinskaya ulitsa. When all the invitees gathered at the stop, they were prompted to take a ride on the trolley bus. After travelling from one bus stop to another, the viewers received paper cards with inscriptions: "WE'RE LEAVING AT THE NEXT STOP. Collective Actions. "After getting off the trolley bus at the next stop (Kozitsky pereulok), the viewers met other organisers who had been waiting there and received paper envelopes with inscription that said: "THE EXIT took place on 20 March, 1983, at 12:24 (handwritten). Thank you for your cooperation." The cards were then put inside the envelopes.

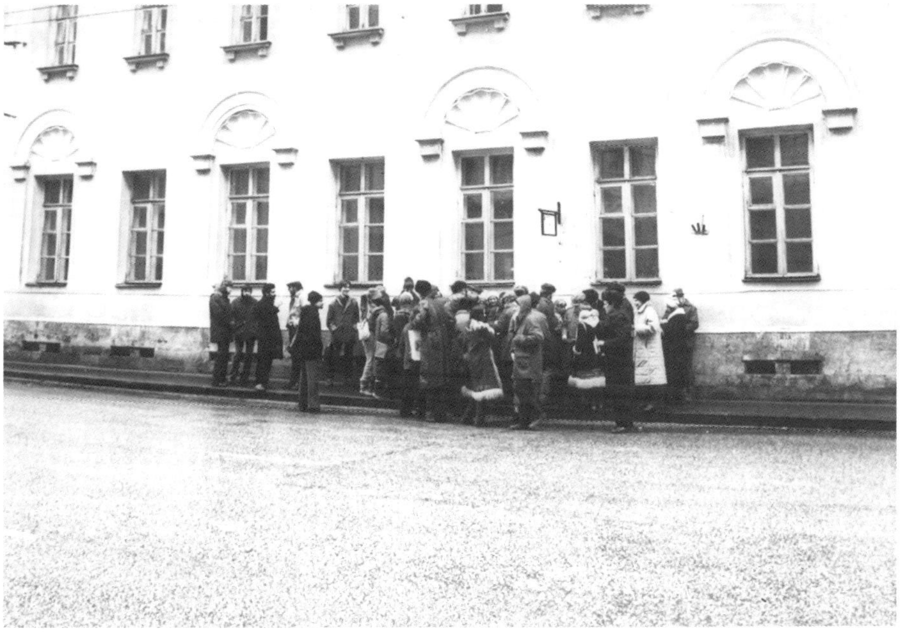

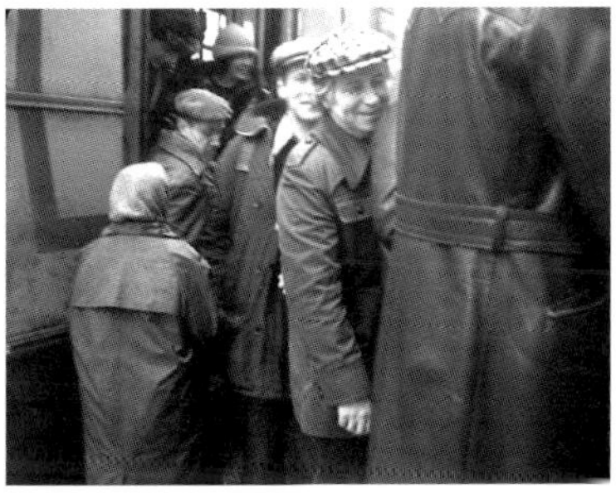

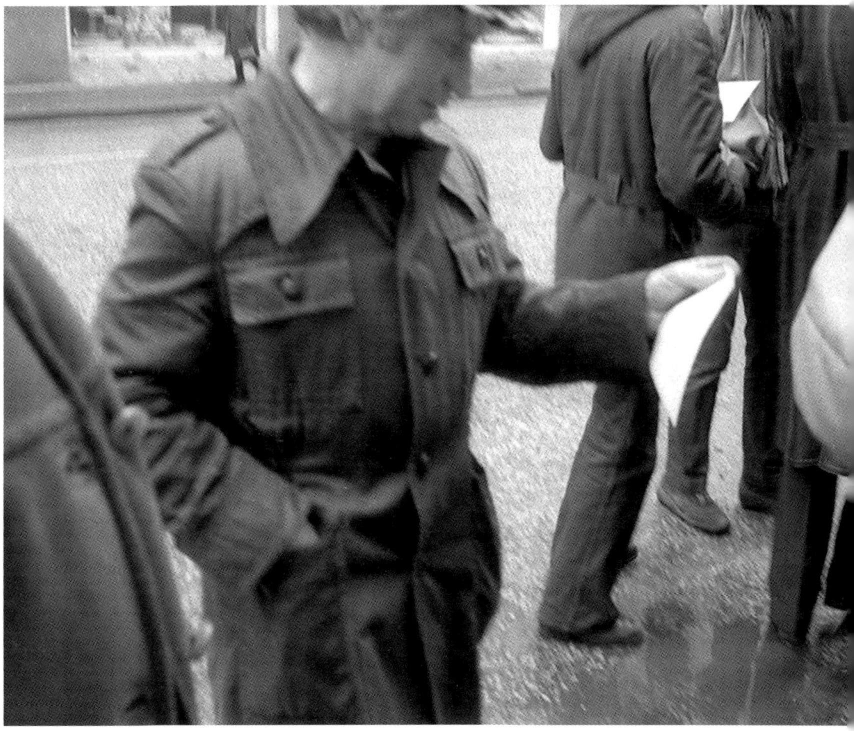

Group–3

Moscow, Rizhksy train
Terminal Square,
24 April 1983.

Collective Actions group:

A Monastyrski, G Kizevalter, N Panitkov, S Romashko, N Alekseev.

Viewers and participants:

I Kabakov, D Prigov, L Rubinstein, L Talochkin, S Bordachev, I Bakstein, V Mironenko, I Pivovarova, I Chuikov, S Gundlakh, A Anikeev, Yu Albert, S Mironenko and five others.

A group of viewers met near Rizhskaya metro station and were brought to a nearby square, some 50 metres away from the point of meeting. There the viewers received envelopes with inscriptions saying "GROUP–3 was assembled on the 24 April, 1983, at 13:24 (handwritten). Collective Actions." Inside each envelope there were two photographs of groups of viewers taken at the actions *The Halt* and *The Exit*, labelled respectively "Group–1" and "Group–2". When the envelopes were labelled, two organisers stood on the group's right and left holding sketch-boards with letters ("GROUP" on the right board and "3" on the left board). A group photo was taken inside this framework.

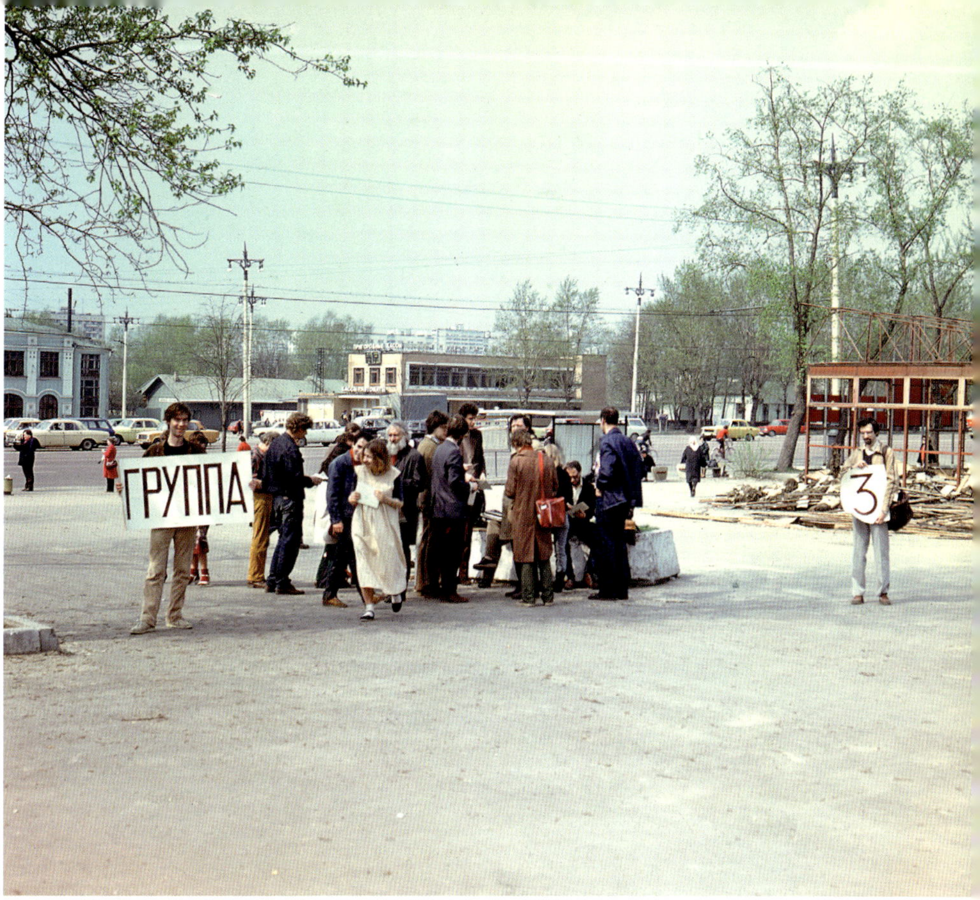
ГРУППА
3

The Russian World

Moscow region, Savyolovskaya railway line, field near Kyevy Gorky village, 17 March, 1985.

Collective Actions group:

A Monastyrski, S Romashko, E Elagina, G Kizevalter, I Makarevich, MK.

Viewers and participants:

I Kabakov, V Sorokin, I Nakhova, I Bakstein, N Abalakova, A Zhigalov, E Zhigalova, M Chuikova, S Anufriev, E Gorokhovsky, Nina, V Naumets, V Zakharov, D Prigov, A Prigov, Yu Leiderman, G Witte, S Hänsgen, I and S Kopystyansky, N Alekseev.

A group of viewers was met on a highway by S Romashko, who offered the guests to proceed to the field along a path trod in deep snow. It is important to notice that Romashko followed the group in the rear. When the viewers approached the centre of the designated field and stopped by the purple cloth with a white canopy (in its centre there was a tape recorder switched to playback), Romashko turned on the right, away from the trail, and began walking along the line of the forest towards the plywood hare standing on the forest's verge 70 metres away from the audience's position. The hare's contour (three metres high) was established facing the field, its side facing the audience: from the viewers' position it looked like a pole or a shield protruding from the snow.

While Romashko was trudging through deep snow towards the hare figure, escaping the audience's attention (as he was moving along the forest's line and avoiding the audience's line of sight), the viewers were listening to a recording consisting of noise produced in the course of assembling and installing the hare figure (recorded two hours prior to the action). Besides that, in the course of Romashko's moving the viewers could observe Monastyrski's motionless figure, standing 70 metres away from the purple cloth, opposite to it and facing the audience. While standing in a position opposite to the cloth and divided from the audience by snowy wild land (Monastyrski took his position before the audience's arrival by avoiding the line, so there was no visible trace of his footprints on the snow), Monastyrski was evenly reeling white thread on the "soft handle"—a prefabricated object made of a thick cardboard circle with an outstretched handle; on one of its sides an image of a dial plate with hands was glued, while the other was formed by a red circle with a silver five-bladed star in the centre; on the disk's handle there were 200 metres of white thread spooled beforehand, so in the course of the action the thread was spooled from another reel over the existing layer of thread. However, the distance between Monastyrski and the viewers prevented the latter from seeing neither the soft handle" nor the process of spooling itself: the spooling was perceived as a vaguely visible rocking motion of a formless object in Monastyrski's hands.

Some six or seven minutes past the start of the movement Romashko reached his position and began gently rapping with his feet on the lower part of the plywood hare, as if shaking snow off his boots. Gradually he applied more and more effort, so that the knocking sound attracted the audience's attention. For three or four minutes Romashko was increasing the kicking the hare with an increasing vigour—first with the toes of his shoes, then with the soles, and finally kicking full force, knocking the hare over. After smashing the hare, Romashko dragged it beyond the forest's verge and disappeared from sight.

As soon as Romashko disappeared in the forest with the hare, Monastyrski turned the "soft handle" with the red circle facing the audience (its reverse side with dial-plate was indistinguishable against the background of Monastyrski's overcoat). Having finished reeling the rest of the thread—it took him one to two minutes—Monastyrski started moving towards the audience through the snowy plain. The snow was deep, and it took him no less than seven minutes to reach the viewers' position. On approaching the purple cloth, Monastyrski removed the tape recorder from it and put the "soft handle" red side up. Then he opened the white canopy, discovering under it nine white objects decorated with golden foil and wing-shaped golden furnishings. These objects were: 1— a glove, 2— an enema, 3— a walking-stick, 4— a doll's head, 5— a clothes brush, 6— a rolling-pin, 7— a toy ladder, 8— a black bag with cardboard dripping pan inside, 9— a folder titled *The Book of Nothingness*. These objects were then put inside cardboard boxes with labels saying "CA The Golden Asp (then the object's name in brackets)" and given to those viewers who had pieces of cardboard (given to them beforehand) with the appropriate objects' names. Kabakov received an individual tenth box labelled "CA The Golden Asp (the flask)" and was asked not to take out the flask (the box with the flask inside was buried in snow until given to Kabakov).

After the distribution of the objects the tape recorder with the taped construction of the hare was switched off, and the viewers were prompted to make their way back to the highway.

After leaving the forest, the viewers found themselves on a snowy plain where a white hare, three metres high, stood facing them. He had a golden line across his belly, imitating the outline of his head. Under the line there was a label identical to those on the cardboard boxes: "CA The Golden Asp (the golden asp)".

Having photographed the objects near the hare, the latter was knocked down to the snow, and the viewers were prompted to put the boxes on him. Then Romashko and Monastyrski dragged the hare with boxes on it to the field some ten to 15 meters away from the audience. Monastyrski took the flask out of the box (the flask was painted white and filled with black gasoline) and broke it with a stick; black gasoline was poured over the white objects and boxes. Then Romashko threw a lit match, the gasoline ignited, and the boxes and objects burst into flames. At this moment a tape recorder was switched on (one of the action's organisers carried it on him), set to play back a recording of various railway announcements, such as "Train so-and-so arrives at platform number so-and-so at designated time" (the recording was made at Kursky railway terminal). When the objects on the hare stopped burning, Monastyrski and Romashko began throwing snow over them and soon buried the whole hare.

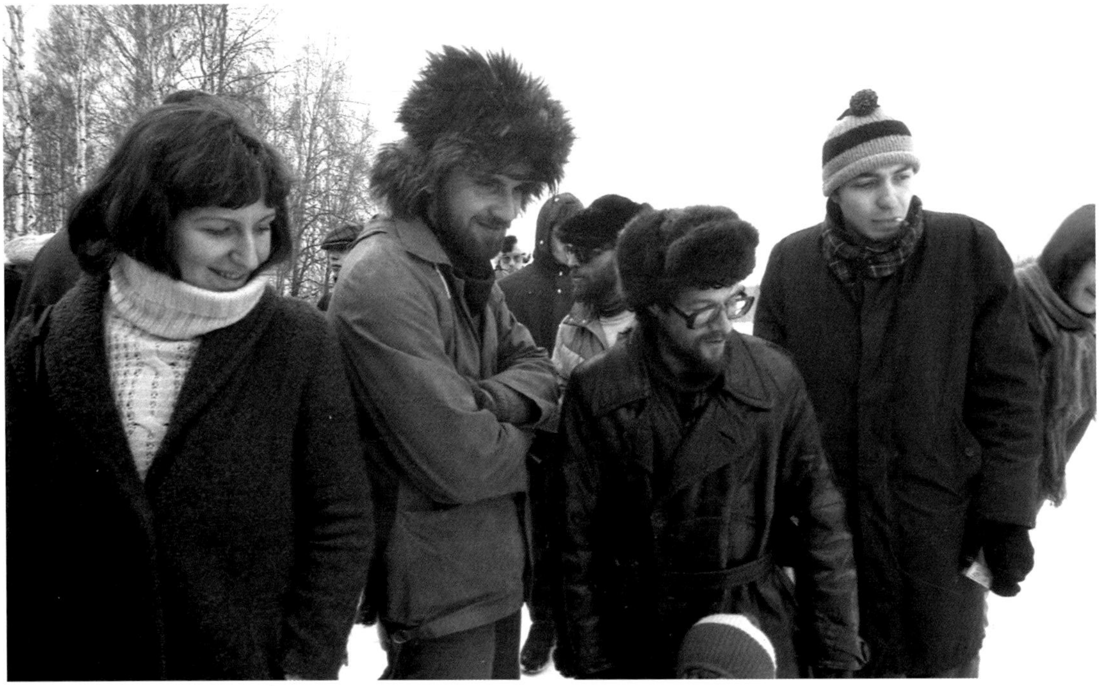

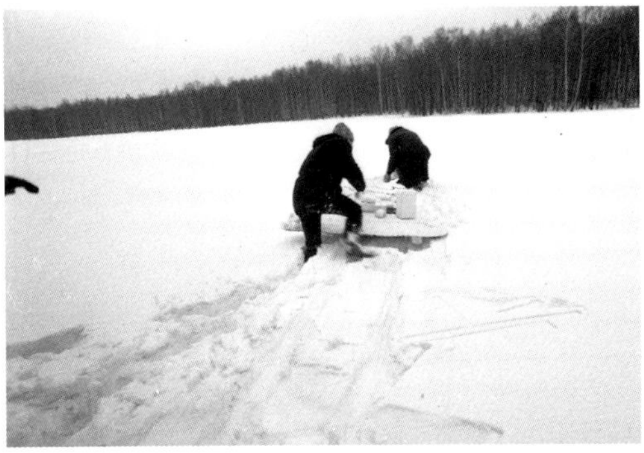

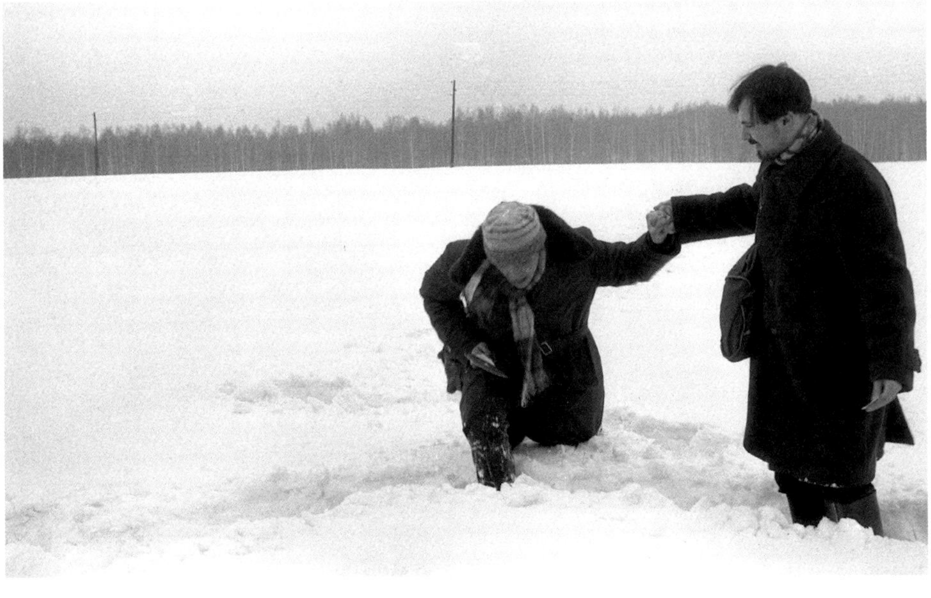

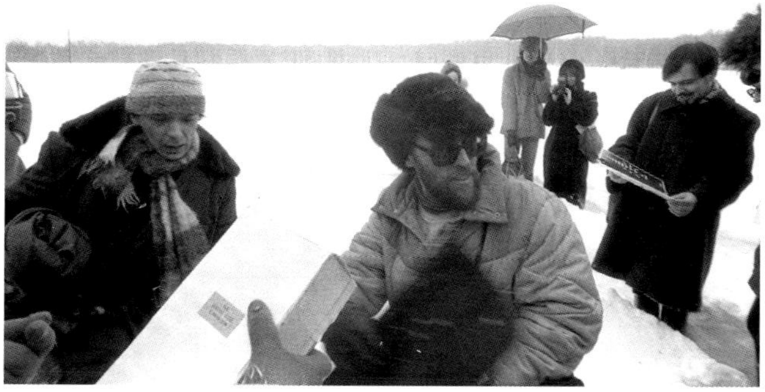

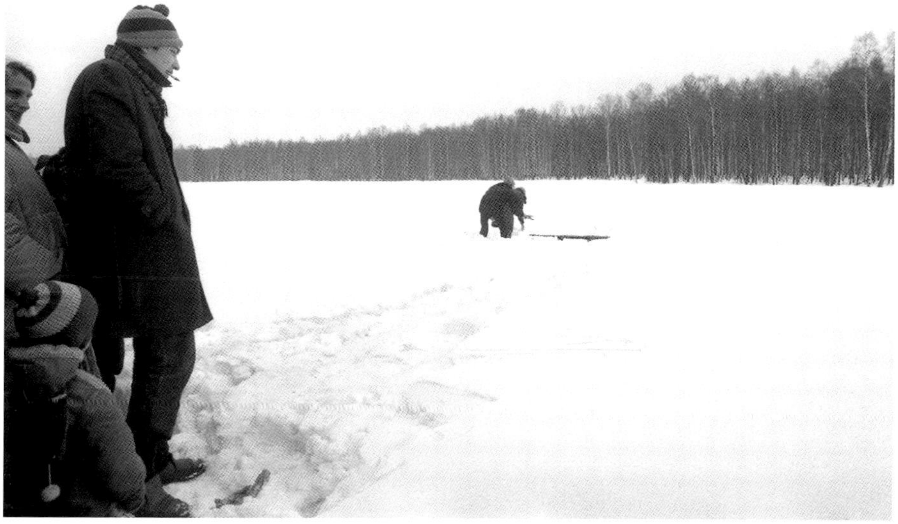

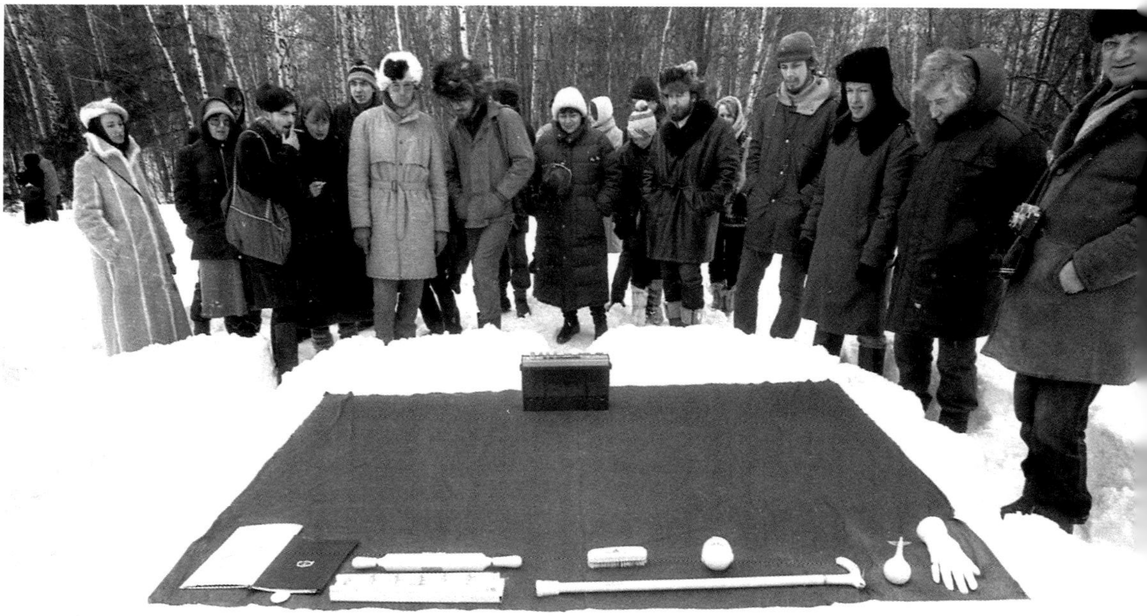

The Voices

Moscow, 4 January, 1985.

Collective Actions group:

A Monastyrski, S Romashko.

Viewers and participants:

I Kabakov, Vs Nekrasov, I Bakstein, V Sorokin, Yu Leiderman, A Zhigalov, N Abalakova, D Prigov, V Mochalova, L Rubinstein, S Hänsgen, S Letov and three others.

On the day before the action Monastyrski and Romashko recorded their conversation (45 minutes) which concerned the last year's action titled *Description of an Action* and the forthcoming *The Voices* during which the recording was to be used (see *The Dialogue*). In the course of the action, which took place indoors (at Monastyrski's apartment), Romashko and Monastyrski put on headphones and while listening to the recorded conversation, they started simultaneously vocalising it for the audience. Romashko repeated Monastyrski's words on the cassette, and *vice versa*.

At the same time a recording of I Kabakov's voice made during *Description of an Action* was being played back through speakers. After finishing vocalising the dialogue, the participants took off the headphones and switched off the tape recorder playing back I Kabakov's spoken report. Then Monastyrski read aloud the text prepared for the action titled *The Voices* (see text *With a Wheel in One's Head*).

The visual set-up of *The Voices* consists of a black box and three electric torches which are switched on and which jut out of the box. The box is then placed behind a balcony door, and a piece of black rubber cable is extended from a bathroom through an open window into the box. In order to conceal the box (and torches) it is placed on the floor in a space where it is not immediately noticeable.

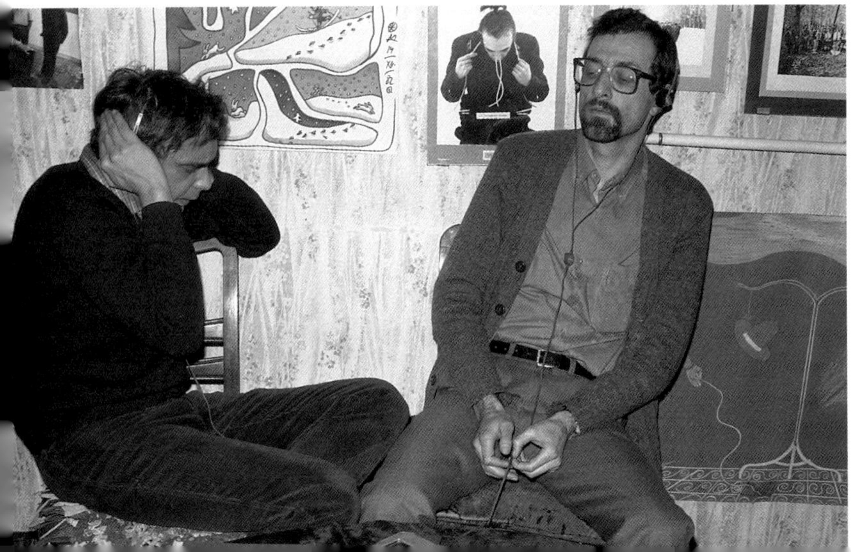

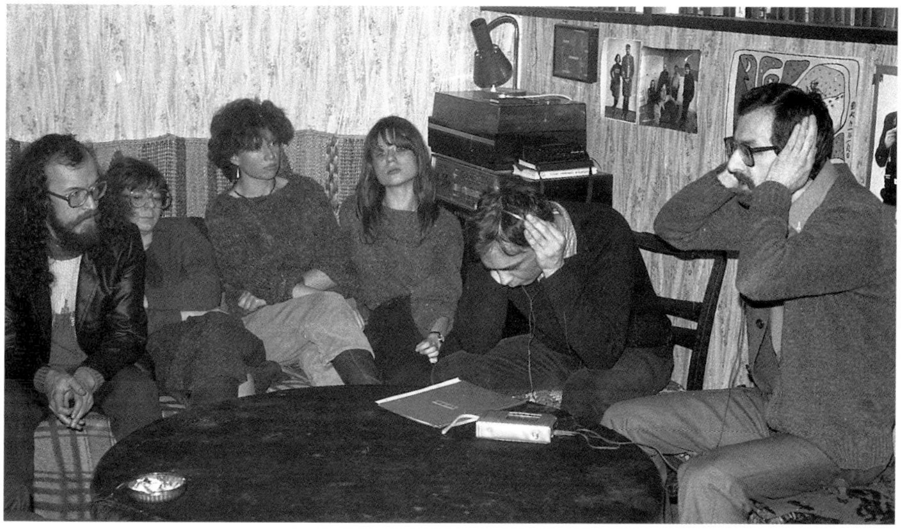

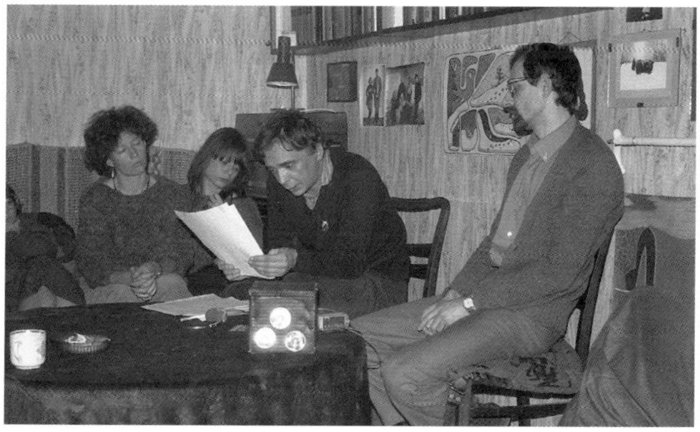

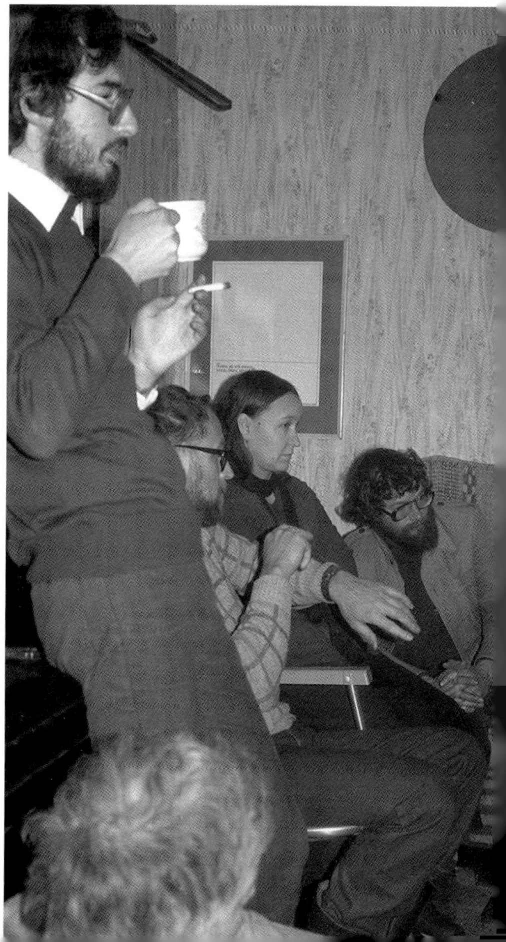

To I Makarevich
(Music of the meteorites)

Kyevy Gorky, 18 March, 1989.

Collective Actions group:

A Monastyrski, G Kitzevalter, E Elagina, S Romashko, N Panitkov, S Hänsgen.

Prior to Makarevich's arrival a black box (202 x 67 x 55 centimetres) with a circular hole on its upper side (21 centimetres in diameter) was installed at the action's scene. The box's base, with attached skis, was covered with snow. Inside the box there was a burning kerosene stove with a whistling kettle heating on it. Ten metres away from the box there was an armchair.

After approaching the scene Makarevich comforted himself in the armchair. 20 minutes later the kettle began to boil, the whistle sounded and clouds of steam poured from the hole in the box's upper side.

15 minutes later the water in the kettle had boiled away, and the whistling stopped. Makarevich approached the box and opened it. Then he discovered a rope attached to the box's front side and pulled it away from the scene.

In the course of the whole action a tape recorder hidden some 15 to 20 metres away from Makarevich's position (behind his back) produced the sound of a dog's barking.

Before the action's start a large lump of black paper with pieces of silver and golden tinfoil glued onto it was strung up between the trees on the field's side, invisible from the action's scene.

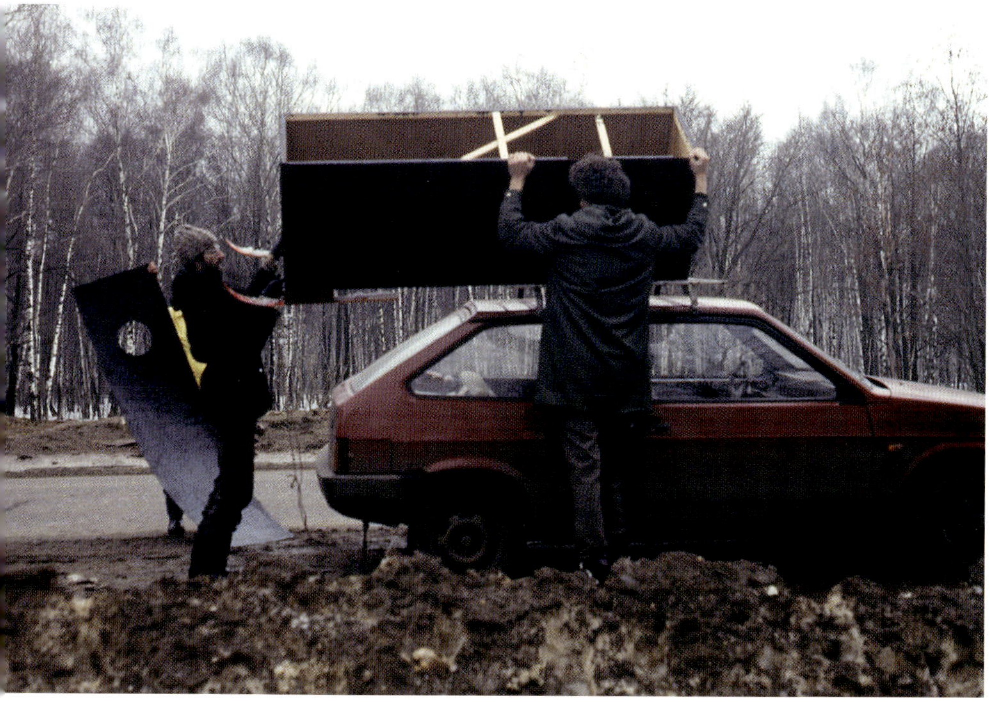

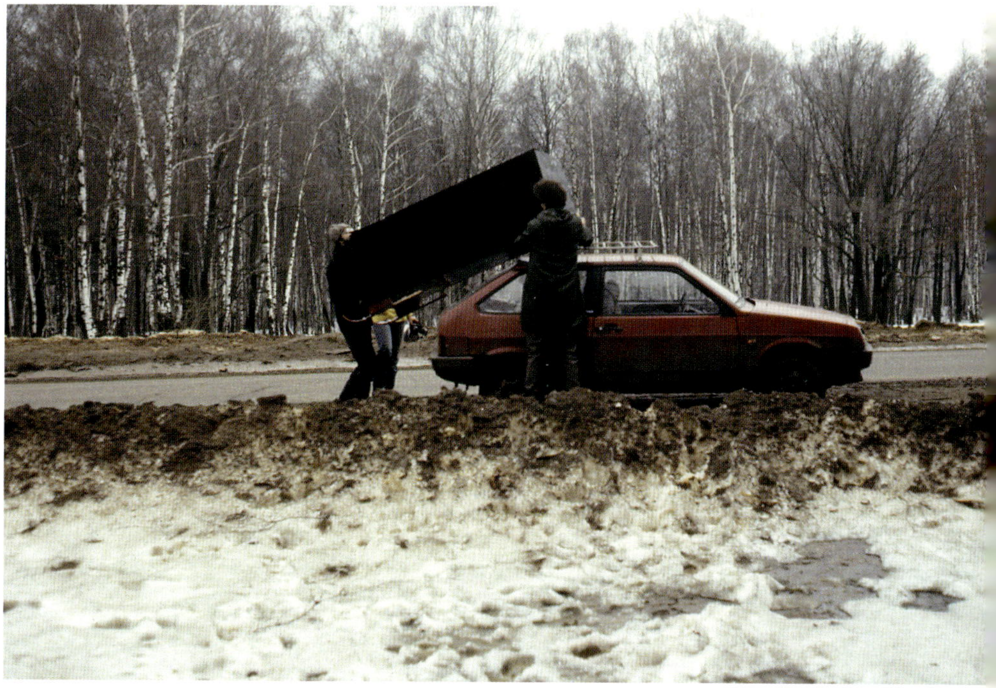

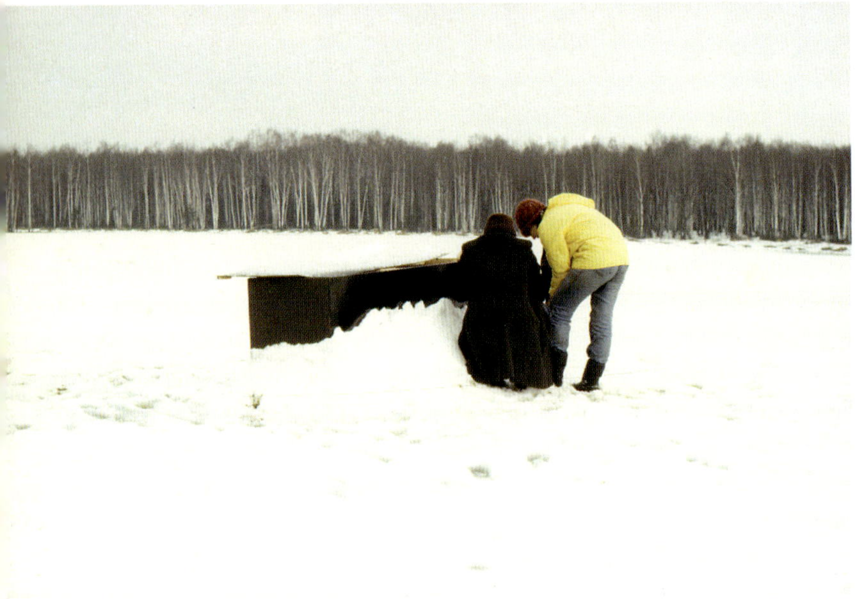

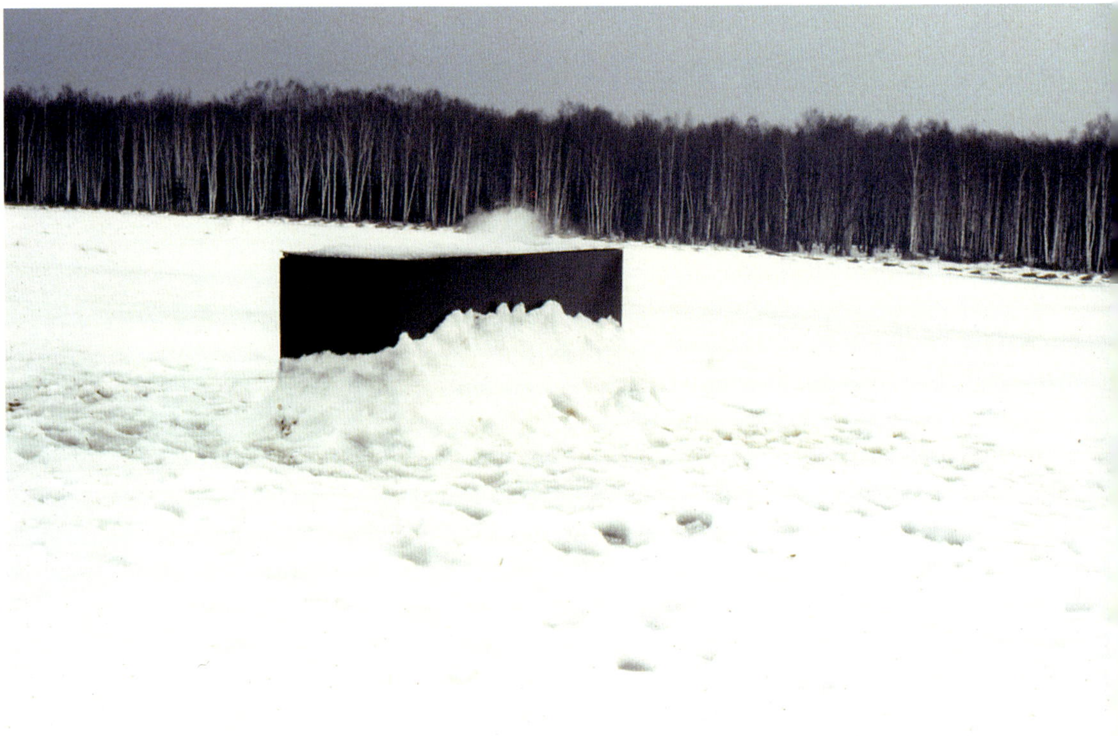

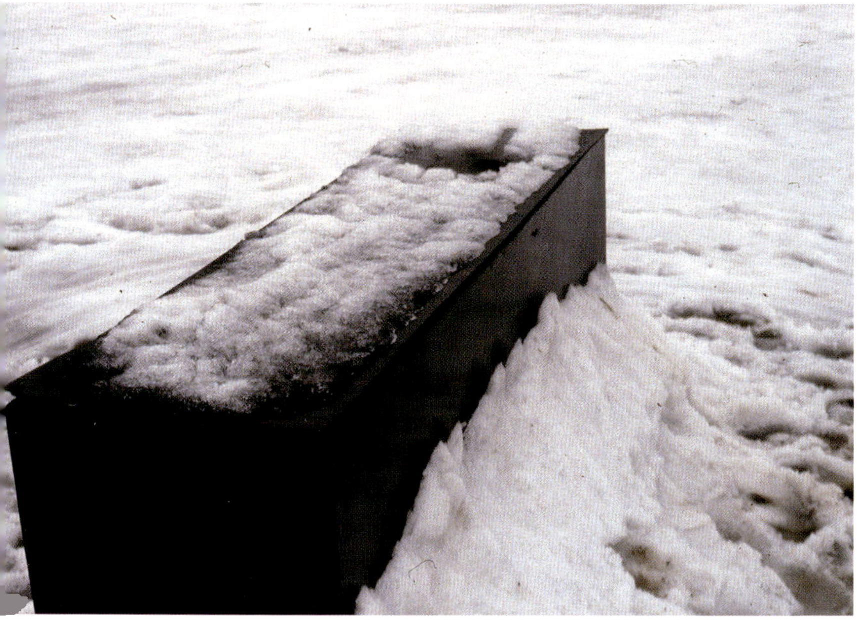

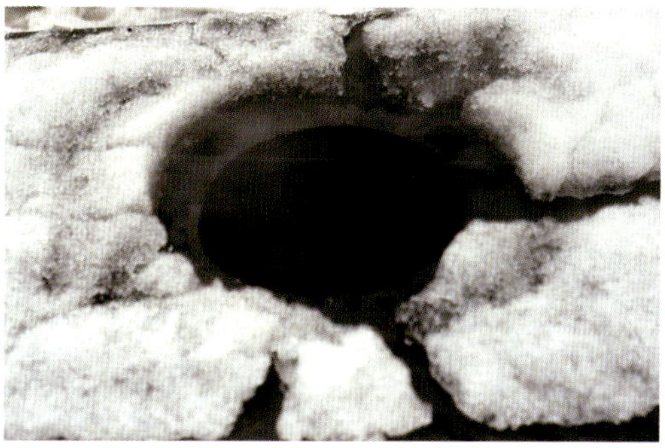

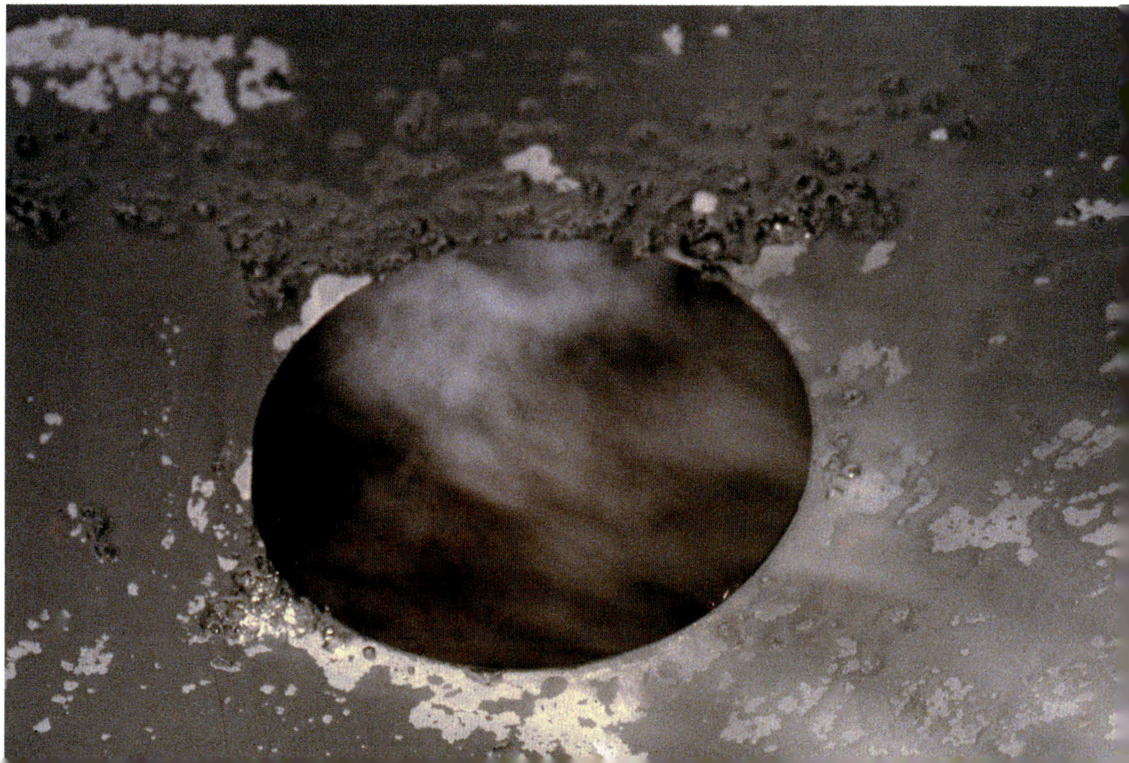

Rope

Moscow region, Losiny Ostrov, 11 March, 2007.

Collective Actions group:

A Monastyrski, N Panitkov, E Elagina, S Hänsgen, S Zagny, M Sumnina, D Novgorodova, I Makarevich.

Viewers:

M Riklin, Yu Kisina, Yu Leiderman, V Zaharov, M Prudominskaya, Yu Albert, O Sarkisyan, D Machulina, S Kalinin, M Krekotnev, Yu Ovchinnikova, I Buruy, M Leykin, A Zaytceva, G Medvedev, A Zhilyaev, S Ogurtcov, N Busheneva, I Trushevskiy, V Egorov, V Uzbashev, A Leksina.

The place for this action was found using the Google Earth software (a circular field, 260 metres in diameter, within the Losiny Ostrov region, approximately 1.5 kilometres east of the place where the action *Fisherman* took place in 2000).

The viewers (22 people), together with the organisers, began by moving through deep snow and, avoiding impenetrable foliage they traveled into the depths of a forest via a cutting through the trees. They travelled for about two kilometres until a field was reached. In the centre of this snowy field, was a white cardboard box and on top of this was a CD player, which played a recording entitled "German Romantics", a work composed by S Zagny especially for this action (69 minutes long).

Alongside the perimeter of the field and attached to trees were 21 portraits (A3 format paper attached to slightly larger cardboard sheets) of 22 German Romantics (the Brothers Grimm constituted one portrait). They were arranged in the following sequence:

Ludwig Achim von Arnim, 1781–1831, Jacob Grimm, Wilhelm Grimm, Friedrich Schleiermacher, 1768–1834, Ludwig Tieck, 1773–1853, Friedrich Schlegel, 1772–1829, Adelbert von Chamisso, 1781–1838, Joseph von Eichendorff, 1788–1857, Bettina von Arnim, 1785–1859, Heinrich von Kleist, 1777–1811, Clemens Brentano, 1778–1842, Ernst Theodor Amadeus Hoffmann, 1776–1822, Wilhelm Hauff, 1802–1827, Jean (Johann) Paul Friedrich Richter, 1763–1825, Johann Joseph von Görres, 1776–1848, Friedrich de la Motte Fouqué, 1777–1843, August Wilhelm Schlegel, 1767–1845, Novalis (Friedrich von Hardenberg) 1772–1801, Ludwig Uhland, 1787–1862, Eduard Mörike, 1804–1875, Karoline von Günderrode, 1780–1806, Wilhelm Heinrich Wackenroder, 1773–1798.

Small holes were made in the right lower corner of each of the cardboard portraits and two metre pieces of the rope were installed. This was done for each of the portraits except Kleist's portrait, which was 6 x 6 cm and enclosed in a metal frame under glass. Once all the portraits had rope attached, two viewers (Leiderman and Medvedev) were asked to walk around the field and to gather in all the ropes (i.e. to remove the rope from the portraits) and to bring them to the centre of the field where the box and CD player were located.

The ropes (20 pieces) were placed inside the box. The recording "German Romantics" was changed to "It's Better than World War II" (47:54) (a recording of a dialogue between Monastyrski and Panitkov, recorded for this performance the day before). Once this was done the viewers started to make their way back through the forest. The CD player, still playing the second recording, was passed through the chain of participants (each kept the player for about two minutes). The portraits of the German Romantics were left in the field.

At approximately 250 metres from the end of the forest and amidst the cutting into the forest was a spindly tree. The box used in the action was attached to this tree at a height of two metres. On one side of the box a big sign in black letters proclaimed the word: "ROPE". Pieces of rope had been taken out of the box in advance, and were handed to the viewers as a 'factography' along with laminated sheets (A5 format) with signed portraits of the Romantics (there had been no signatures on the portraits suspended in the field). Approximately half of the portraits distributed to the viewers were the same as the portraits in the field with the others painted by different artists and showing the Romantics at different ages.

The empty box with the "ROPE" sign was left on the tree. The viewers and organisers departed the forest (the total distance from the clearing in the snowy forest to the field was about five kilometres).

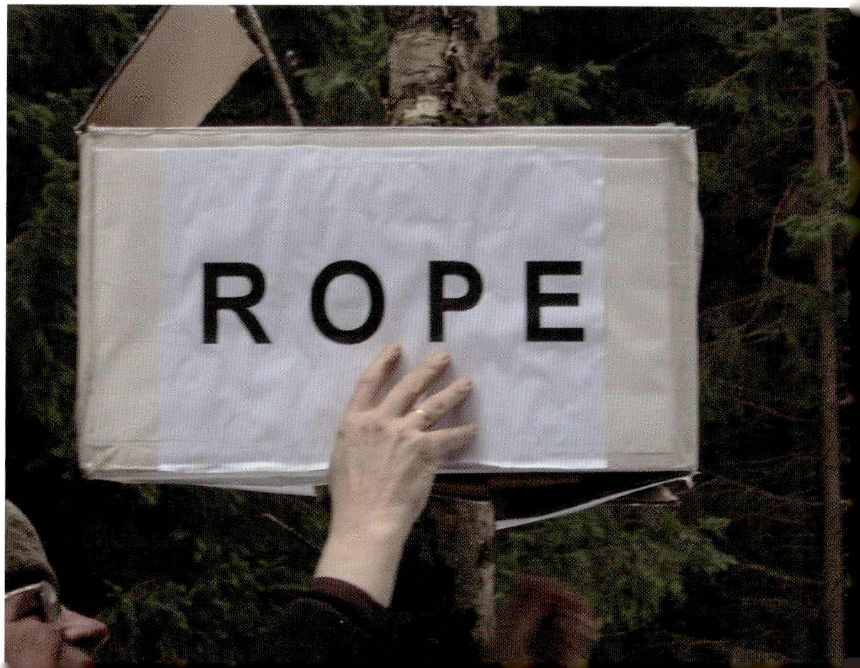

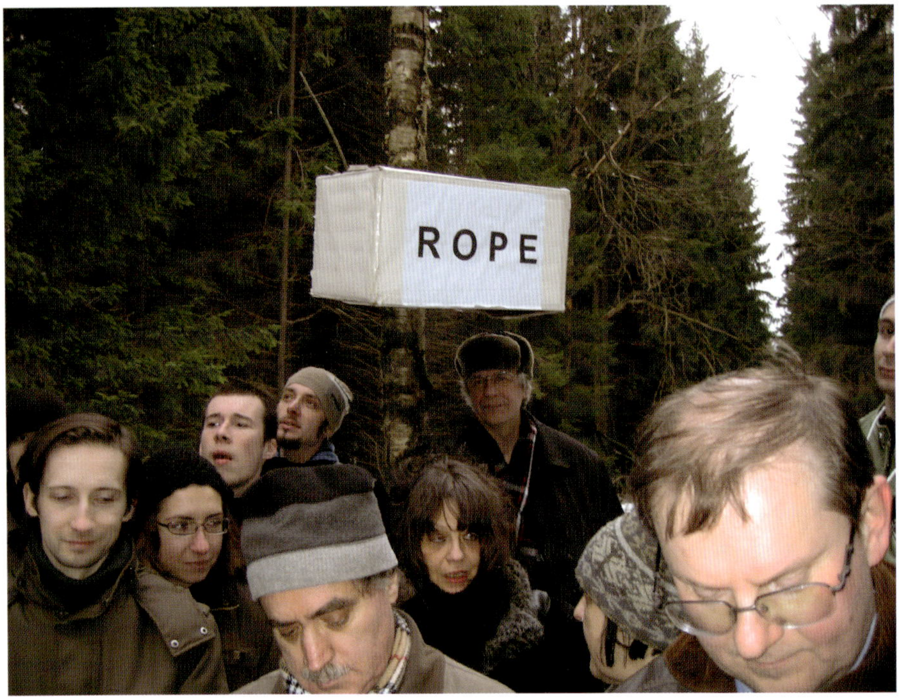
ROPE

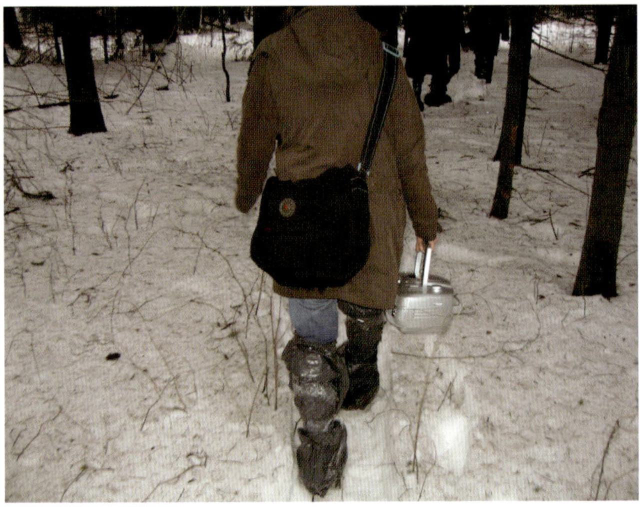

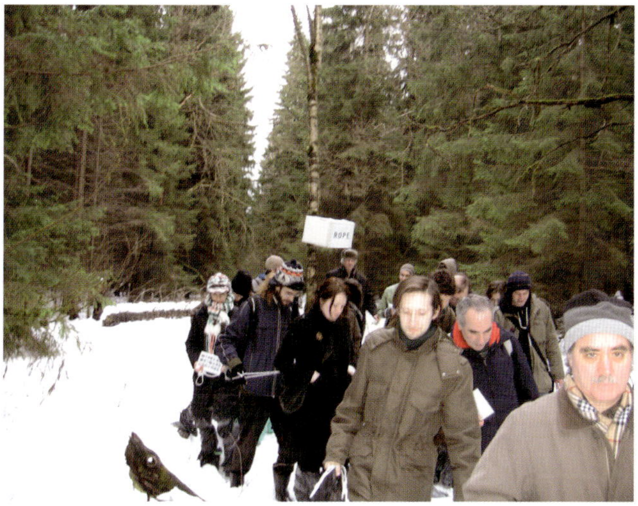
ROPE

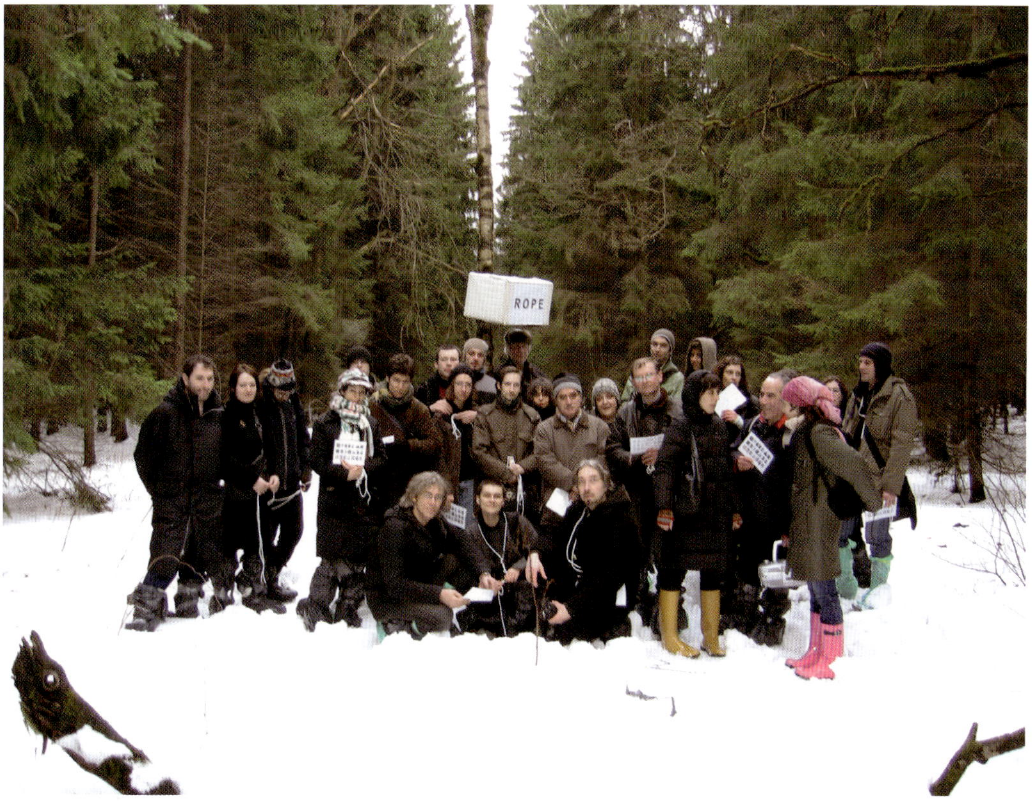
ROPE

Collective Actions and *Trips out of Town* The Aesthetics of Collective Actions

Andrei Monastyrski

On becoming acquainted with the activities of the Collective Actions through an exhibition, most often the foundational aspect of this activity remains hidden—i.e. *Trips out of Town*. Under this title, we published and still publish volumes of documentation about the performances made over the 34 years of the group's work (ten have been published altogether). If the very problem of *Trips out of Town* as a genre with its textual components is not correctly understood, then the whole problematic stratigraphy of documentation—with its descriptions, narrative and discourse—may appear to be merely tedious, bureaucratic psychosis. The question arises, why in fact did some minimal actions in nature give birth to such voluminous "textcretion", and specifically in such a complex and—to an outside eye—muddled form. The point is that on the meta-level of textual criticism (which is indeed a product of this "complexity") in each of these textual layers, only one subject is discussed, and experienced—the subject of the border between town and non-town ("out of town").

It is difficult to adequately translate from Russian into any other language the very phrase *"poezdki za gorod"* (trips out of town), since in this region the town does not constitute that stable textological element of socio-topographical description, which it constitutes in the Western discursive context. When someone says that he is travelling "out of town" in Russia, everyone understands what he means, although no localisation in the process of this telling-understanding takes place. It might refer to anything at all—a *dacha*, village, river, forest, some sort of worker's settlement or even just a smaller town (if the act of leaving takes place from Moscow, for example). In other words, the semantic *field* of the concept "out of town" is very blurry, indeterminate, and, as such, in the psychological sense mentally charged and erogenous. Out of town, the very 'out of town-ness' here is more of a metaphysical, and if not 'transcendent' then at least a 'transcendental' character (taking this term in the sense of an "applied, instrumental transcendence" used for mental conceptions and efforts).

It is clear that under such circumstances—since "out of town" is conceptually paired with "town"—the city itself is metamorphosed. Actually, this whole problem of the border between the "town" and the "out of town" can be explained more simply, phrasing it using the legal term of the process of urbanisation, "enclosure".

But in this case it would simply become the well-known historical perspective and analogy, whilst the textual aspect would be 'overwhelmed' and destroyed by such a 'forceful' and 'clear' concept. Whereas in our case, with *Trips out of Town* as a genre, we are dealing with a relatively nuanced textological treatment of the very presence of the as-yet still developing relationship "between town and village" (it was using this exact phrasing, by the way, that this problem was described—from the 1920s onwards—in the official Soviet ideological discourse. There was constant discussion of the "merging of town and village").

And so, when certain spaces have yet to take on their more or less 'completed aspect' (in this case these spaces are the "out of town", and the "town"), there arises a heightened emotional (i.e. non-functional) relationship to these space-'objects', which are described using all kinds of 'seductive' metaphors—they are compared to something, their definitions shimmer, the contours of these spaces vibrate and so on. As a result of all this, a kind of *plot* appears, in actual fact—a 'novel'. And so *Trips out of Town* constitutes this kind of 'novel' with relatively complex story lines, episodes, 'characters in progress' and so on.

Plots can be written in various manners—naturalistic, romantic, philosophical—whichever. We wrote it in a 'structural-metaphysical' manner, sort of 'speculatively-exaltedly', since, as it seems to me, this manner is isomorphic to the actual state of affairs: after all, these two spaces—out-of-town and town—really do remain, to this day, in the condition of abstract relations, in a condition of uncompleted moments of contact between the two. And in this "plot of contacts" there are a lot of "empty spaces", pauses, expectations—in other words that very same minimalism, in the style of which the majority of our actions are made.

The tension in the linguistic field between town and out-of-town, the breadth of this field were what gave birth—through the united efforts of the members of Collective Actions and their viewer-interpreters—to the textological *field* of the ten volumes of our *Trips out of Town*. The dual meaning of the word "field" plays a relatively important role here—after all, the main actions of "contact" in this story took place on an actual field. That is why this real field, on which certain aesthetic manipulations took place, easily metamorphosed, first into the linguistic, and then into the textological ('novel').

It is curious to note that the main 'erotic' intrigue or attraction—specifically now on a textological level—emanated from the "town" as a character in the 'novel'. After all, in the title *Trips out of Town* the town itself is not named, or rather: from whence are the trips out of town made? Although the implication is—and it was the case in actual fact—that the trips were made from the town to "out of town". In other words in contrast to the usual process of urbanisation, according to which it is more of a case of displacement towards the town, in this case, the plot was built around the opposite—it was the "out of town" that was thought of as the object of desire (which, for example, I Kabakov always emphasised in his accounts of the actions) and it was only later (only in the Second Volume) that any actions were undertaken in the town, in which the town in some way laid itself bare, de-metaphorised itself and in some sense 'took on a face' and became a 'character' in this story. It could be said that a relationship was achieved, with boundaries, albeit complicated, but boundaries nonetheless.

Any sustained relationship requires serious *stylistic* efforts, and the 34 years of work on this particular plot within the framework of Collective Actions, and then beyond this framework, is a relatively long duration for a 'novel'. That is why style played a significant role for us, and often a painful one, affecting for the members of the group's relationships with one another. Style in its widest sense can be understood as the ability to manipulate the knowledge, the experience, that has been accrued by others. At the same time, style is a kind of restraining of feelings, if we apply it to character traits. For us, dealing with a difficult and tense plot, Buddhism for example, was very important as a mental style, and minimalism as an aesthetic one. Most probably it was these two styles that took on the function of a kind of 'restraining' factor, guaranteeing the textological duration of the plot. But at the same time in any plot certain "bright spots" appear, certain enlivening "flashes", for which we made use of the discursive-plastic practices of romanticism, psychedelia, post-structural 'schizoanalyse'.

In this short text I do not have the goal of examining the entire 'literature' of *Trips out of Town*—literature in every sense, in both the sense of 'bibliography' and of plot. I simply wanted to point to the textological aspect of *Trips* in its 'pre-emptive' meaning in relation to Collective Actions' literature.

The source of the visual plastics, the visual spaces of performance in *Trips* deserves a separate examination. I will only say that the source of this visuality should be sought—amongst other things—also in the phenomenon of "speech", marked by the poetical-textological singularity of "voice" in its gradual transgression from the pictographic to the hieroglyphic, and then into spatio-depictive propositions, taken as a broad spectrum—from abstract—"empty" (geometrical) spaces to architectural discourse. I could refer any reader who might be particularly interested in this problematic to my poetical-aesthetic research in *Elementary Poetry*, 1975, and to my articles of the late 1980s about the architectural discourse of the VDNKh and several other urban spaces in Moscow, Volume Four of *Trips out of Town*).

I am purposefully individualising my remarks here regarding Collective Actions since each member of the group could and should have their own view on the group's work. Yet at the same time, and this is perhaps the most important thing that I would like to say here, personally for me the plot of Collective Actions is not the same as the plot of *Trips out of Town*, the textology of which I imagine to be wider (both in the spatial and the temporal sense) than the already existing literature of Collective Actions.

[redacted]

The aesthetic discourse of Collective actions was always built, to a large extent, not on the actual acts of art (what was shown to the viewers during the performance) but, rather, on the *accompanying* materials: the parameters of the trip to the "place of action", the departure from it, certain secondary events that did not relate directly to the plan for the actions and so on. In other words, the discussion and commentary also included those zones of practice where art does not yet dominate the everydayness of life. For example, a group of viewers gathers at the train station in order to travel to an action by Collective Actions. The journey to the place of action might stretch to an hour and a half—about 40 minutes on the suburban train, then waiting for the bus, then about 20 minutes on the bus and about 20 minutes' walk to the field. In this hour and a half of displacement out of town from Moscow, it would seem that there is no art. And yet, in some sense, there already is—after all, the viewers already know about the event that awaits them, they have been united into a *group* with a defined aim: to travel to a field, in order to view an action. Having gathered at the station, they have already entered into the preliminary demonstrative zone of the action. All of these preliminary zones, the zones of "after the action" and so on were included by us in the structure of the aesthetic discourse by the inclusion of large 'pauses' within the events, the actions, from the very beginning of Collective Actions' work. We call these pauses during the performance's unfolding the "empty actions", and describe them as "extra-demonstrational time in the flowing of events". For example, some viewers gather on the edge of the field. A participant comes out of the woods, walks a little way across the field towards the middle and lays down in a hole. He is no longer visible. Time stretches on. Two minutes go by, five minutes, ten. The field is empty. Where is the participant? Is he lying in the hole or has he crawled away somewhere? Is the action still going on or did it end long ago, in the moment when the participant lay down in the hole? The viewers have no idea.

Take another example; a group of viewers gather on a sunny April day on an empty snowy field. Under the snow, a bell is ringing. Nothing else happens. The viewers leave the field. The bell is left behind to ring. Is the action over or not? After all, the bell is still ringing! The viewers do not know this. It only becomes clear afterwards, when they become acquainted with the *descriptive text* of the action and with the commentaries relating to it. It is these elements of the "not-happening" that we call the "empty action". Similar kinds of pauses were used by Cage (think of his composition "4.33"). There is a lot of "empty expectation" in Kabakov's albums and in his large 'empty' works.

These pauses have their own paradigmatic line, their own rhythm. But they are built not in relation to other—event-based—elements of the actions, but on a wider horizon of the occurring, on the border between art and life, the point where life is in the state of *awaiting* art, and art, in its turn, awaits life. Of course, this is a situation of 'uncertainty'—from a psychological point of view. But from the point of view of aesthetic discourse as a constituent part of theorising, this uncertainty, which is permanent, becomes a *problem*, the source for the construction of aesthetic instruments, through which the contemplative possibilities of art are examined.

And so, these pauses within the action actualise other pauses, and specifically those occurring prior to the event of action, those that follow it and those spaces of processing material where the commenting, discussing, evaluating and so on, take place. These spaces 'before' and 'after', and the factographic spaces are in fact the principal object of aesthetic interest of Collective Actions. It is specifically in them that the true 'event-ness' of our "actions" unfolds—and not simply on the field in front of the viewers. Our 'artistic' elements, from which the actions are constructed, can equally be found both in art and in everyday life, for example—"group", "person in the distance", "walking", "departure", "noise", "light" and so on. Sometimes it can be quite difficult to separate the things that take place according to the plan of action, from the things that take place in the same place, at the same time, simply by themselves, on the level of the everyday. We could say that elements of Collective Actions' actions are citations from real life, 'ready made', taken from the free zone of incidental perceptions: "a person appeared from around the corner, walked across the field, disappeared in the forest, a cyclist went by, the wind bent the tops of the trees" and so forth.

In my articles examining the discourse of Collective Actions, I call this "free zone of incidental perceptions", the exhibitory sign-field, examining it in relation to the demonstrational sign-field, which includes all of these spatial-temporal events, planned by the artistic operation of the action. In our actions it is specifically this exhibitory field that is examined, whilst the demonstrative field (the artistic event itself) is posited as a system of observational positions, 'viewing platforms', from which the contemplation of exhibitory spaces takes place. What is more, this enlightenment, as a rule, takes place after the event, not during the action itself, but in the text—in the debates, articles, commentaries and so forth.

The activity of Collective Actions can equally be ascribed to literature (the novel), to the visual arts (the history of performance) and to music (audio-discourse). At various points in time, one or another of these readings of the materials of the Collective Actions group becomes 'dominant'. Collective Actions never made art in the sense implied when some sort of result-yielding activity is spoken of, or the creation of concrete art works. The meta-position of Collective Actions is an aesthetic practice, an aesthetic discourse. For us, it was always the process that was important, and not the result. This is easy to understand if one is ready to distinguish *poesis* (or *melos*) from poetry (or music) itself, having correctly placed the contemplative accents—the spatial and the temporal (space and time are the true 'heroes' and 'characters' of *Trips out of Town*, and not the viewers or us, the authors and creators of the actions).

EARTH WORKS

Andrei Monastyrski, 1987

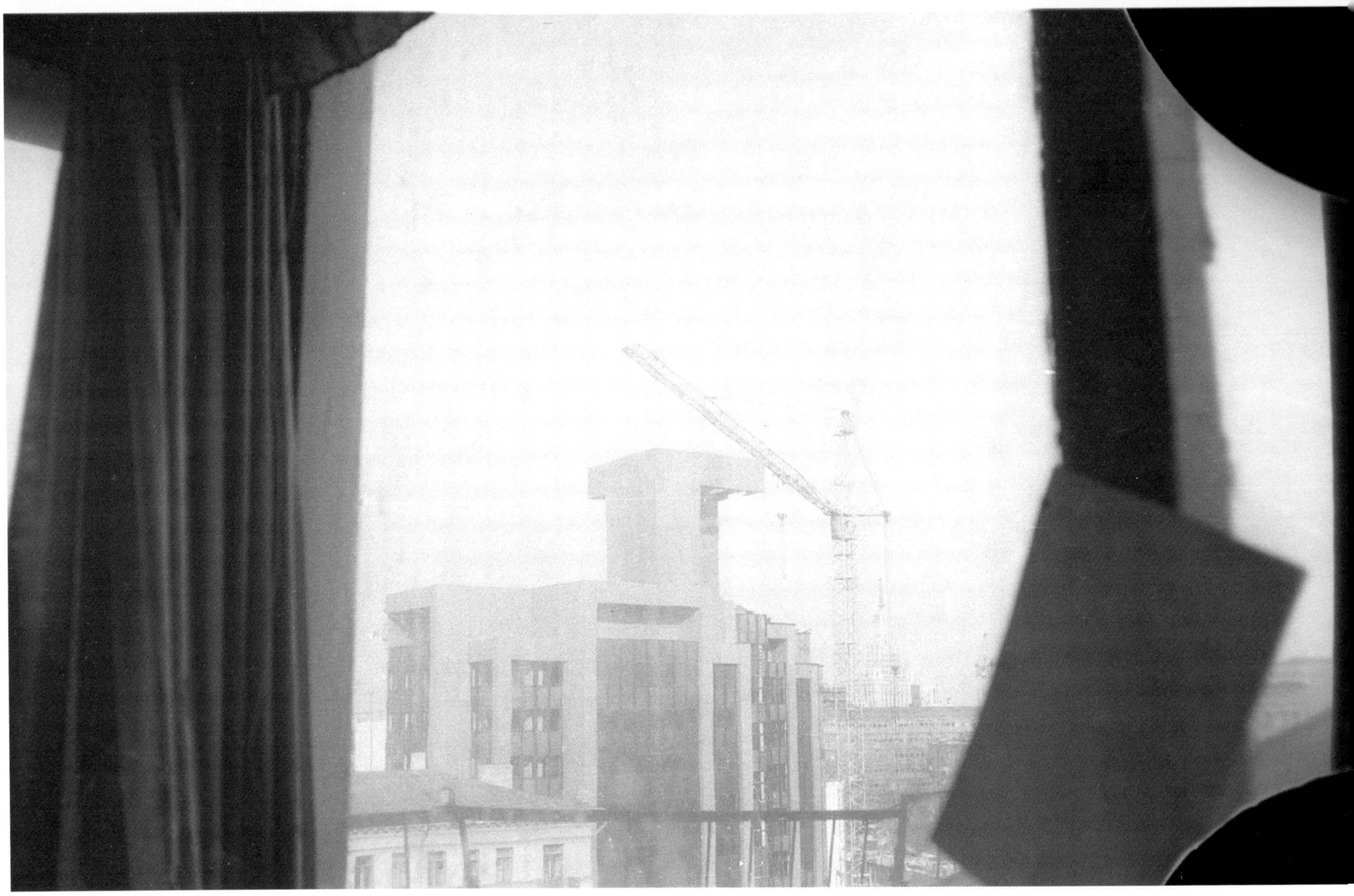

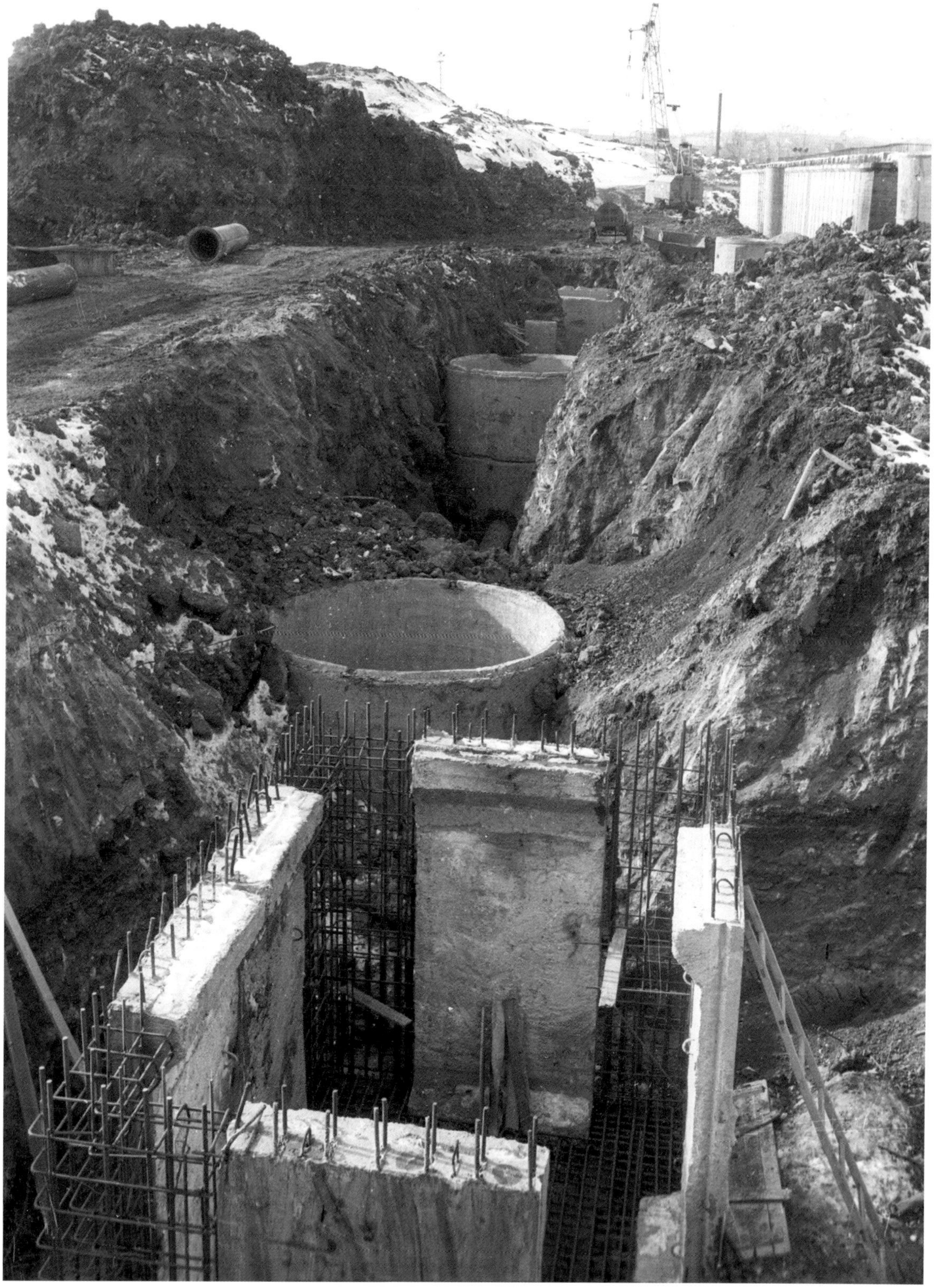

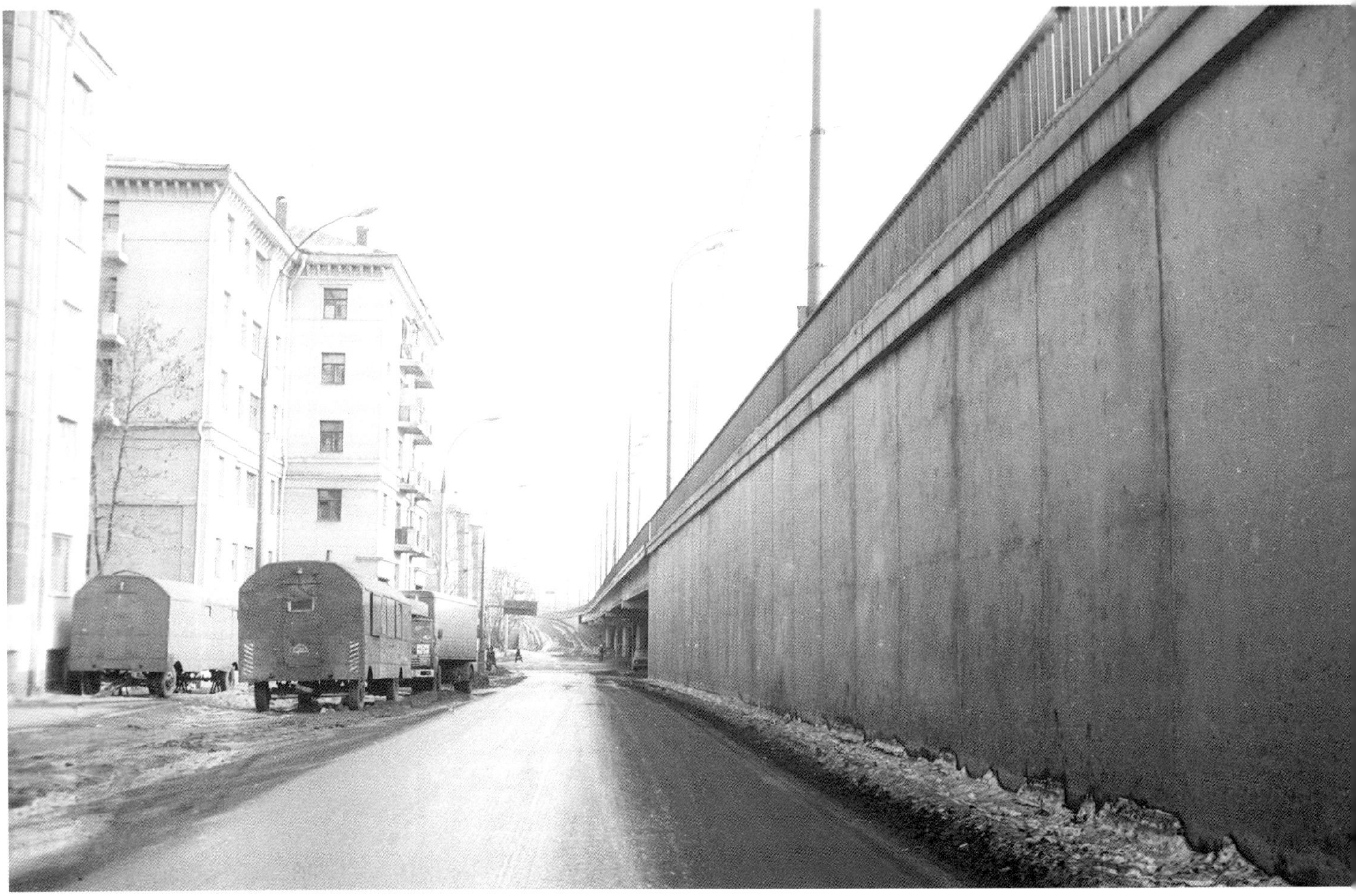

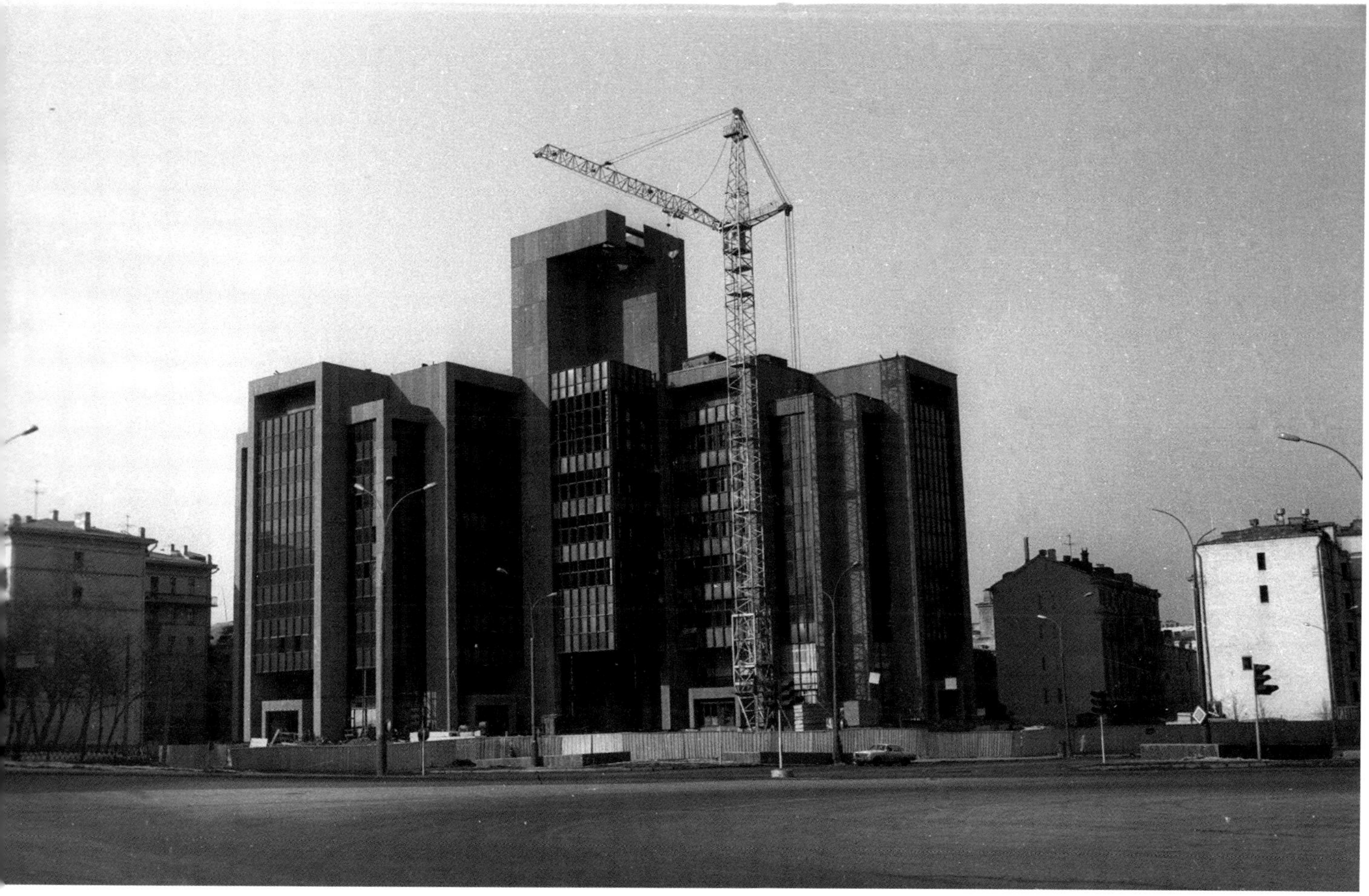

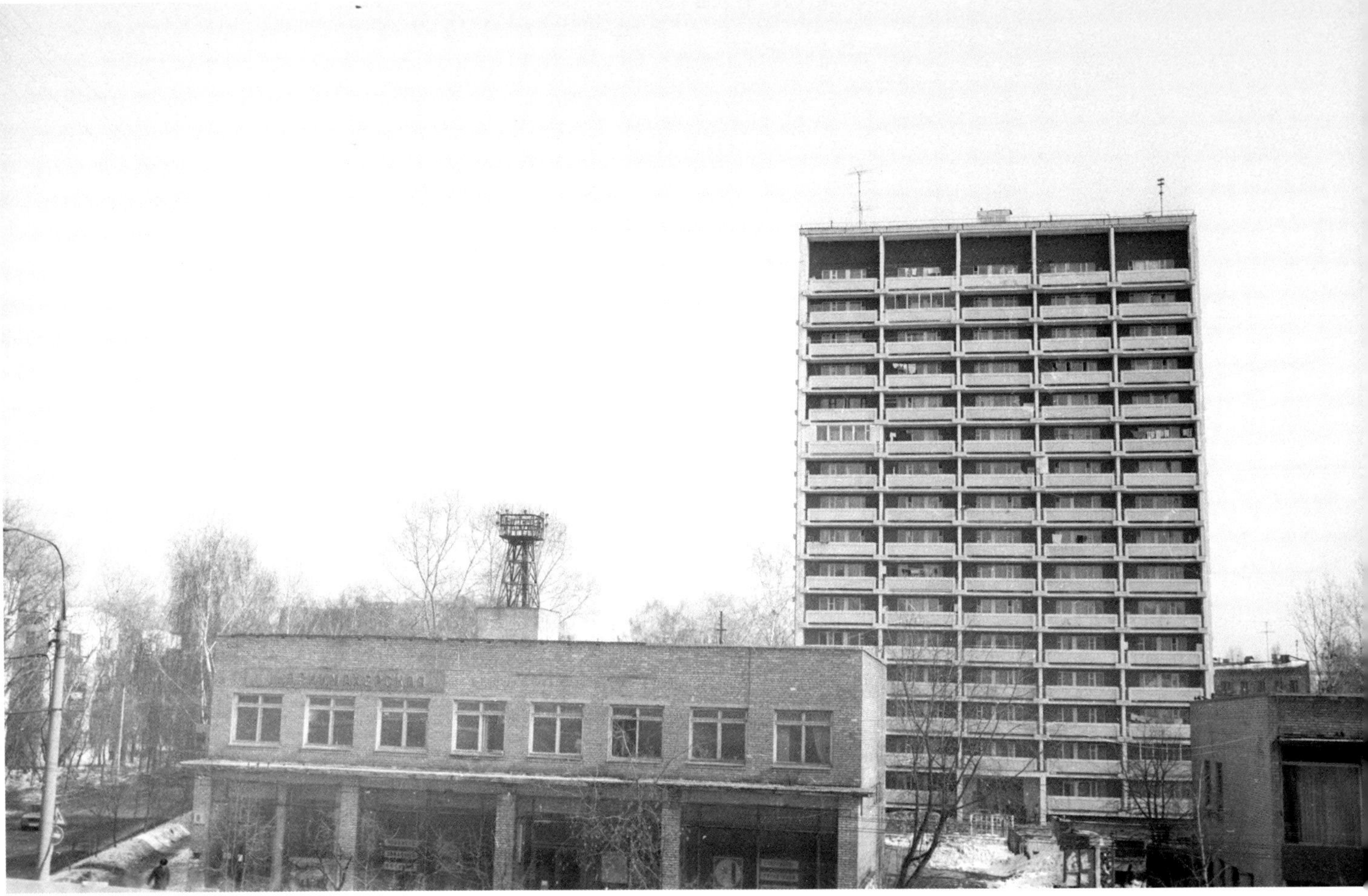

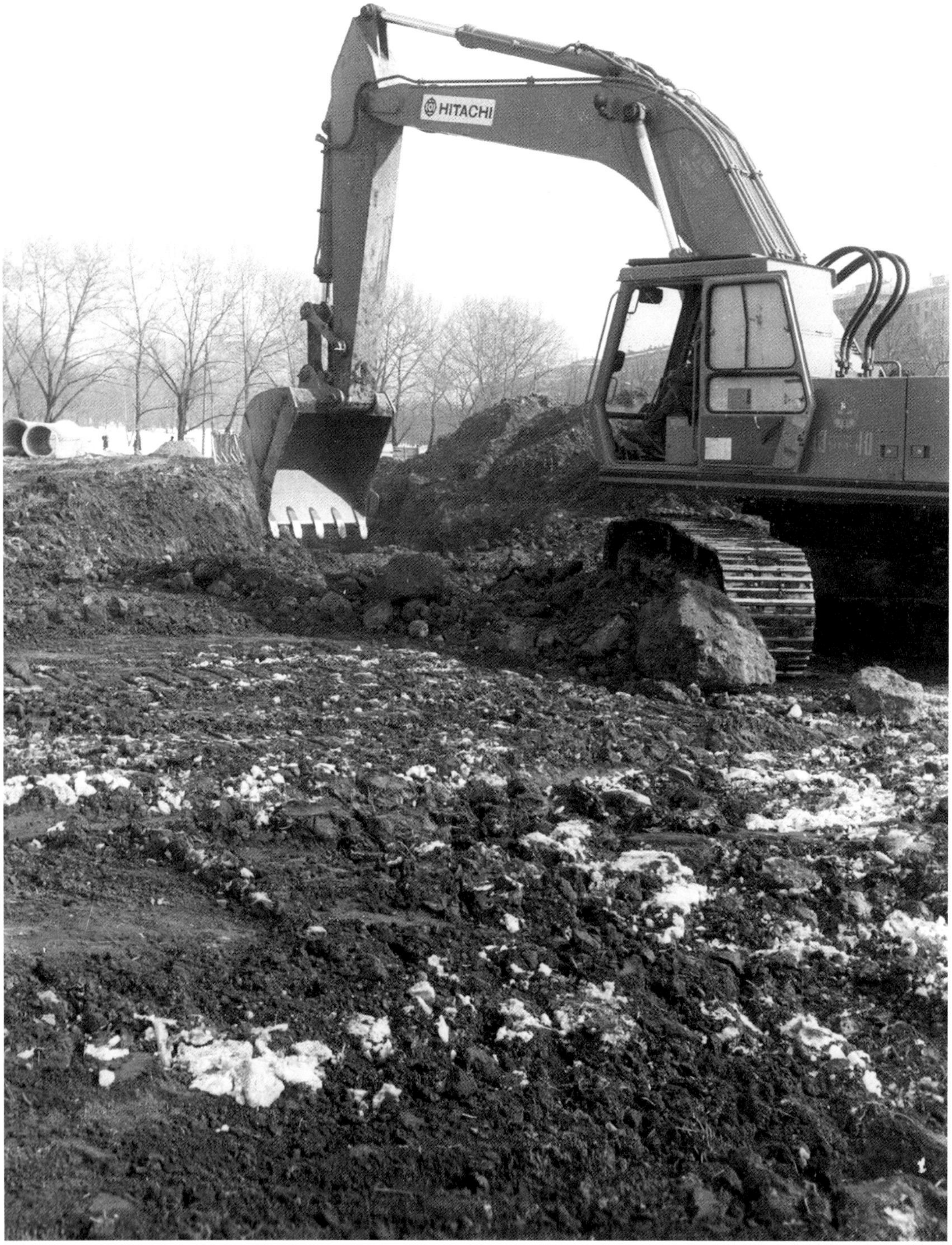
HITACHI

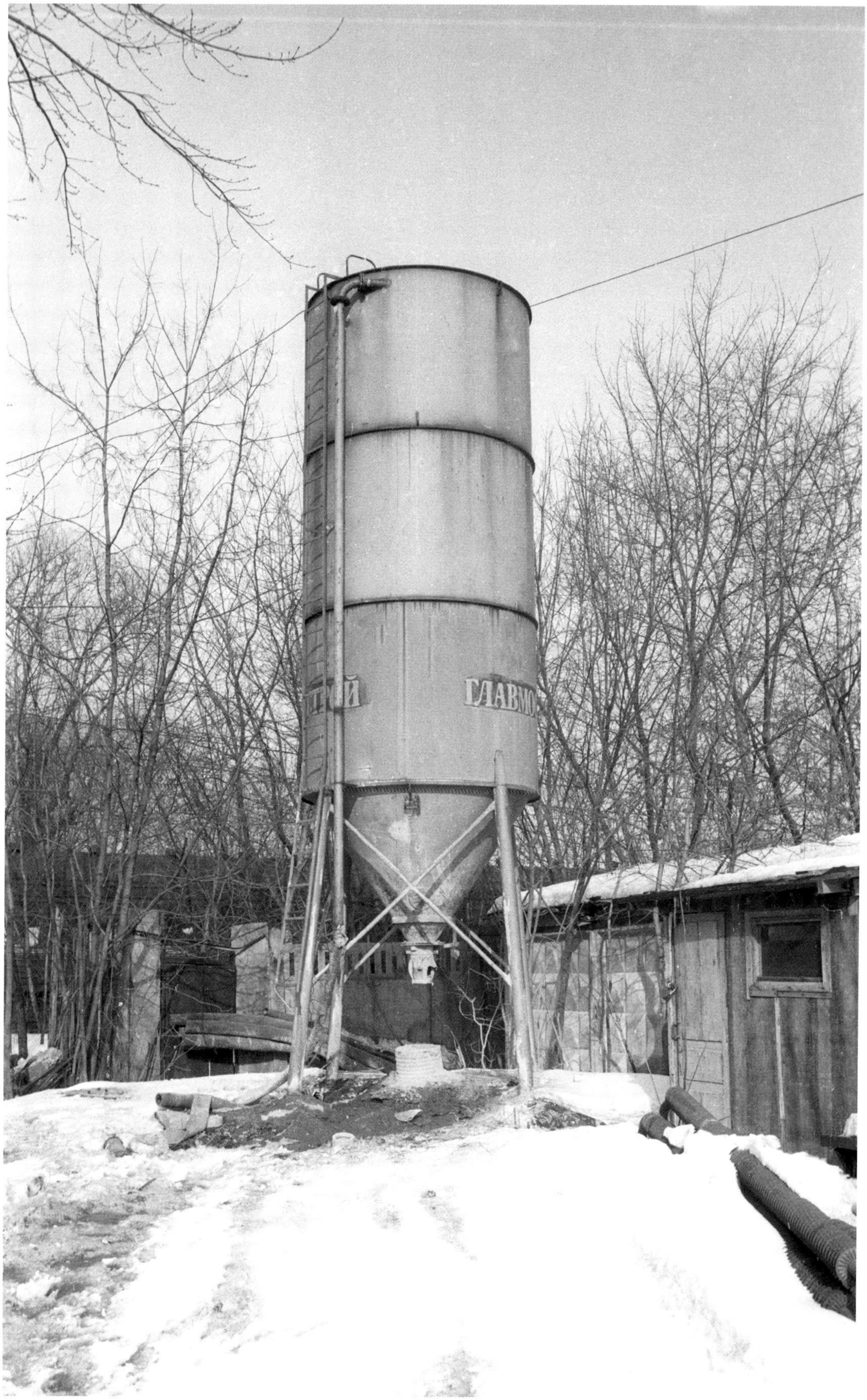
ГЛАВМО

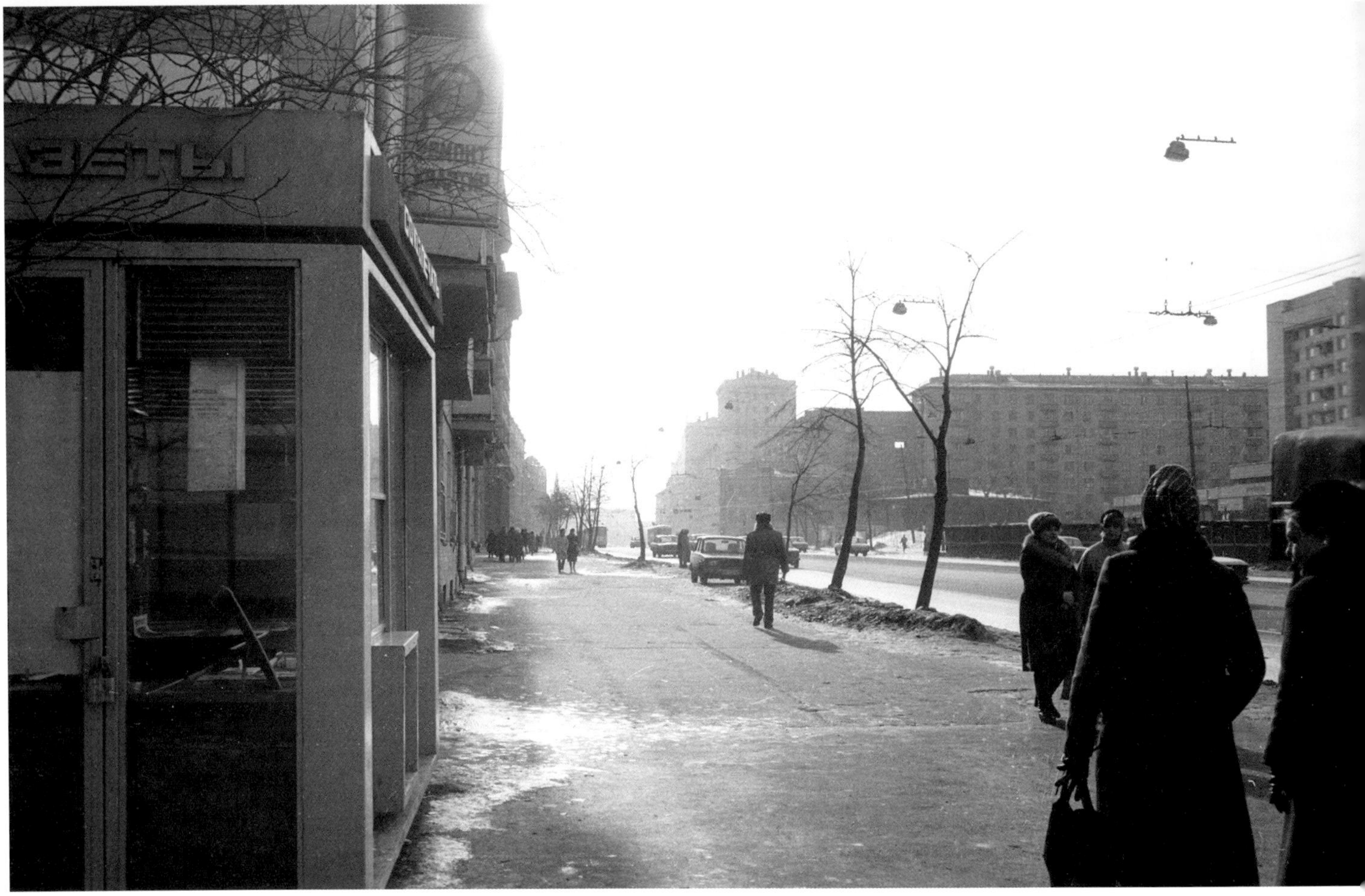

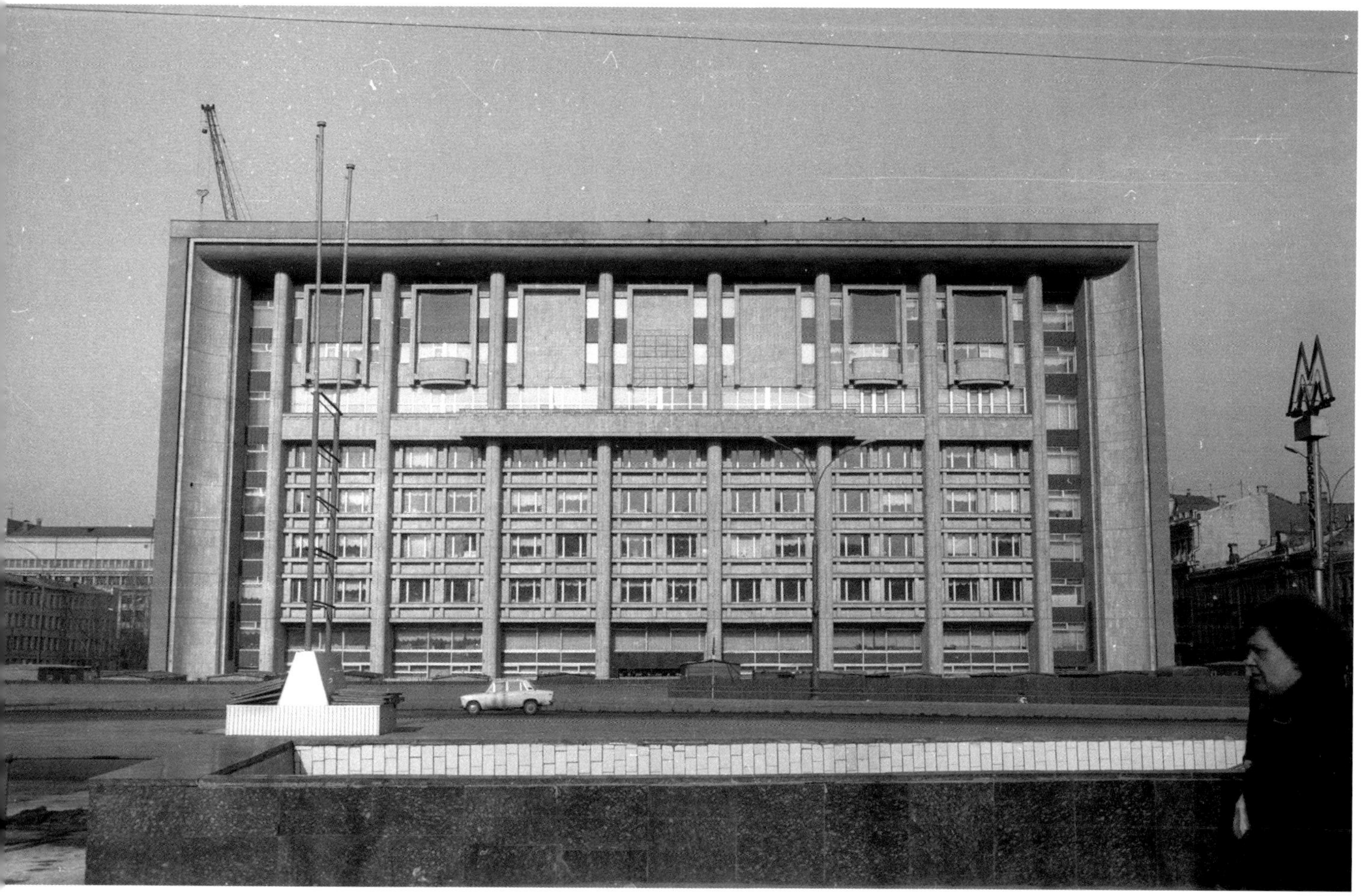

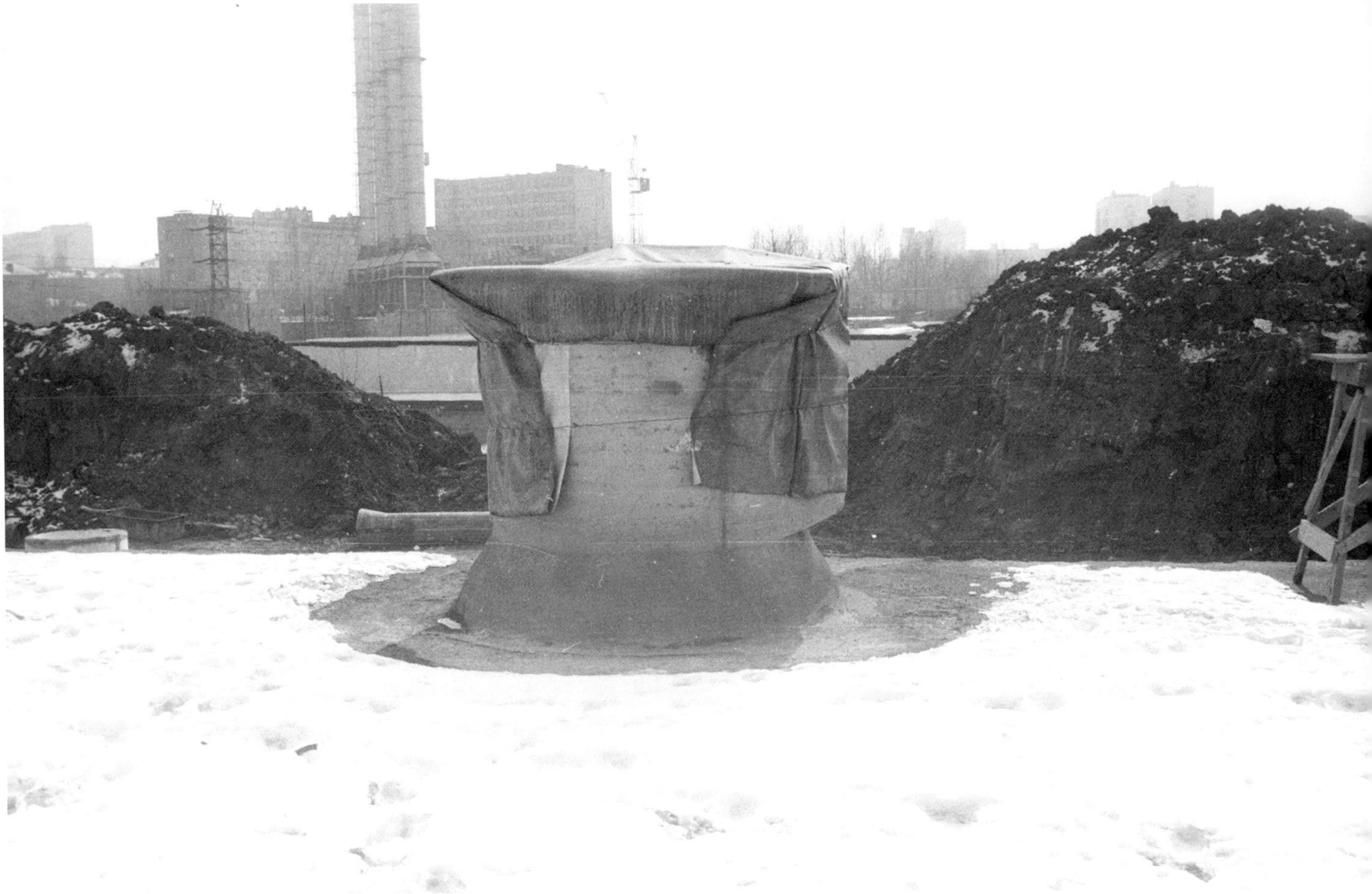

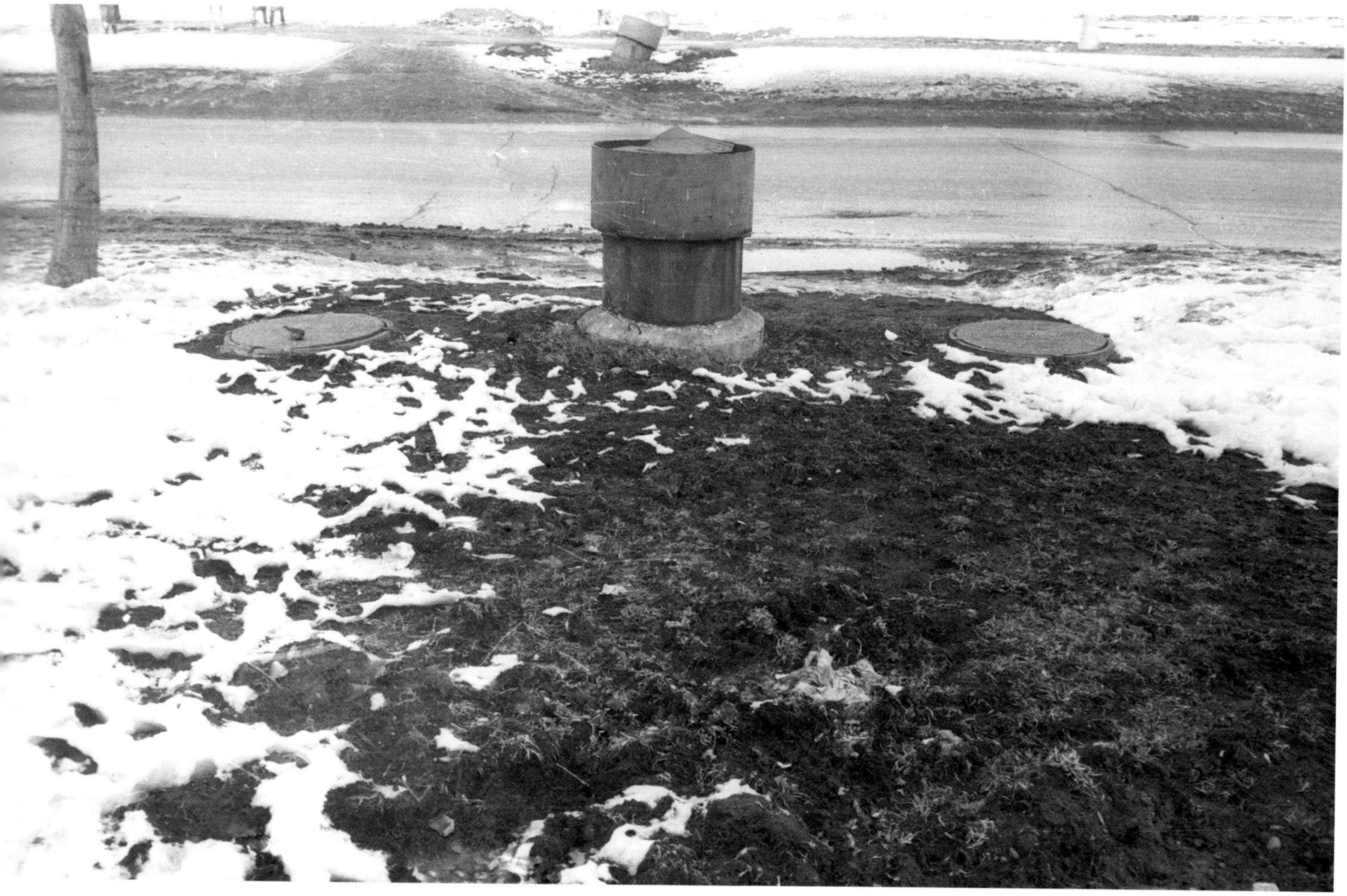

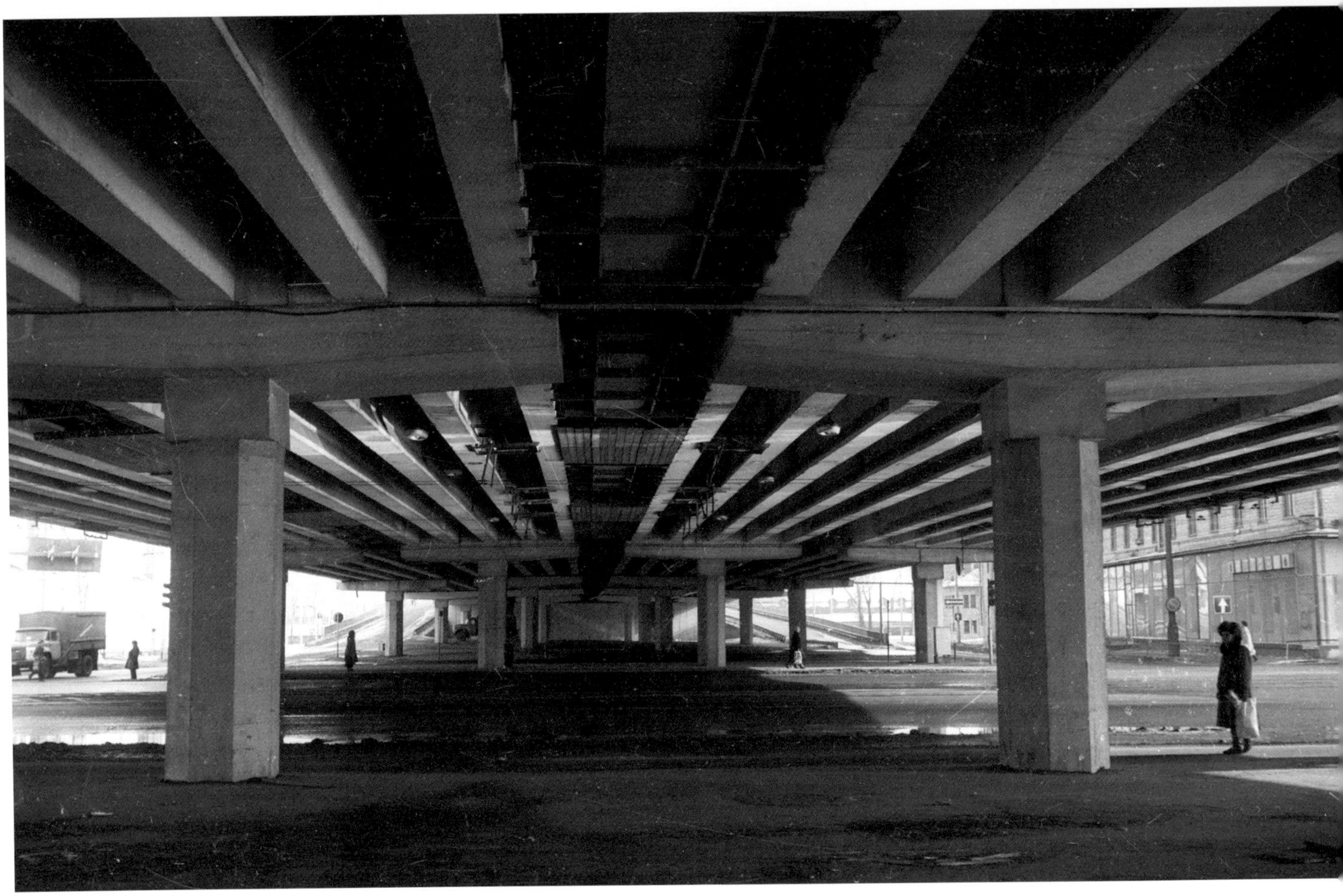

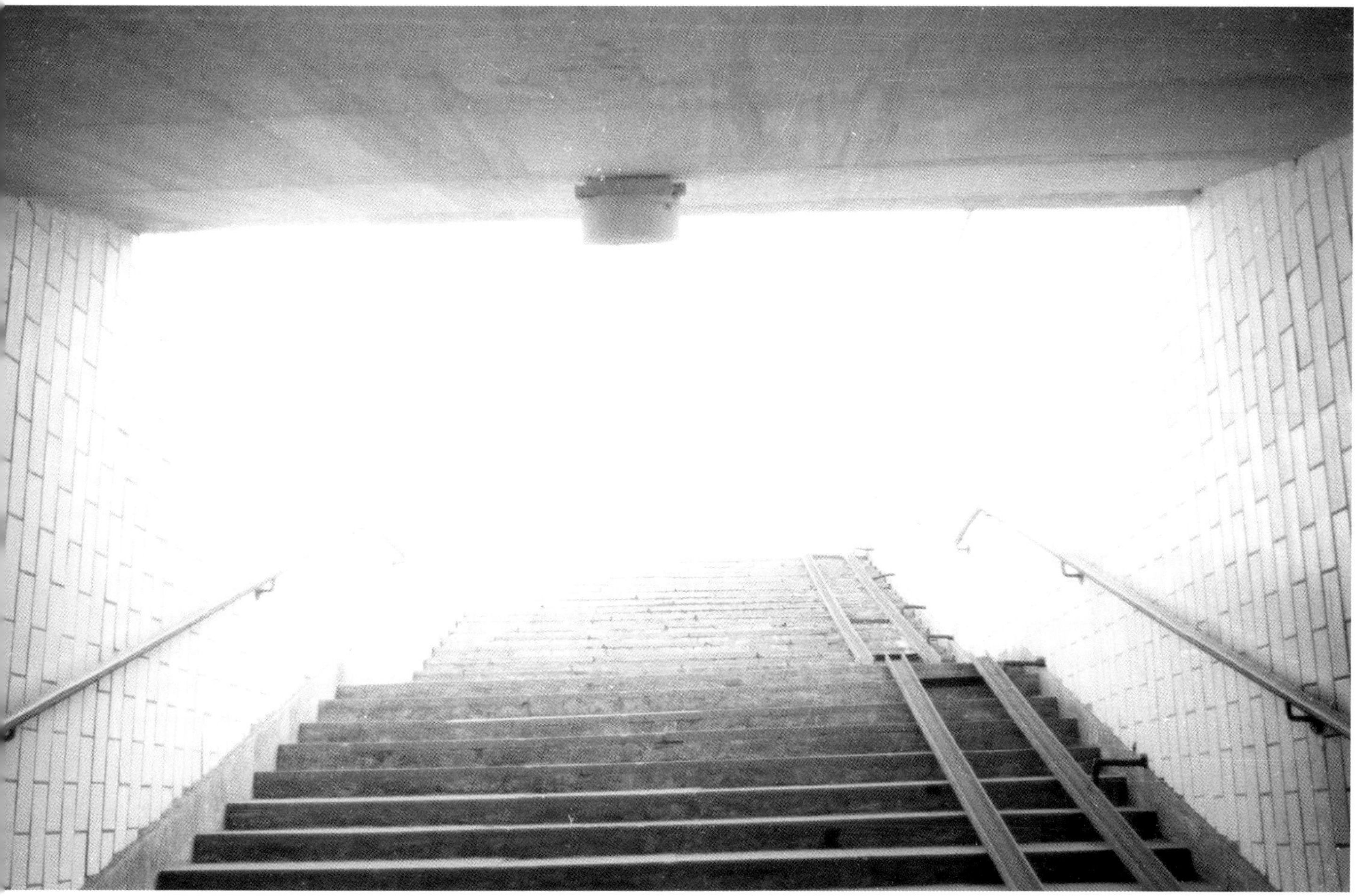

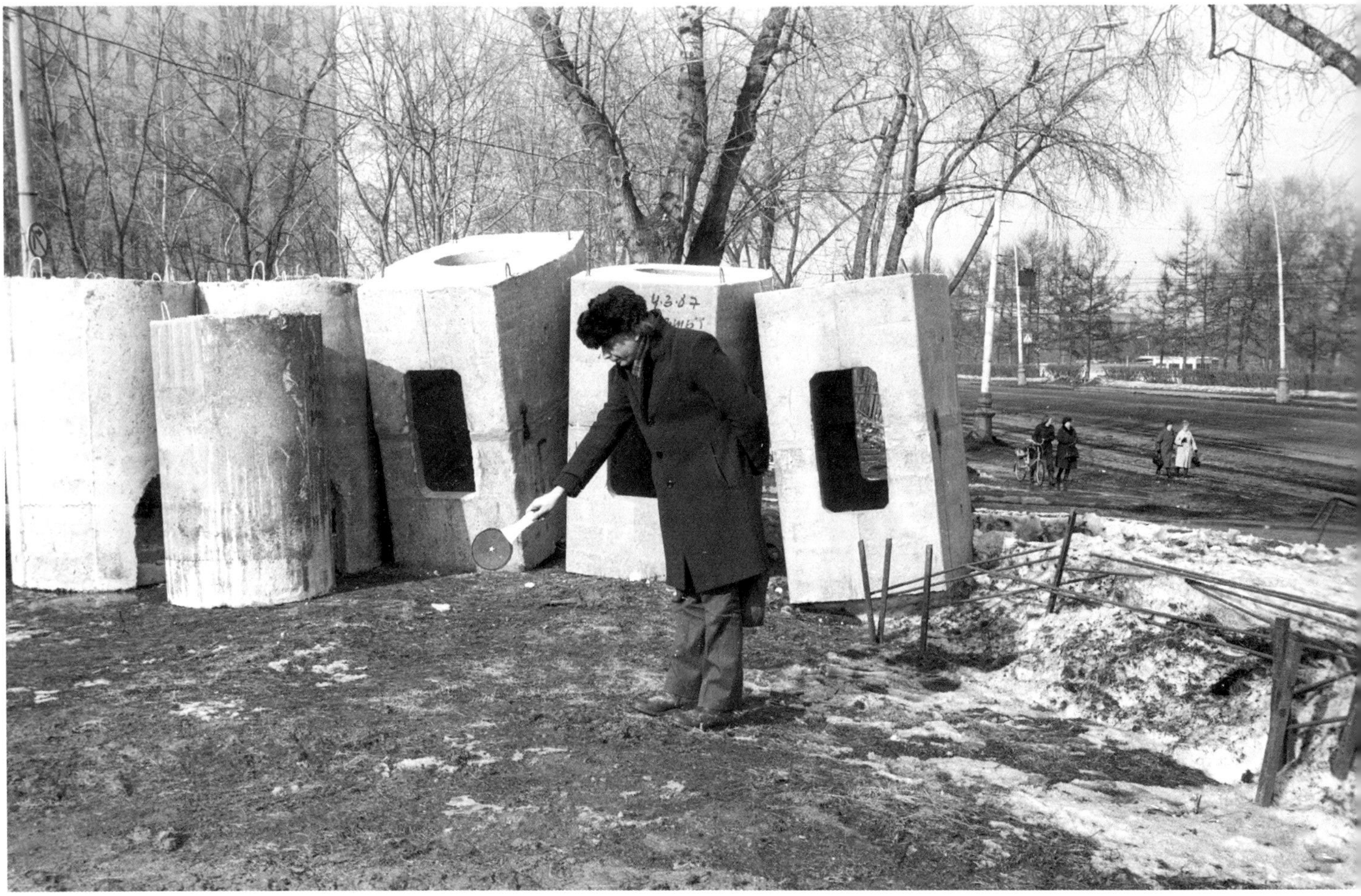
4.3.87

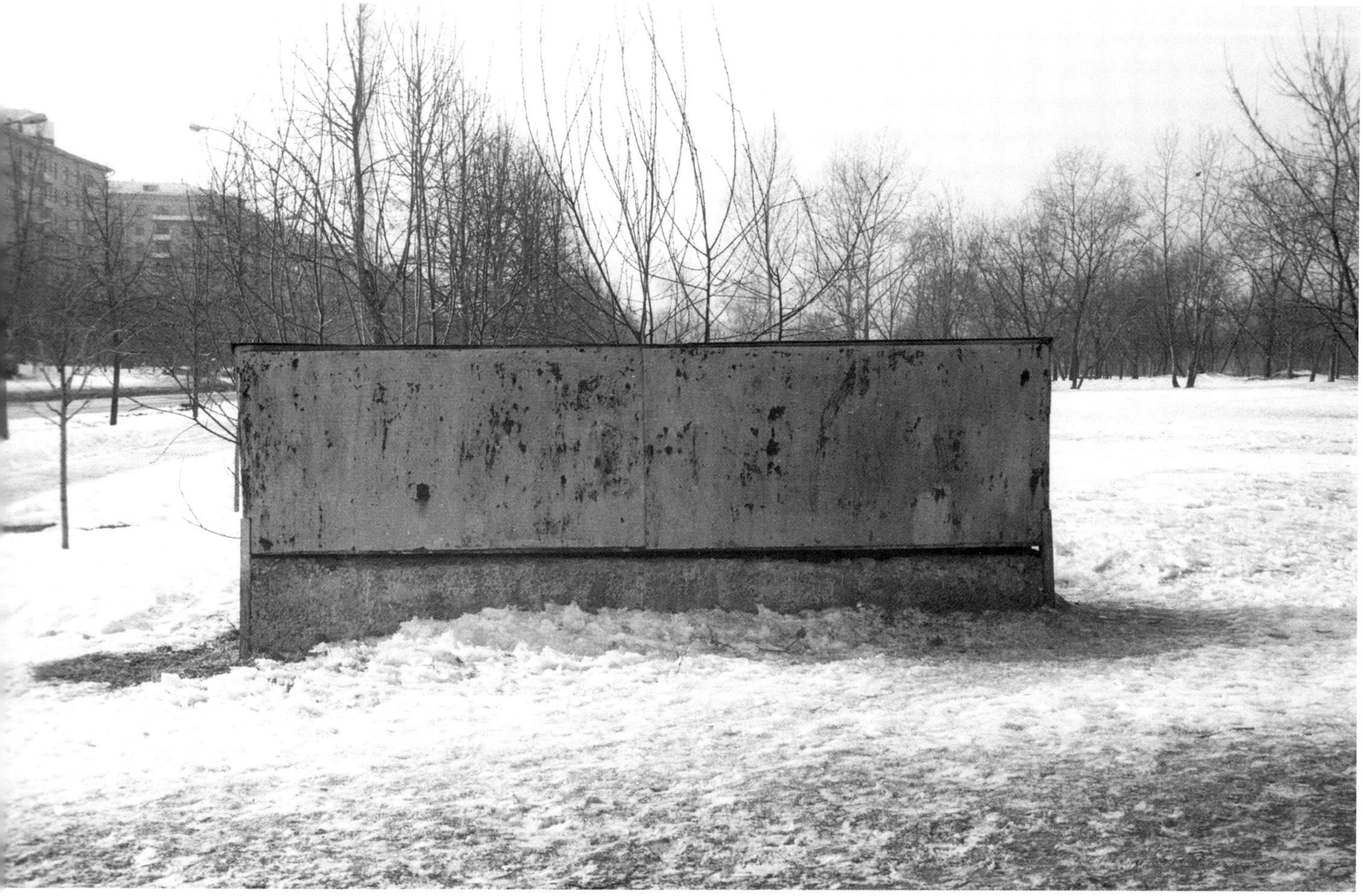

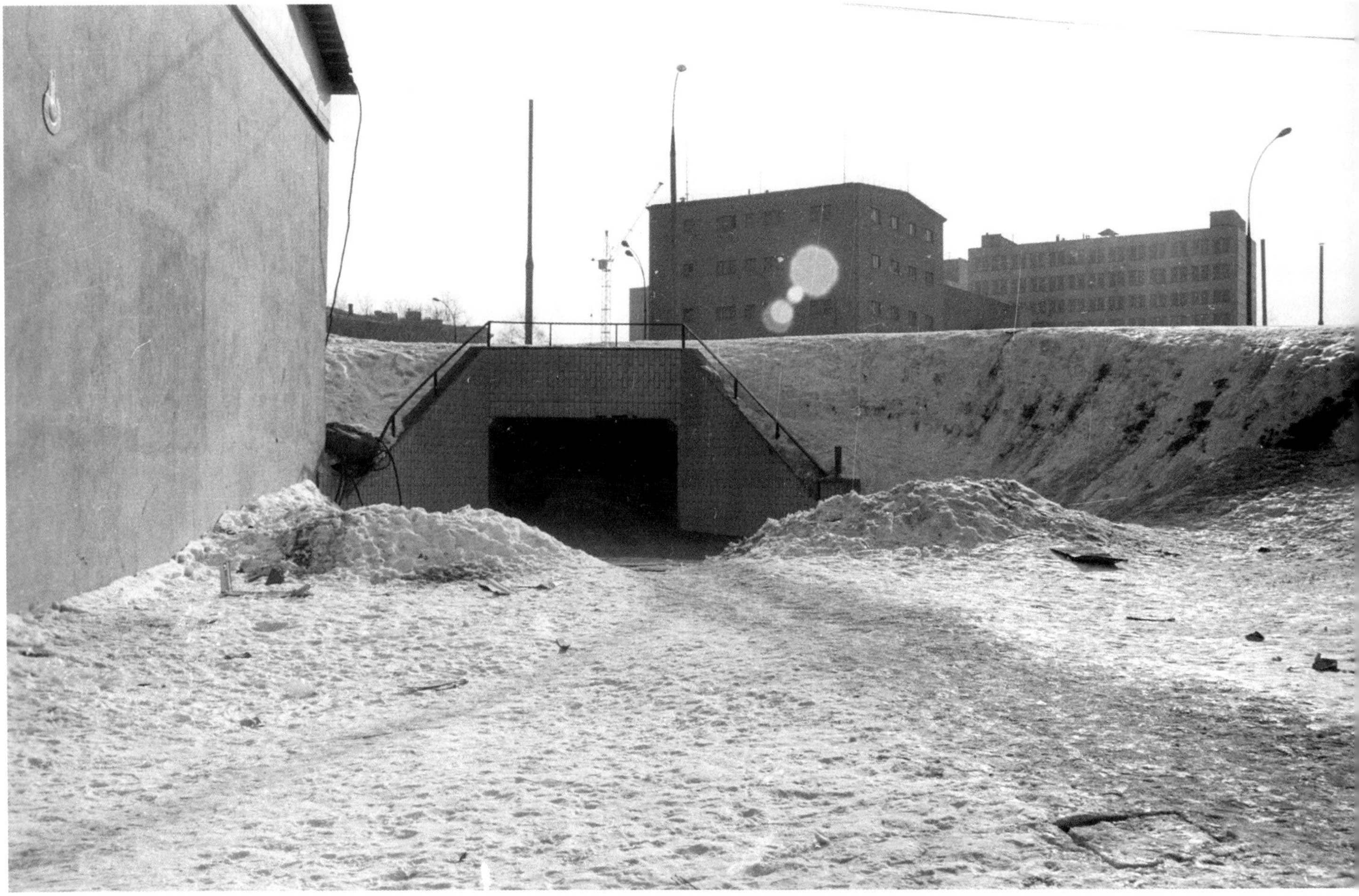

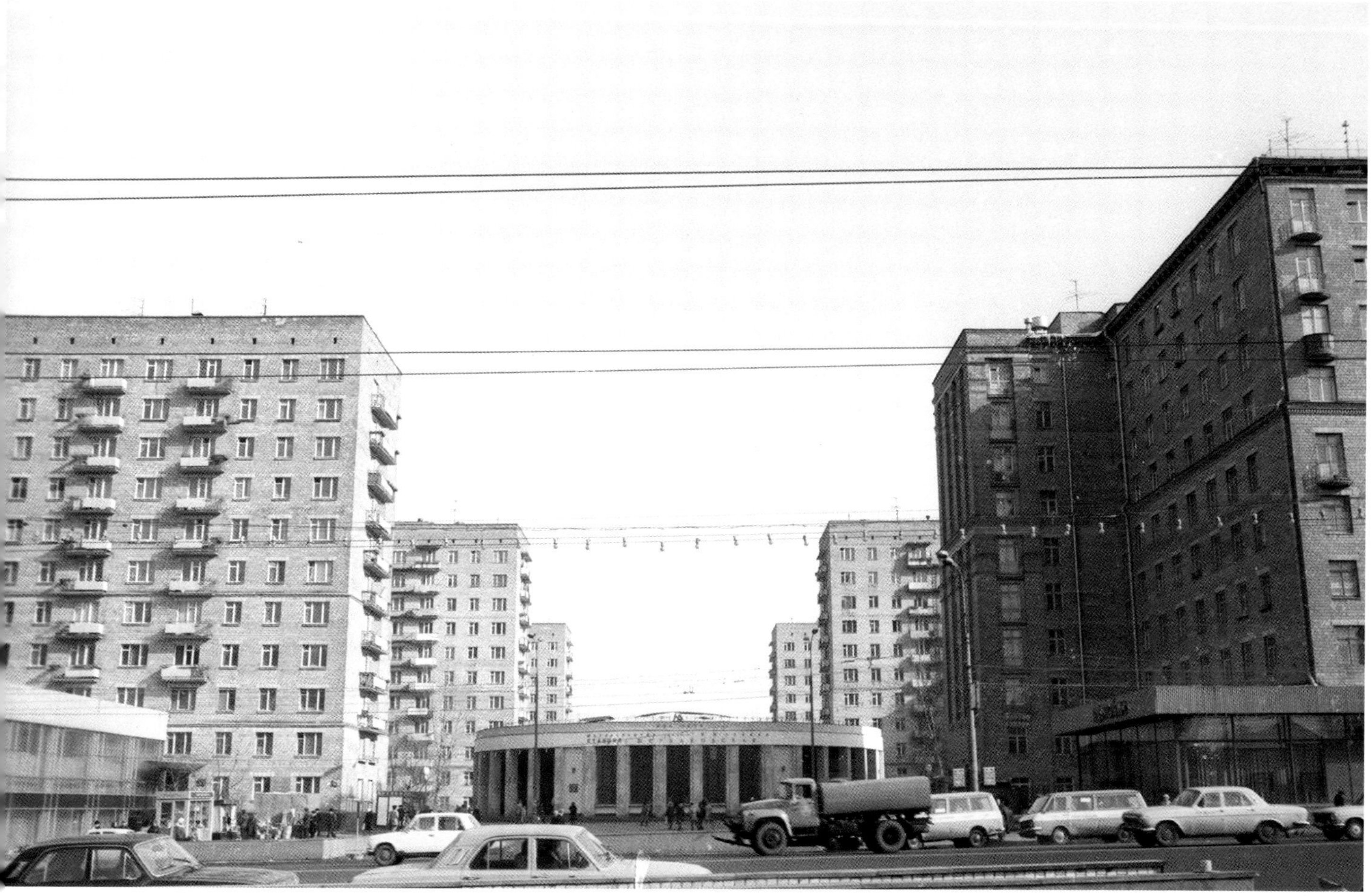

VIDEOS FROM PODJACHEV'S YOUTUBE CHANNEL

Andrei Monastyrski, 2010–2011

In a mystical place of Moscow—examine lighthouses

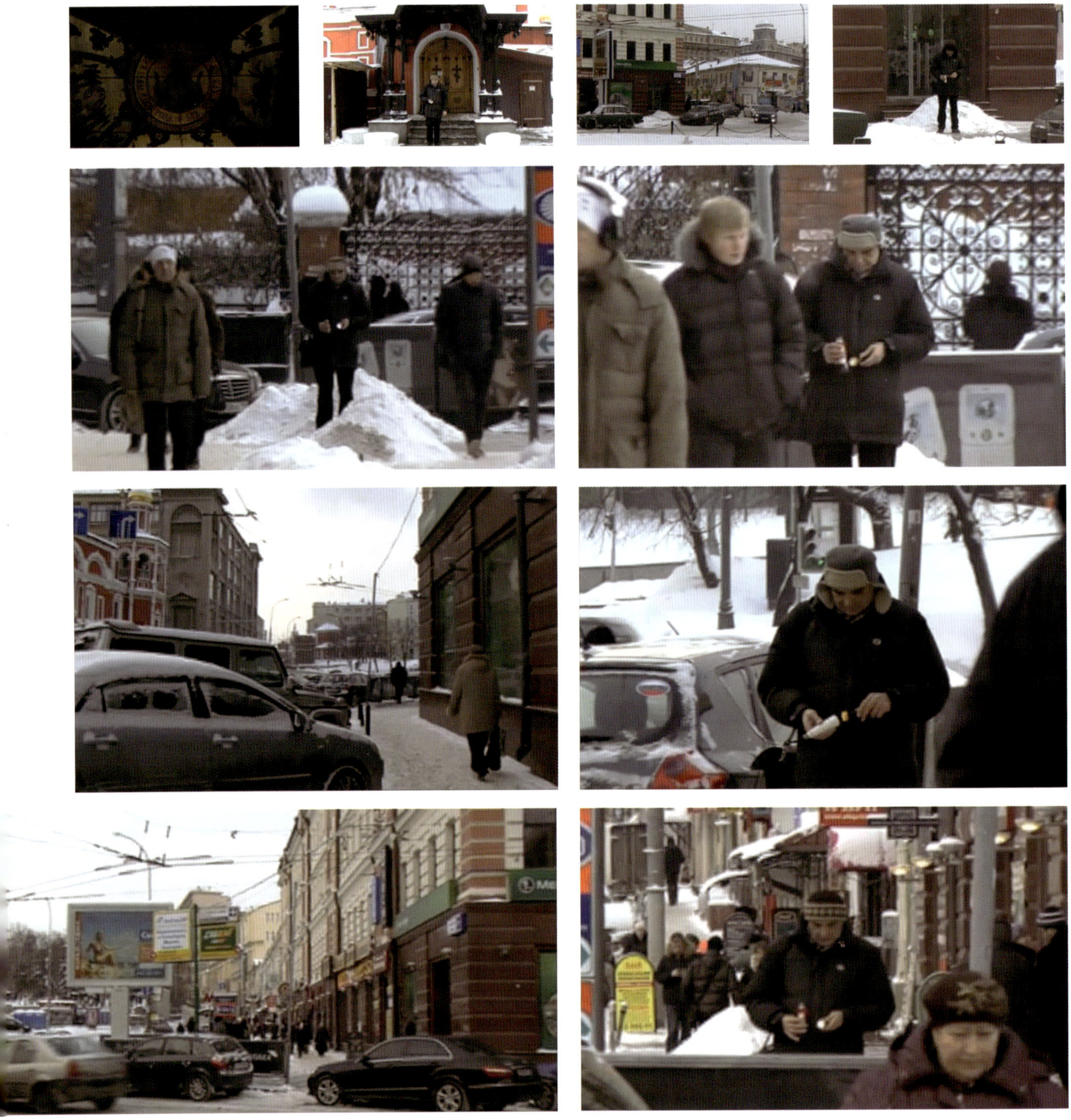

The blue strip in front of the towers

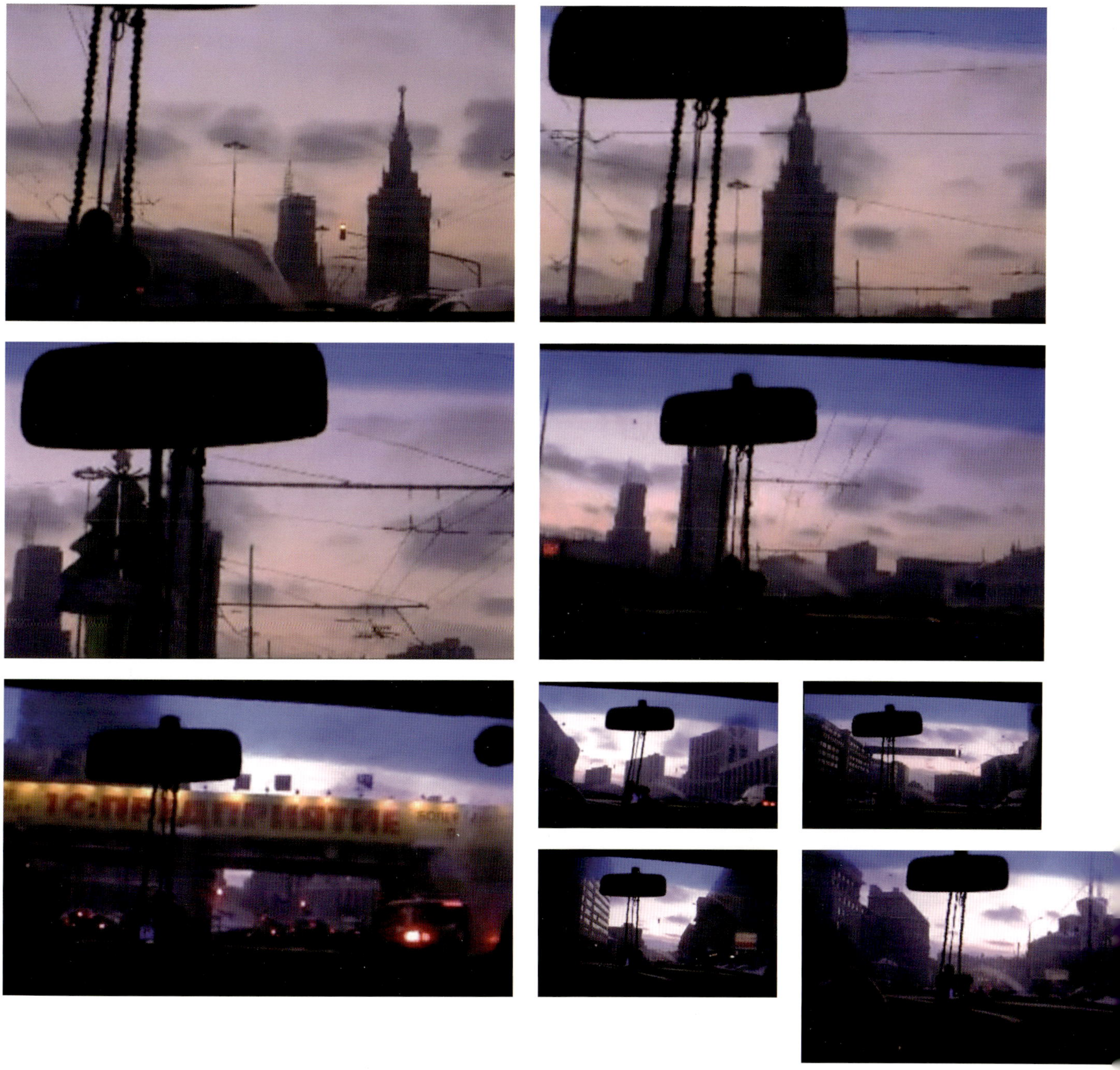

Pass through the cemetery with a rooster

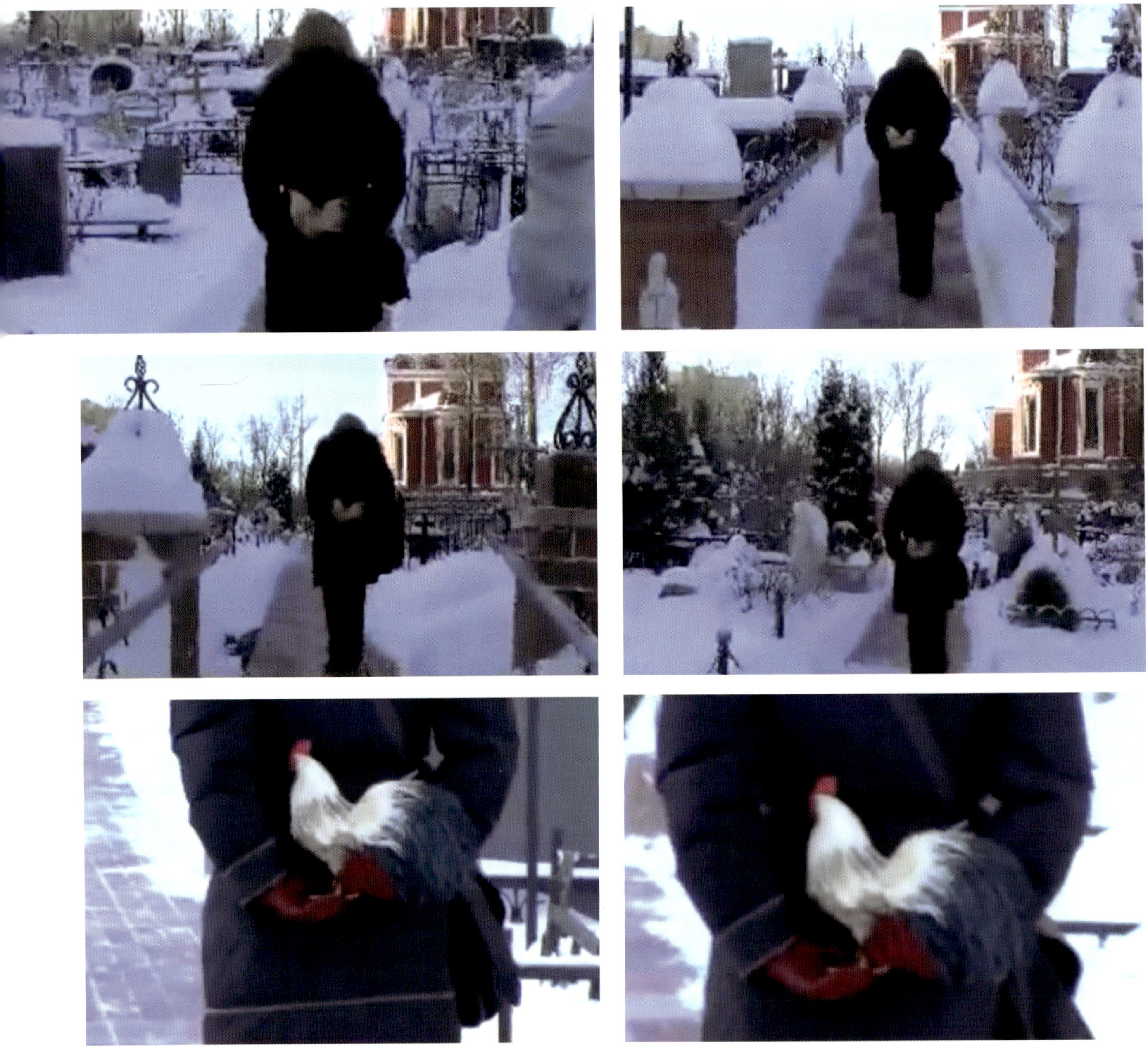

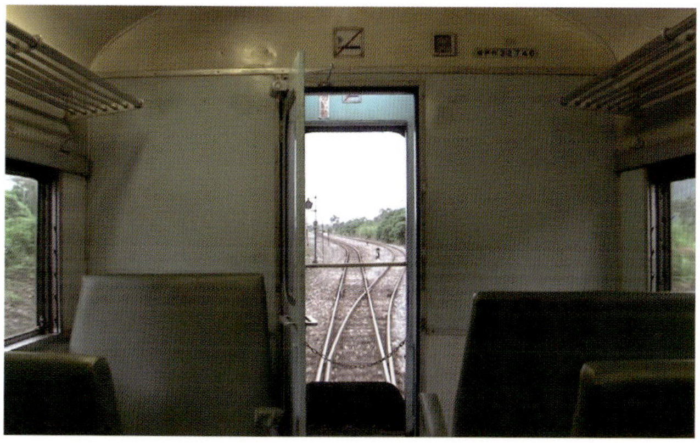
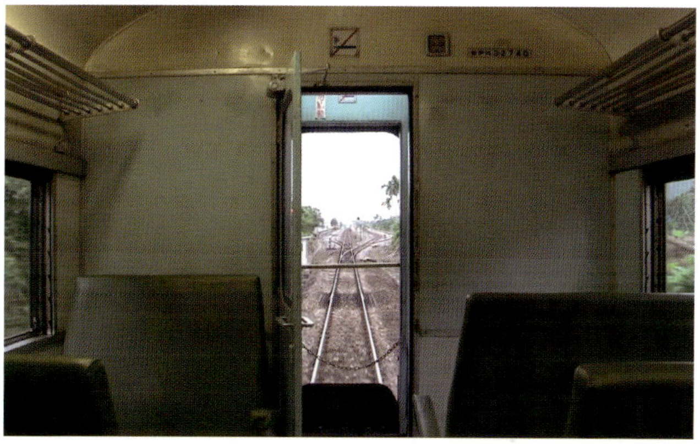
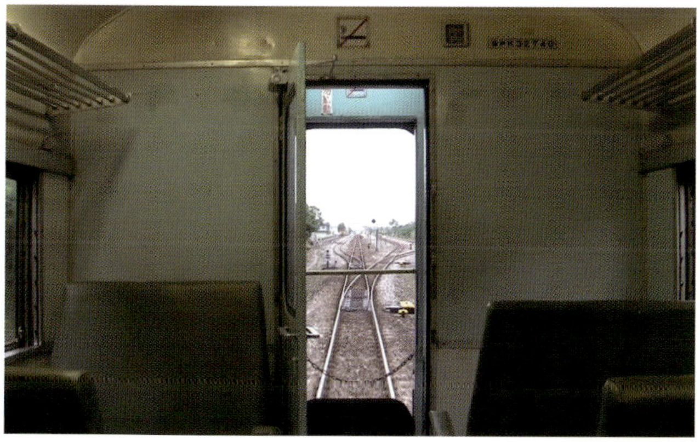
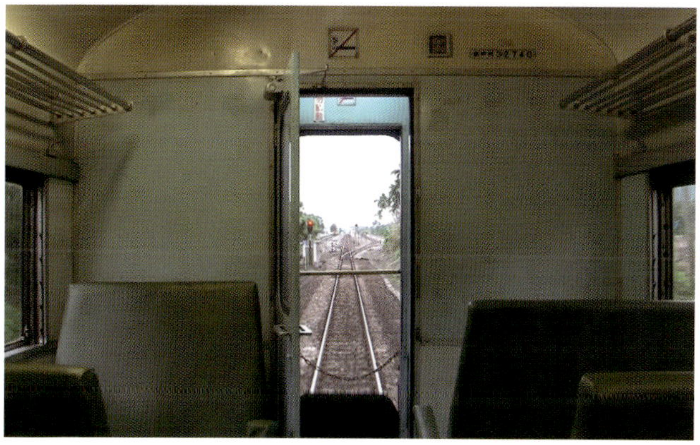
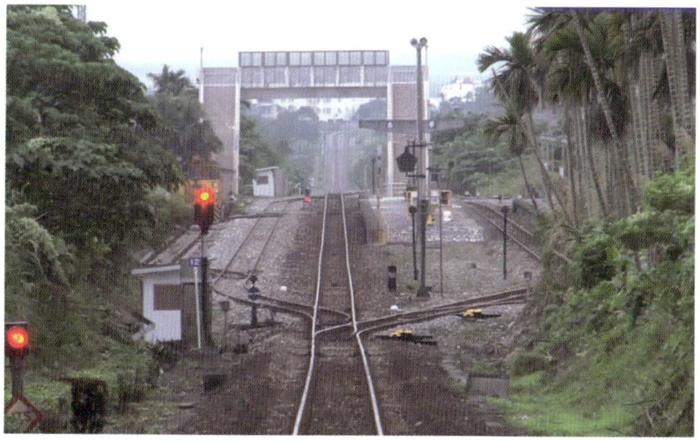
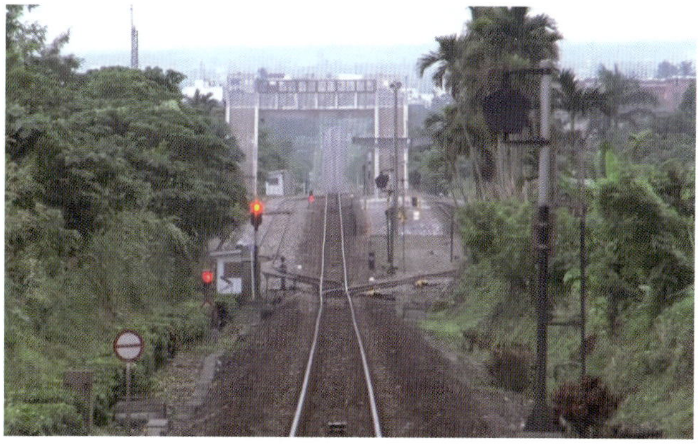
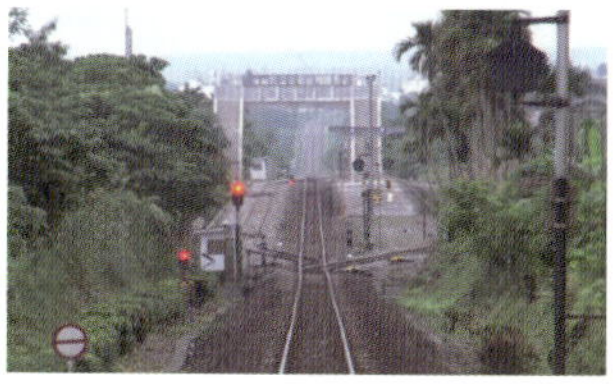
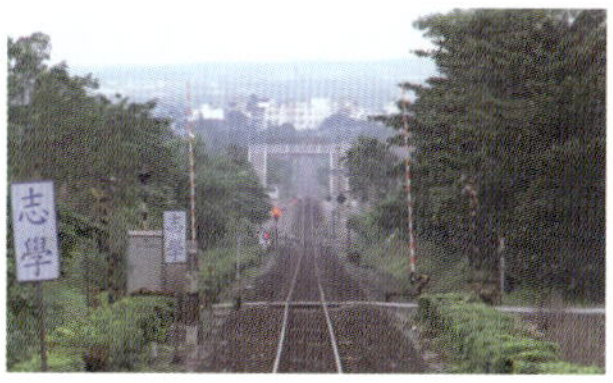

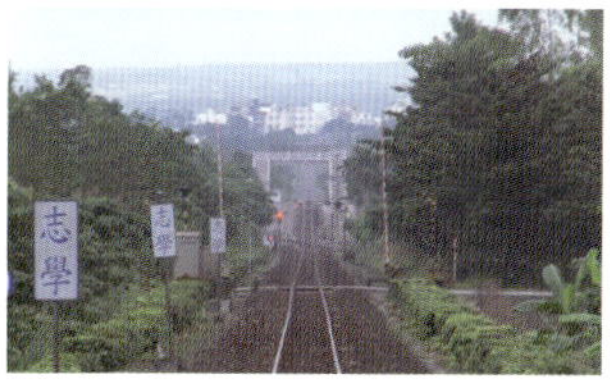

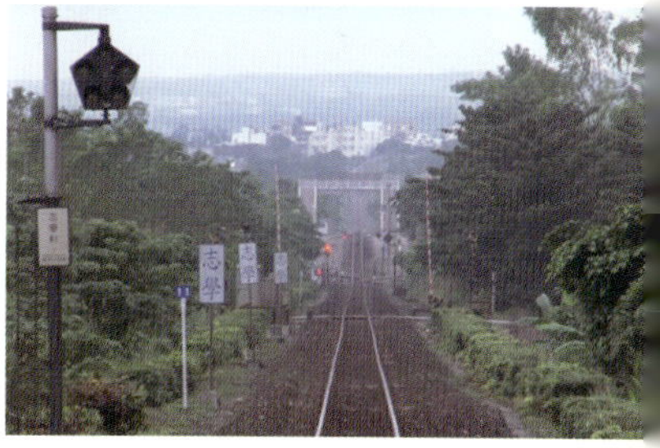

Videos from Podjachev's YouTube Channel

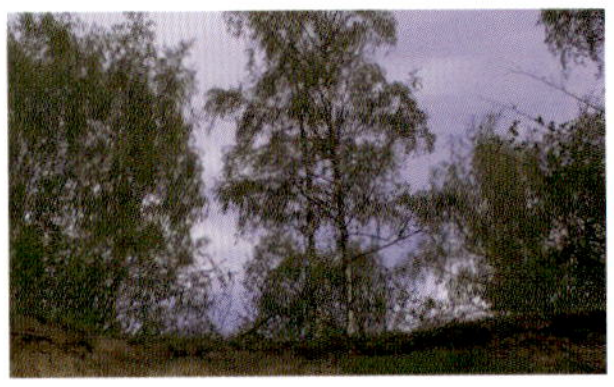
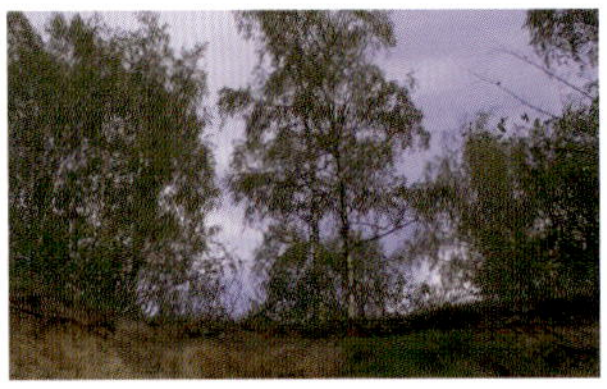
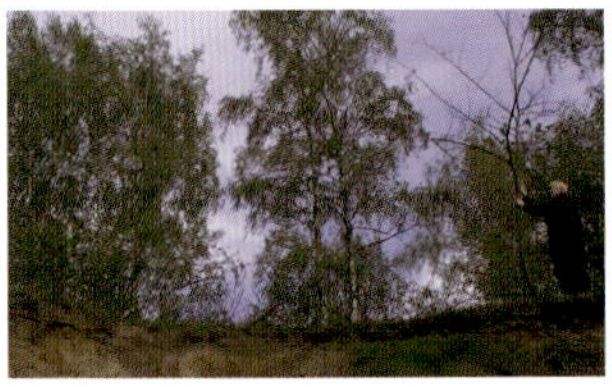
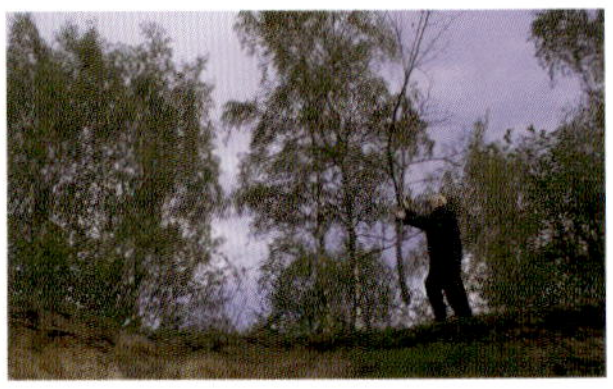

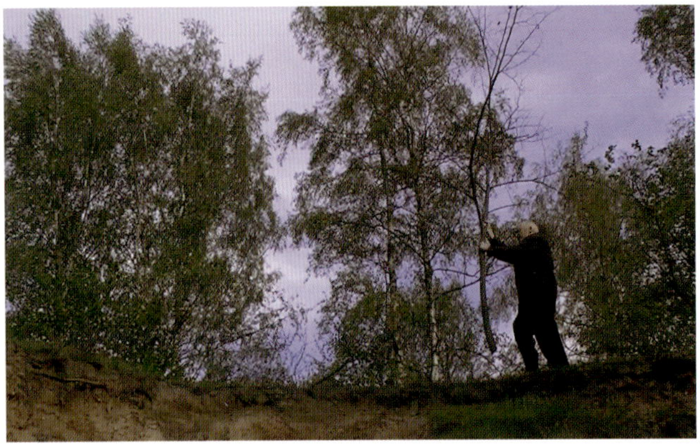
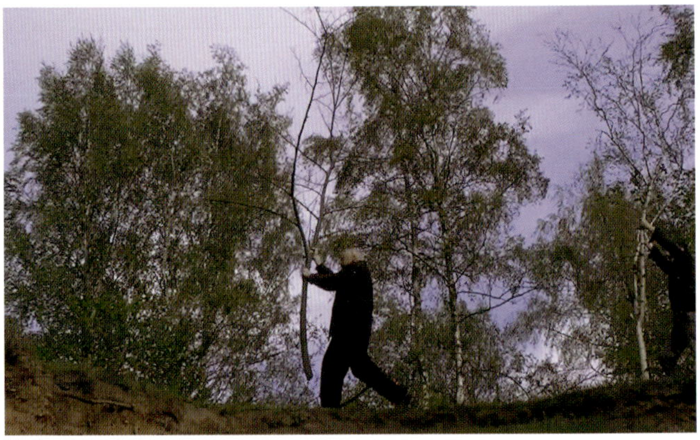

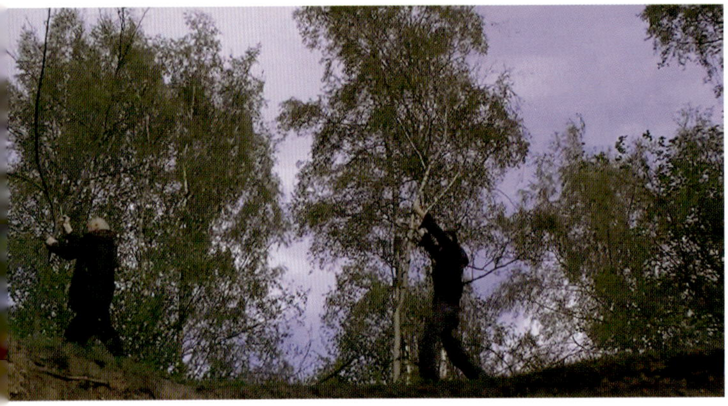
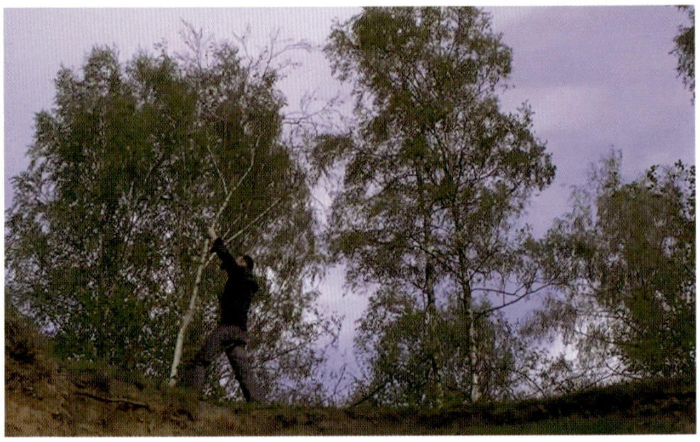

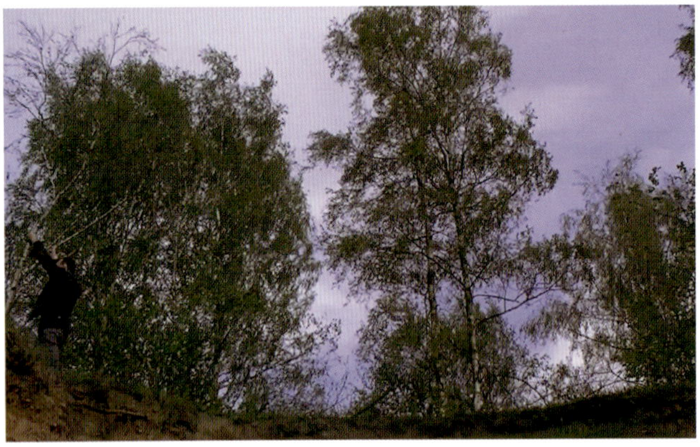
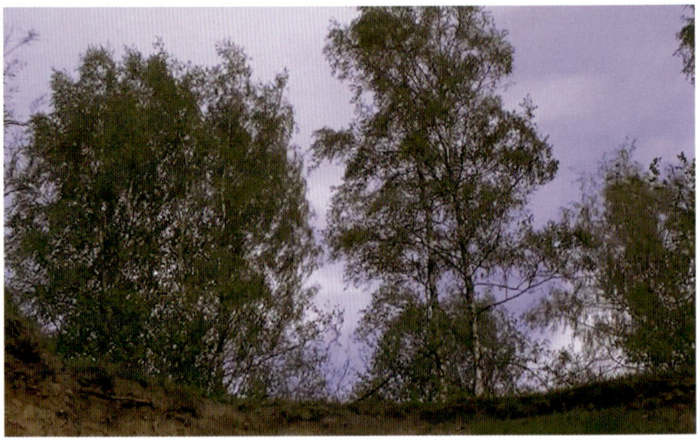

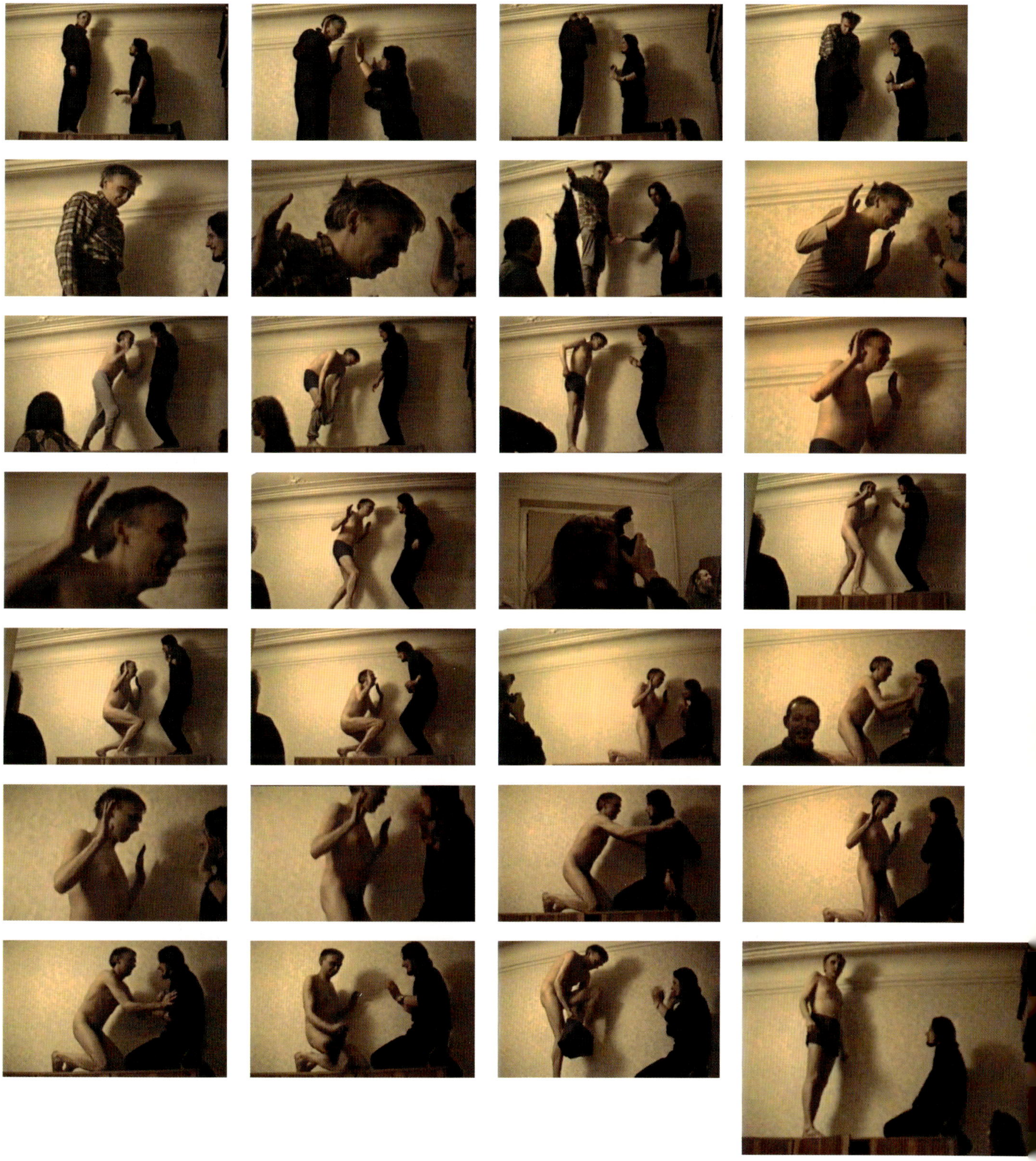

The communist—writer S Podjachev calls for extra-terrestrials

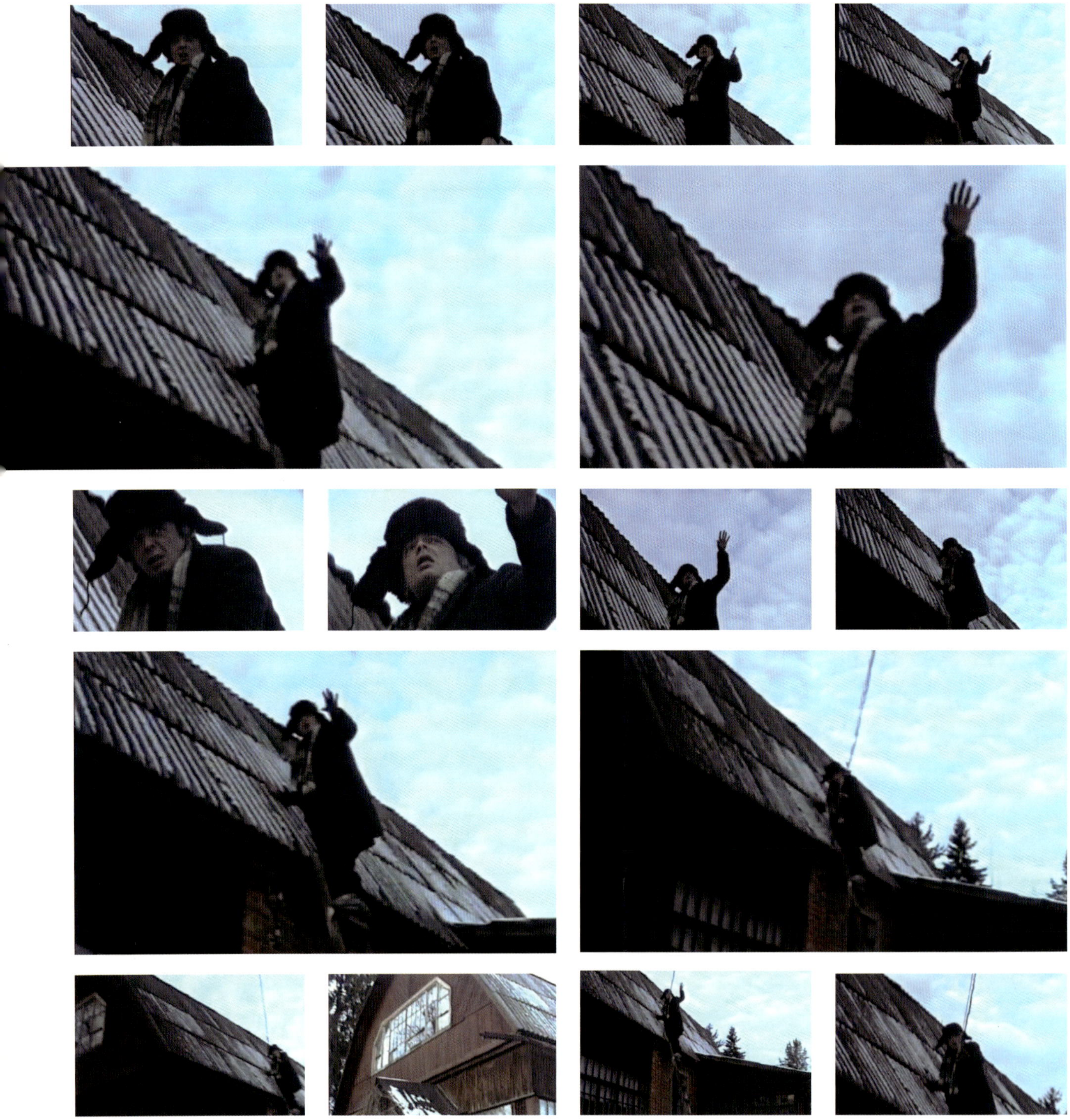

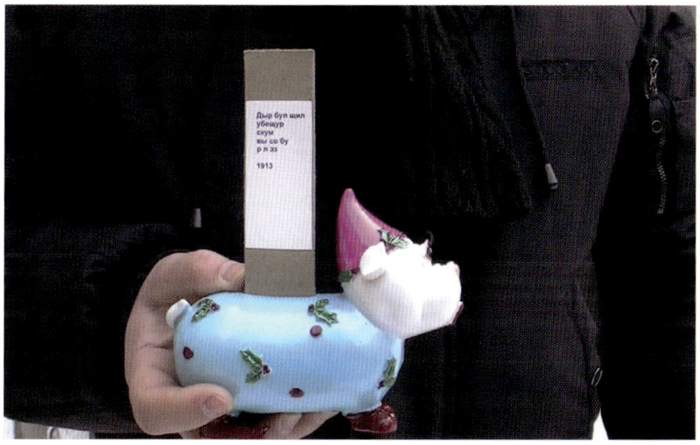
Дыр бул щыл
убешур
скум
вы со бу
р л эз
1913

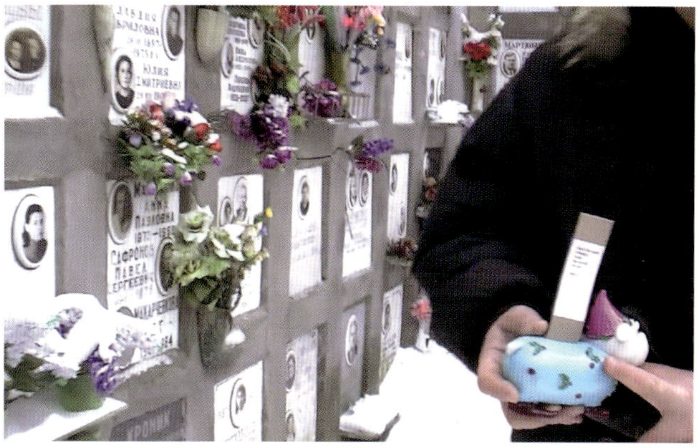

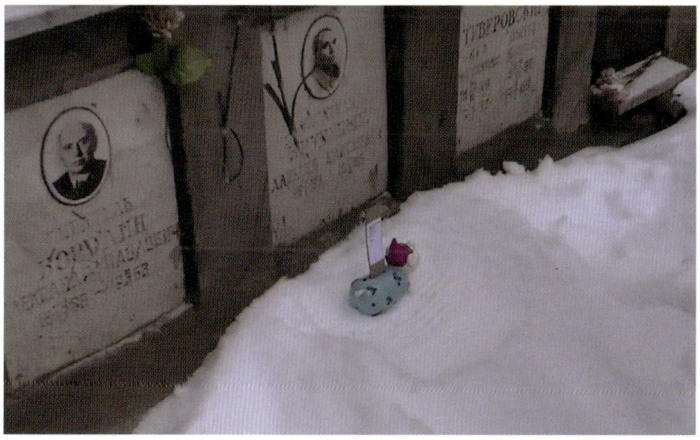

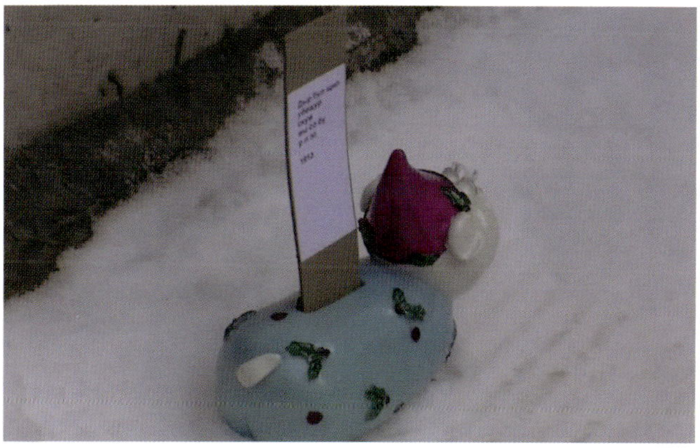

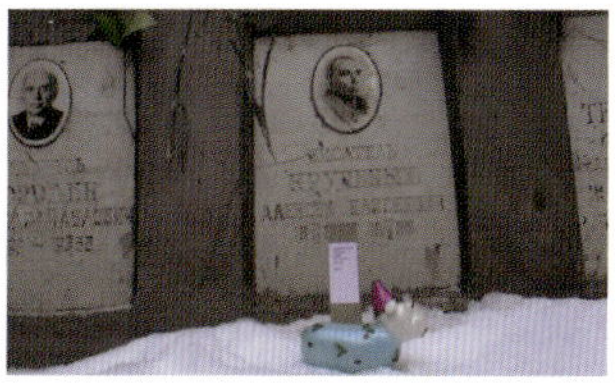

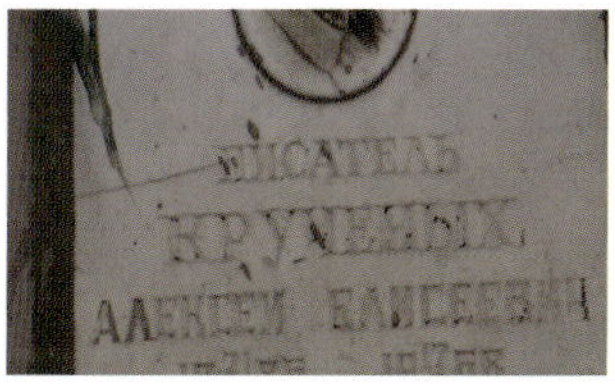

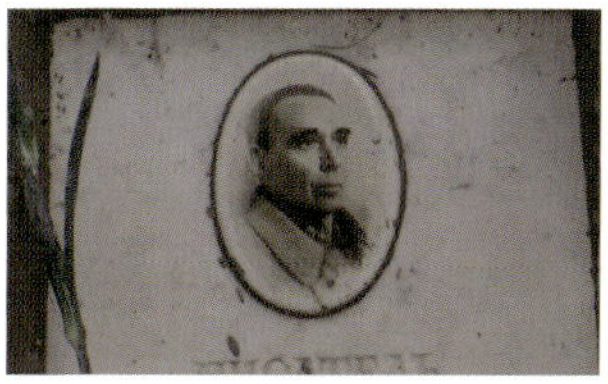

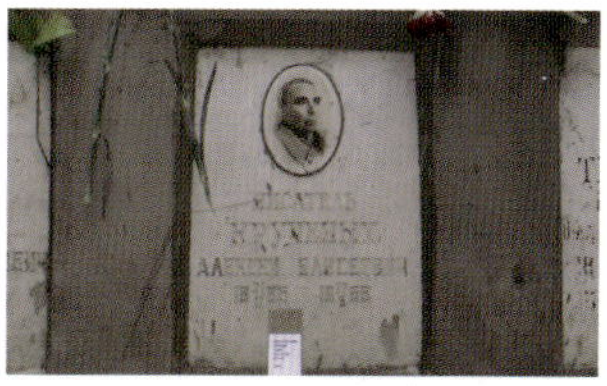

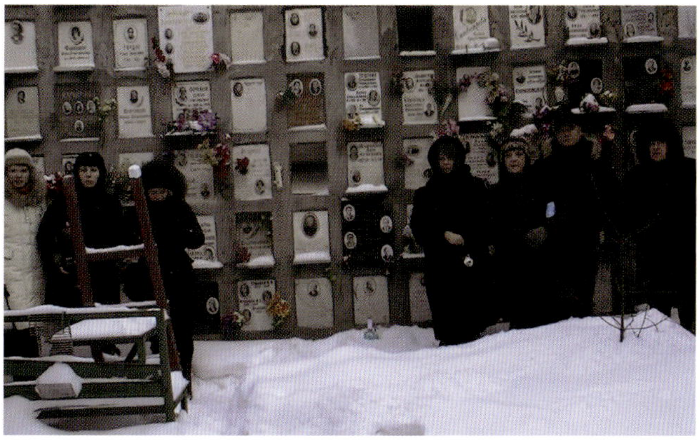

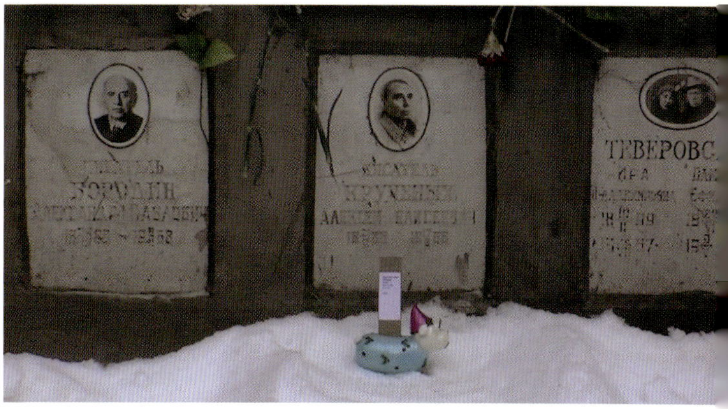

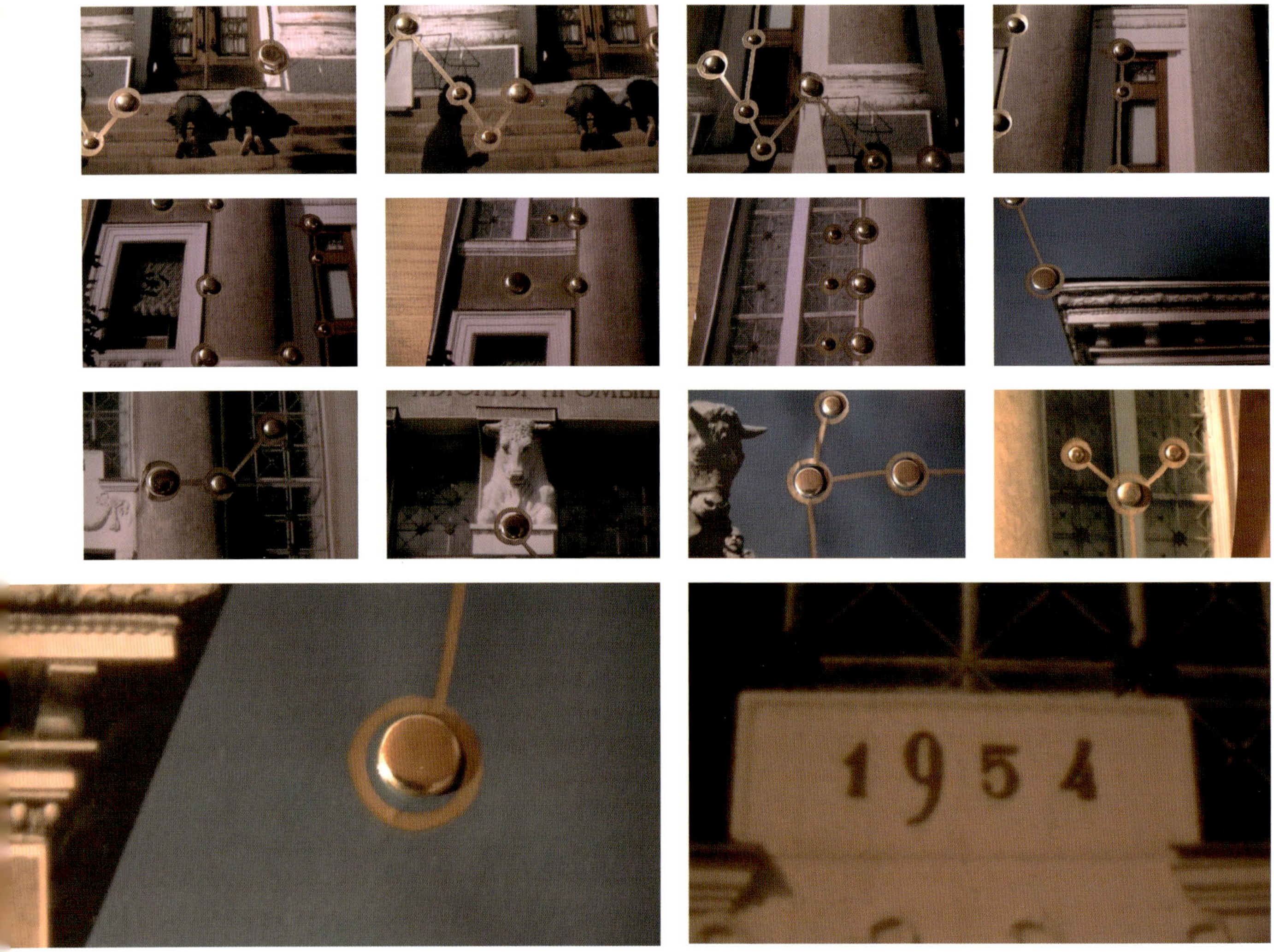
1954

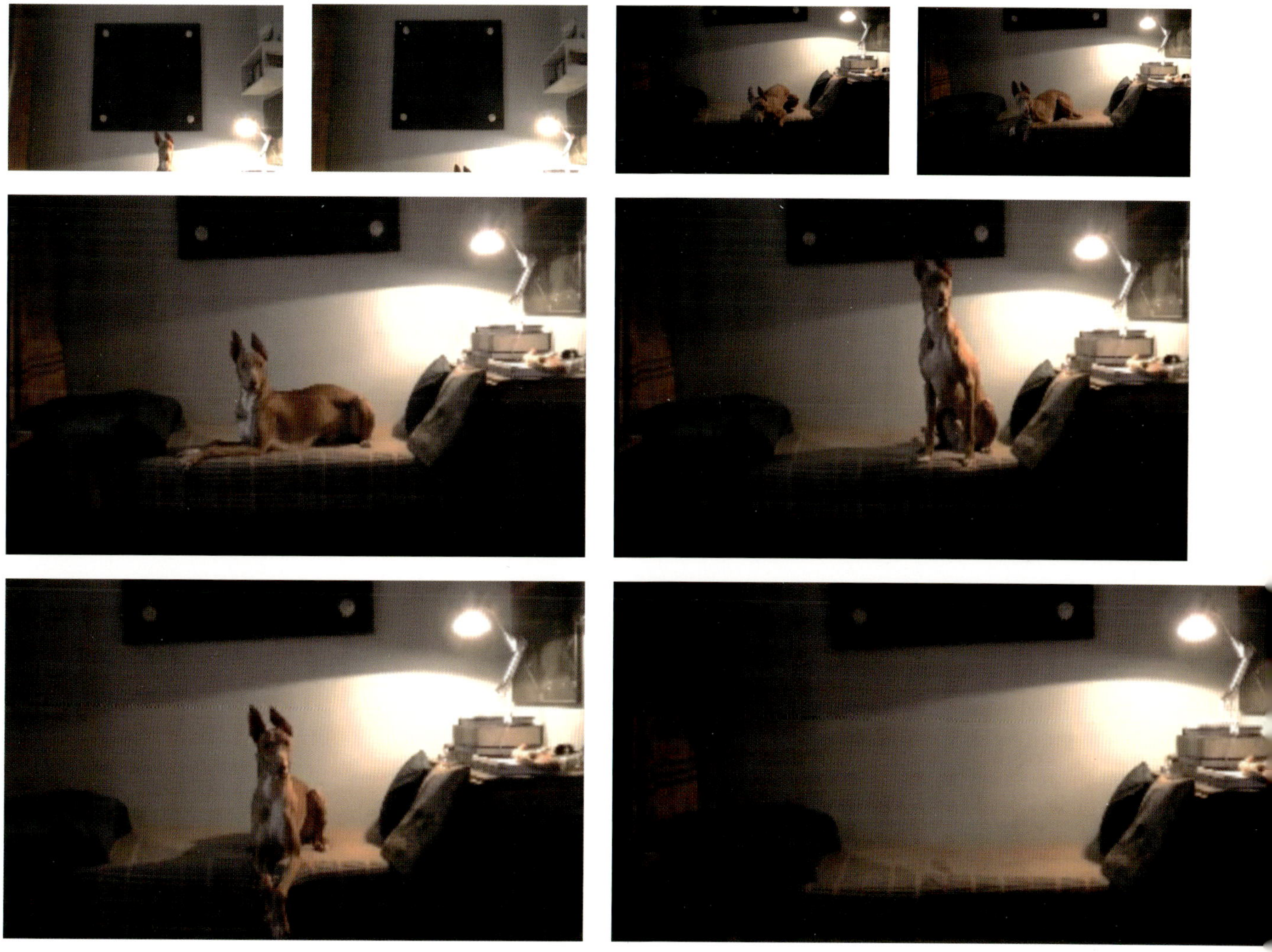

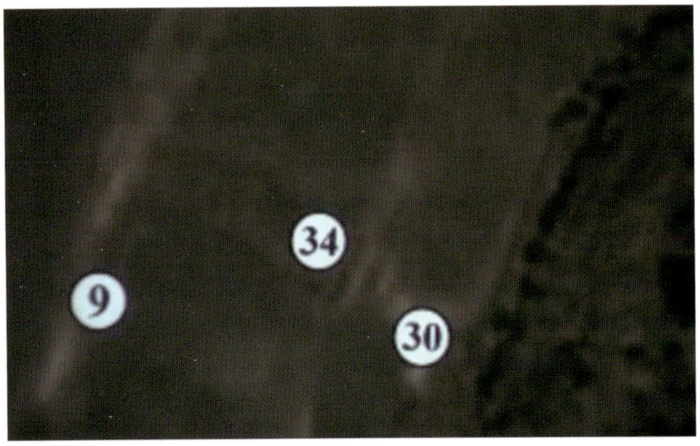
34
9
30

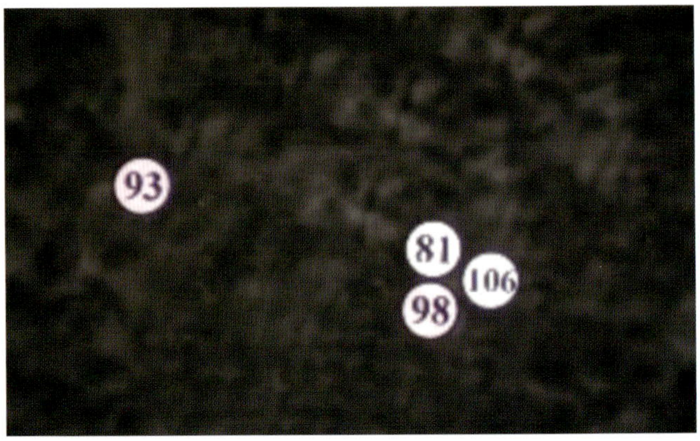
93
81
106
98

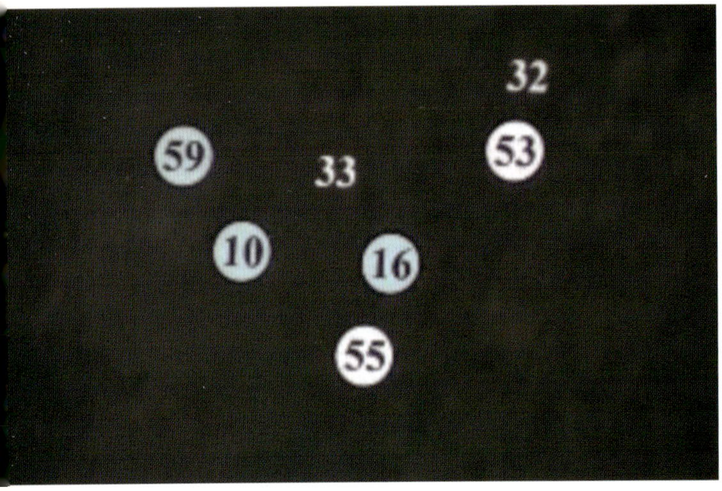
32
59
33
53
10
16
55

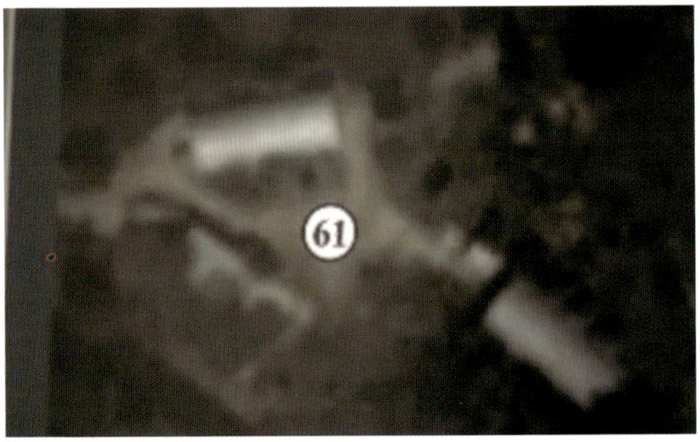
61

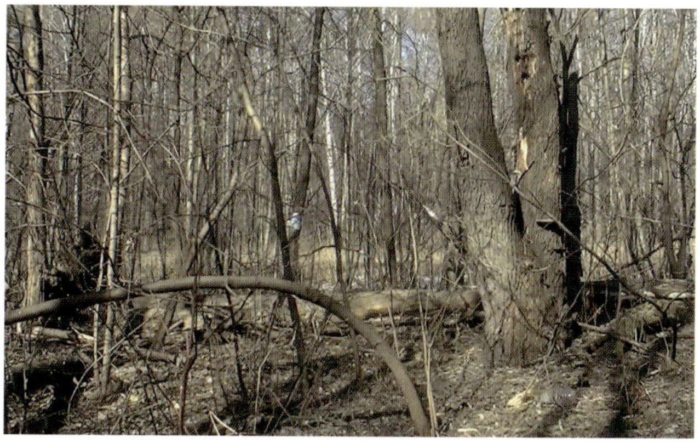

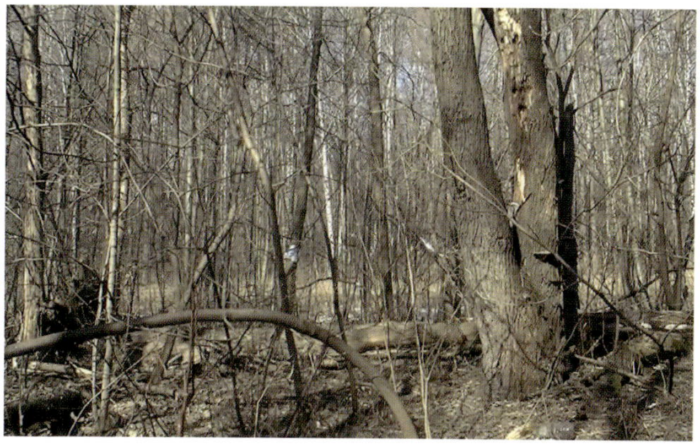

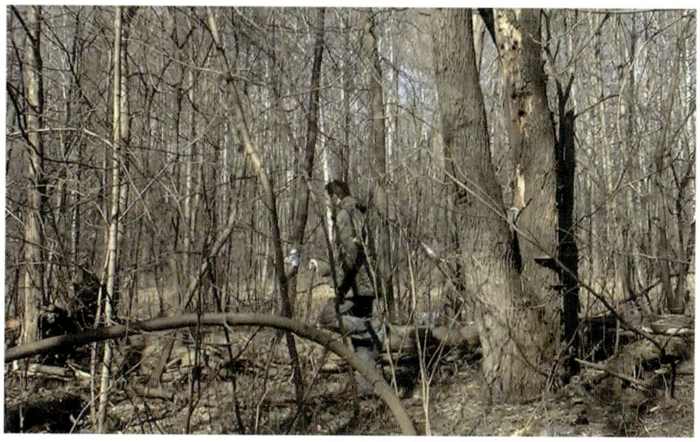

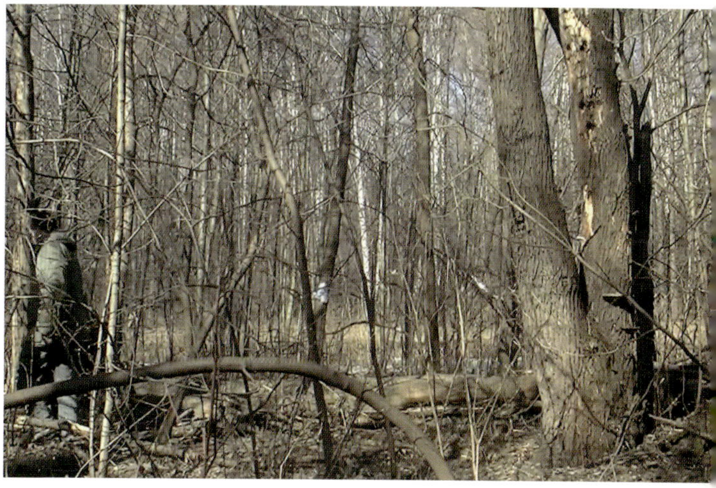

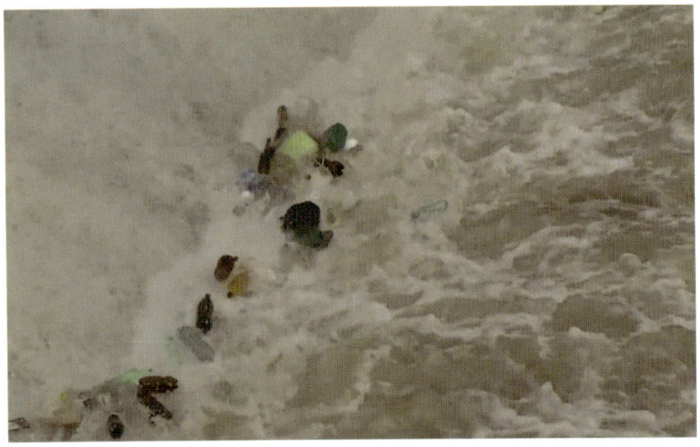

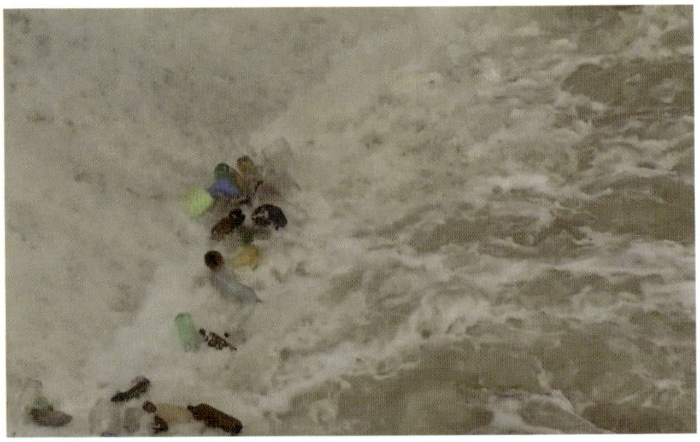

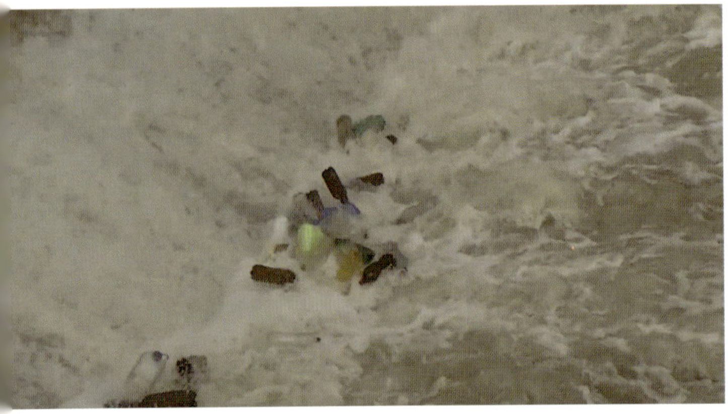

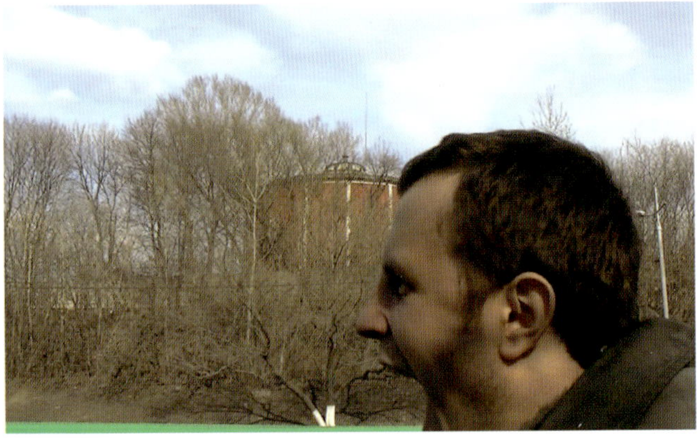

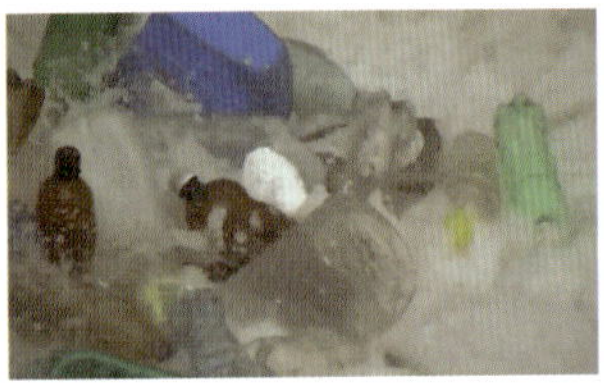

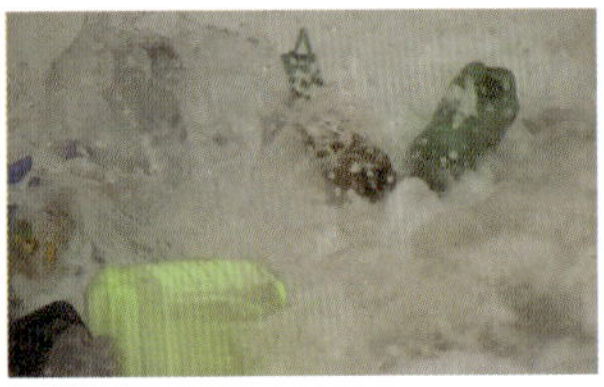

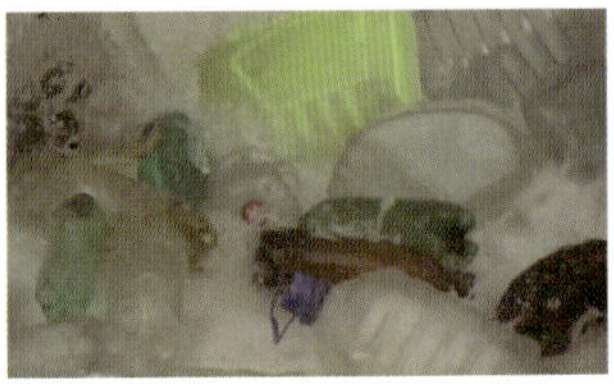

Moving forward of Panitkov

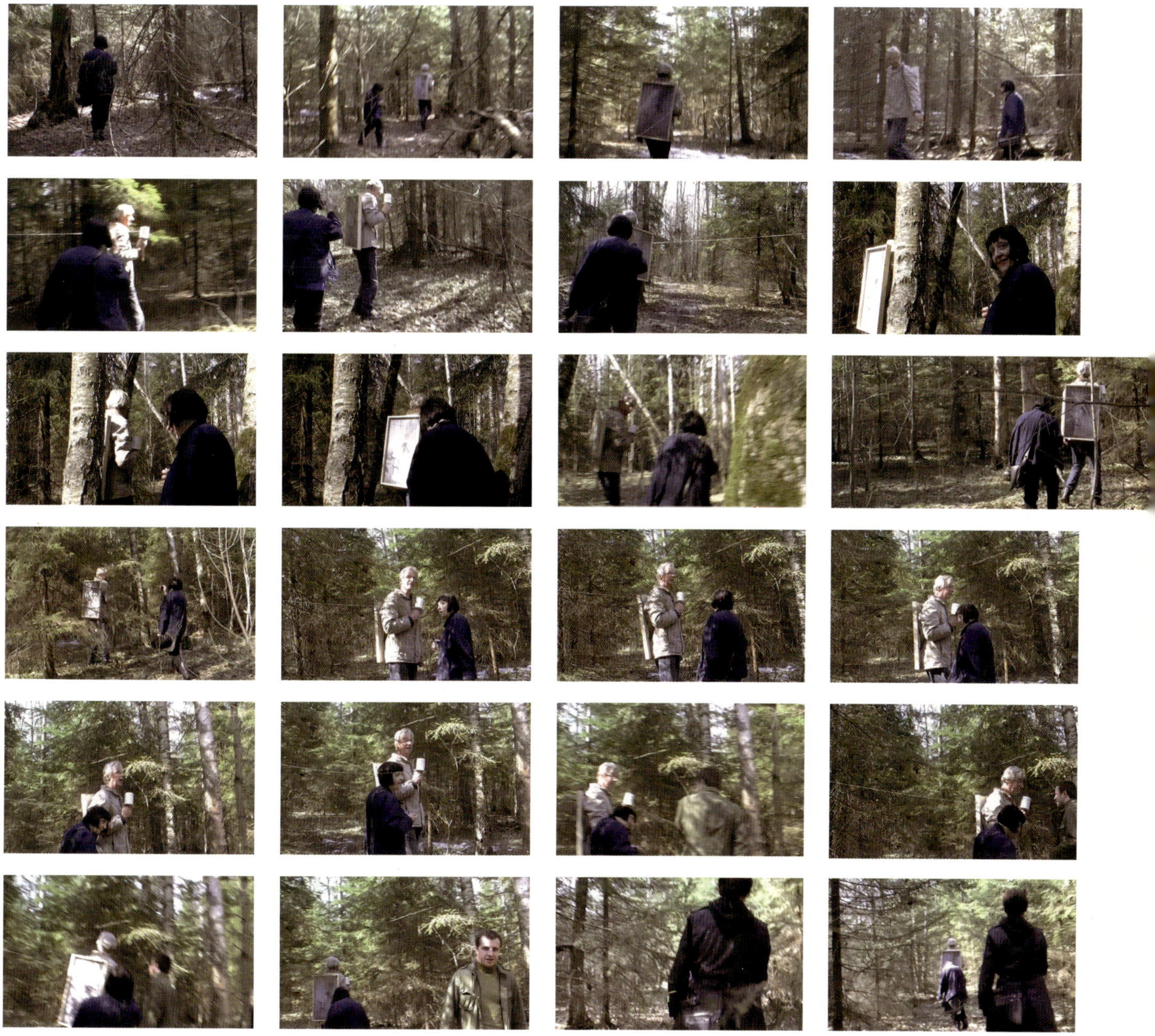

O, Cover your pale legs!

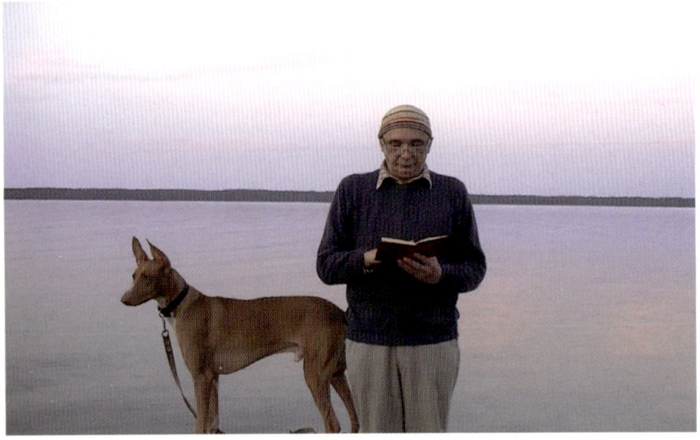
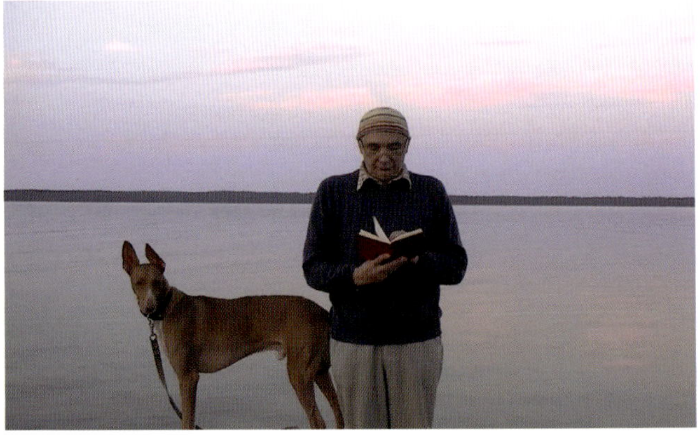
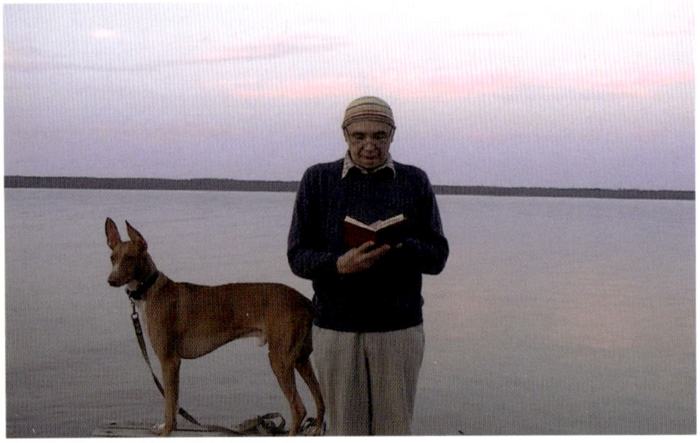
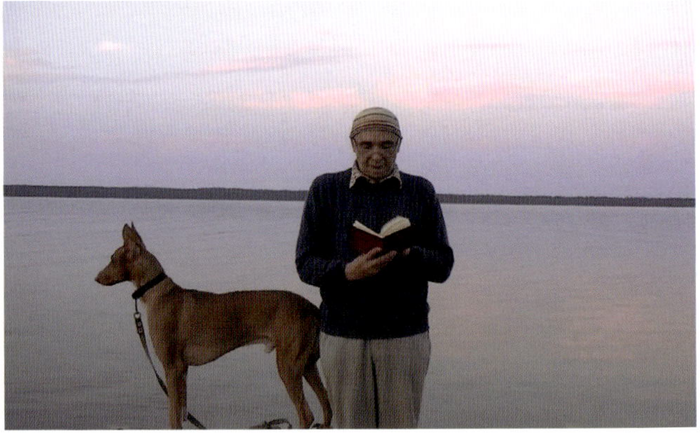
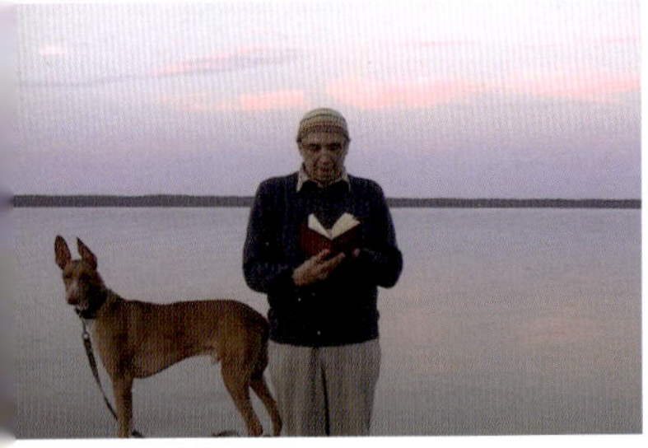
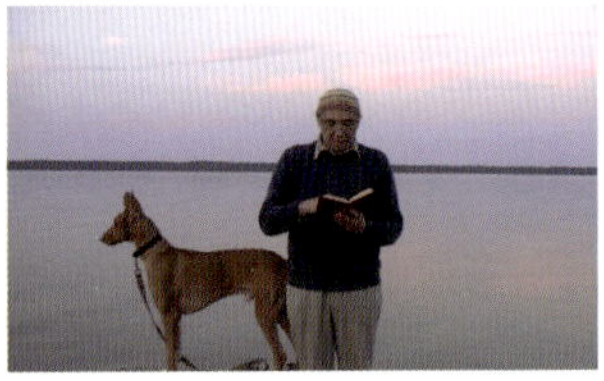
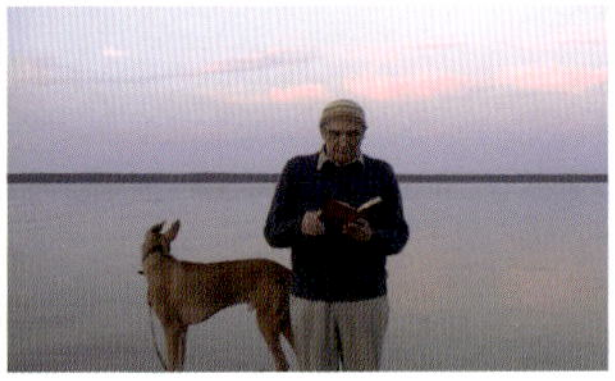
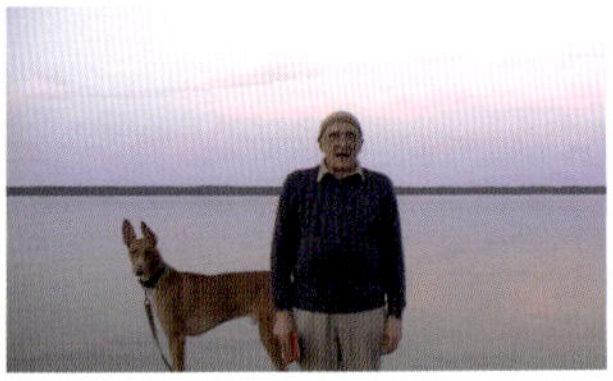

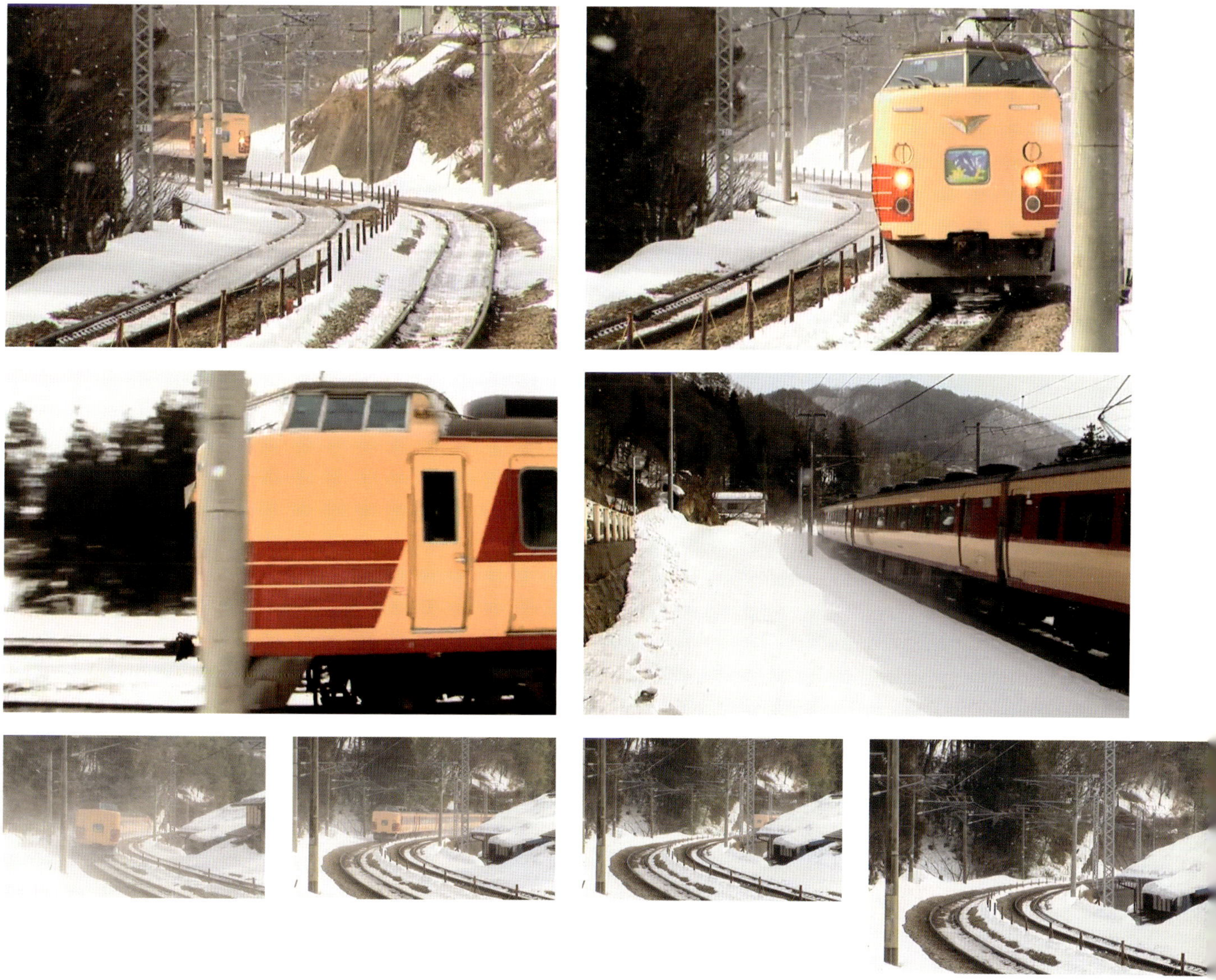

Andrei Monastyrski (Sumnin)

	1949	Born in Petsamo, Murmansk region, USSR.
	1980	Graduated from Moscow State University, Moscow, USSR.
	1976–present	Member of the Collective Actions (Kollektivnye Deystviya) group.
	1981	Compiling of the first MANI (Moscow Archive of the New Art) folder.
	1980–1989	Compiling of the Trips out of Town (in Five Volumes) of the Collective Actions group.
	1986–1990	Compiling of the Five Volumes of MANI (Moscow Archive of the New Art) folders.
		Lives in Moscow, Russian Federation.
Selected Solo Exhibitions	1990	Particular Histories (with Conrad Atkinson), Proletarsky District Exhibition Hall at Peresvetov Lane, Moscow, USSR.
	1991	Art Situation at the MANI Museum, MANI Museum (N Panitkov's country mansion), Lobnia, Moscow region, USSR; Artists' Studio in Bolshaya Bronnaya ulitsa, Moscow, USSR.
		Neighbourhood of the Regina Gallery, Regina Gallery, Moscow, USSR.
	1994	Unterschriften, Kunstwerke, Berlin, Germany.
	1995	Andrei Monastyrski, Pavel Peppershtein, Paszti-Bott Gallery, Cologne
	1996	The Limb, XL Gallery, Moscow, Russian Federation.
	1998	Gosagroprom. Obscuri Viri Gallery, Moscow, Russian Federation.
	2000	70s and Other Works, Navicula Artis Gallery, St Petersburg, Russian Federation.
	2004	Mouse Hunting (with Vadim Zakharov), Stella Art Foundation, Moscow, Russian Federation.
	2005	Earth Works, Stella Art Foundation, Moscow, Russian Federation.
	2007	Winter of 1983 – 2008, Moderna Galerija, Ljubljana, Slovenia.
	2008	Tallinna Kunstihoone, Tallinn, Estonia.
	2010	Moscow Museum of Modern Art, Moscow, Russian Federation.
Selected Group Exhibitions	1977	La Nuova Arte Sovietica: Una prospettiva non ufficiale, la Biennale di Venezia, Venice, Italy.
	1981	Russian New Wave, Contemporary Russian Art Center of America, New York, USA.
	1982	First AptArt Exhibition, AptArt Gallery (N Alekseev's apartment), Moscow, USSR.
	1984	AptArt in Tribeca, Contemporary Russian Art Center of America, New York, USA.
	1985	AptArt. Moscow Vanguard in the 80s, Washington Project for the Arts, Washington, USA.
	1986	Arts of Today, International exhibitions. Hotel Hilton, Budapest, Hungary.
	1987	Art of Today, II International exhibitions, Budapest Galeria, Budapest, Hungary.
		Creative Atmosphere and Art Process. First Exhibition of the Avantgardists' Club, Proletarsky District Exhibition Hall at Vostochnaya Street, Moscow, USSR.
		Retrospection 1957–1987, Hermitage Amateur Society, Exhibition Hall at 100 Profsoyuznaya, Moscow, USSR.
		Object 1, Exhibition Room on 28 Malaya Gruzinskaya, Moscow, USSR.
	1988	Ich lebe—Ich sehe. Kunstmuseum, Bern, Switzerland.
		Second Exhibition of the Avantgardists' Club, Proletarsky District Exhibition Hall at Peresvetov Lane, Moscow, USSR.
	1989	Expensive Art (Exhibition of the Avantgardists' Club), Moscow Palace of Youth, Moscow, USSR.
		The Green Show, Exit Art, New York, USA; Dunlop Art Gallery, Regina, Canada; Mendel Art Gallery, Saskatoon, Canada.
	1990	Towards an Object, Sadovniki Gallery (Krasnogvardeisky District Exhibition Hall), Moscow, USSR. Catalogue, Palace of Youth, Moscow, USSR.
		Schizo-China: Hallucination at Power (Exhibition of the Avantgardists' Club), Construction pavilion of VDNKh on Frunzenskaya Embankment, Moscow, USSR.
	1990–1991	Between Spring and Summer: Soviet Conceptual Art in the Era of Late Communism, Tacoma Art Museum, Tacoma, USA; Institute of Contemporary

	Art, Boston, USA; Des Moines Art Center, Des Moines, USA.
1991	MANI Museum—40 Moskauer Künstler, Karmeliterkloster, Frankfurt am Main, Germany.
	BiNationale (Israelische—Sowjetische Kunst um 1990), Kunsthalle Düsseldorf, Dusseldorf, Germany; The Israel Museum, Jerusalem, Israel; Central House of Artist, Moscow, USSR.
1991–1993	Perspectives of Conceptualism, The University of Hawaii Art Gallery, Honolulu, Hawaii, USA; Clocktower Gallery, PS1, New York, USA; North Carolina Museum of Art, Raleigh, USA.
1992–1993	a Mosca... a Mosca, Villa Campoleto, Herculaneum, Italy; Galleria Comunale d'Arte Moderna, Bologna, Italy.
1993	La 45. Biennale di Venezia, Venice, Italy.
1994	Fluchtpunkt Moscau, Ludwig Forum, Aahen, Germany.
1995	No Man's Land, Kunsthallen Nikolaj, Copenhagen, Denmark.
	Kunst im verborgenen. Nonkonformisten Russland 1957–1995, Wilhelm-Hack-Museum, Ludwigshafen am Rhein, Germany; Documenta-Halle, Kassel, Germany; Staatliches Lindenau-Museum, Altenburg, Germany; Manege Central Exhibition Hall, Moscow, Russian Federation.
	Kräftmesse, Kunstlerwerkstatt Lothinger Straße 13, Munich, Germany.
1997	Collective Actions, Exit Art, New York, USA.
1998	Out of Action, Museum of Contemporary Art, Los Angeles, USA.
1998–2001	Praprintium, Staatsbibliothek, Berlin, Germany; Neues Museum Weserburg, Bremen, Germany; Museum fuer literatur am Oberrhein, Karlsruhe, Germany; Oesterreichischen Nationalbibliothek, Vienna, Austria; Minoritenkloster, Graz, Austria.
1999	Global Conceptualism: Points of Origins, Queens Museum of Arts, New York, USA.
	Kunst im Untergrund, Albertina Museum, Vienna, Austria.
2000	L'autre moitié de l'Europe, Galerie Nationale du Jeu de Paume, Paris, France.
	Art of the XX Century, State Tretyakov Galley, Moscow, Russian Federation.
2001	Art Moscow Workshops, Central House of Artist, Moscow, Russian Federation.
2002	In Capital Letters, Kunsthalle Basel, Basel, Switzerland.
	Moscow Minimalism, Art Frankfurt, Frankfurt am Main, Germany.
	The Music in Me, Chapter 1, Gesellschaft für Aktuelle Kunst e.V. Bremen, Germany.
2003	La 50. Biennale di Venezia, Venice, Italy.
	Moskauer Konzeptualismus, Kupferstichkabinett, Berlin, Germany.
2003–2004	Berlin-Moskau/Moscow-Berlin 1950–2000, Martin-Gropius-Bau, Berlin, Germany; State Historical Museum, Moscow, Russian Federation.
2004	KD Group, EK ArtBureau, Moscow, Russian Federation.
	My Kabakov, Stella Art Foundation, Moscow, Russian Federation.
2005	Accomplices, State Tretyakov Gallery, Moscow, Russian Federation.
	International Biennale of Contemporary Art 2005, Prague, Czech Republic.
	Angels of History, Museum van Hedendaagse Kunst Antwerpen, Antwerp, Belgium.
	AptArt 1982–1984, EK ArtBureau, Moscow, Russian Federation.
	Russia! Solomon R Guggenheim Museum, New York, USA.
	Reflection, National Centre for Contemporary Arts, Moscow, Russian Federation; National Centre for Contemporary Arts, Nizhny Novgorod, Russian Federation.
2006	¡Rusia! Museo Guggenheim de Arte Moderno y Contemporáneo, Bilbao, Spain.
	Renegades. 25 Years of Performance at Exit Art, Exit Art, New York, USA.
	The Sun on the Wall, Pavelhaus, Radkersburg Umgebung, Austria; Laikmetīgās mākslas centrs, Riga, Latvia.

		The Vincent 2006, Stedelijk Museum, Amsterdam, The Netherlands.
		Artists Against The State: Perestroika Revisited, Ronald Feldman Fine Arts, New York, USA.
		Venture II, Galerija Gregor Podnar, Ljubljana, Slovenia.
	2007	I Believe! Winzavod Contemporary Art Center, Moscow, Russian Federation.
		Woe from Wit, State Literary Museum, Moscow, Russian Federation.
		Thinking Realism, State Tretyakov Gallery, Moscow, Russian Federation.
		La 52. Biennale di Venezia, Venice, Italy.
		documenta XII, Kassel, Germany.
		Who's got the Big Picture? Museum van Hedendaagse Kunst Antwerpen, Antwerp, Belgium.
		Romantischer Konzeptualismus, Kunsthalle Nürnberg, Nurnberg, Germany.
		Landschaft (Entfernung), Württembergischer Kunstverein Stuttgart, Stuttgart, Germany.
		History of Russian Video Art. Volume 1, Moscow Museum of Modern Art, Moscow, Russian Federation.
	2008	Die totale Aufklärung – Moskauer Konzeptkunst, Schirn Kunsthalle, Frankfurt am Main, Germany; Fundación Juan March, Madrid, Spain.
		Brussels Biennial 1, Brussels, Belgium.
		That Obscure Object of Art, Kunsthistorisches Museum, Vienna, Austria.
	2009	Collection and Archive of Vadim Zakharov, National Centre for Contemporary Arts, Moscow, Russian Federation.
		History of Russian Video Art, Volume 2. Moscow Museum of Modern Art, Moscow, Russian Federation.
		The Another Mythology, National Centre for Contemporary Arts, Moscow, Russian Federation.
	2010	Hide and Seek, Museum of Contemporary Art Chicago, Chicago, USA.
		Archstoyanie 2010, Summer, Nikola-Lenivets village, Kaluga Region, Russian Federation.
		Collection and Archive of German Titov, National Centre for Contemporary Arts, Moscow, Russian Federation.
Collections		Kupferstichkabinett, Berlin. Germany.
		Moderna Galerija Ljubljana, Ljubljana, Slovenia.
		Moscow Museum of Modern Art, Moscow, Russian Federation.
		Museum van Hedendaagse Kunst Antwerpen, Antwerp, Belgium.
		National Centre for Contemporary Arts, Moscow, Russian Federation.
		State Tretyakov Galley, Moscow, Russian Federation.
		Stella Art Foundation, Moscow, Russian Federation.
Awards and Prizes	2003	Andrei Bely Prize, Moscow, Russian Federation.
	2008	Soratnik Prize, Moscow, Russian Federation.
	2010	Innovation—2009 Award (Art Theory and Criticism nomination), Moscow, Russian Federation.

Collective Actions group

Nikita Alekseev

	1953	Born in Moscow.
	1968–1972	Studied at the Year 1905 Art College, Moscow, USSR. (Industrial Graphics and Advertising).
	1973–1976	Studied at the Moscow Polygraphic Institute, Moscow, USSR. (Department of Artistic and Technical Design of Printed Matter).
	1976–1983	Member of the Collective Actions group.
	1979	Co-organizer of the Moscow Archive of New Art, MANI Museum, Moscow, USSR.
	1982–1984	Co-founder and director of AptArt Gallery, Moscow, USSR.
	1987–1993	Lived in France.
		Currently lives and works in Moscow, Russian Federation.
Selected Solo Exhibitions	1984	For the Soul and Body (with Konstantin Zvezdochetov), AptArt Gallery (N Alekseev's apartment), Moscow, USSR.
	1989	Liebe und Tod des Nikita Alekseev, Galerie Roesinger, Cologne, Germany.
	1992	Cross-shaped Songs, L-Gallery, Moscow, Russian Federation.
		Palais de l'arbre balai, La Base Centre d'Art Contemporain, Levallois-Perret, France.
	1994	Heaviness and Tenderness, L-Gallery, Moscow, Russian Federation.
		Two Moons, XL Gallery, Moscow, Russian Federation.
	2003	Antemortem Drawings. Let Every Thing that Has Breath Praise the Lord, Ulitsa OGI Gallery, Moscow, Russian Federation.
	2004	Final Cut, EK Art Bureau, Moscow, Russian Federation.
		Towels. Recollections of Summer, XL Gallery, Moscow, Russian Federation.
	2005	Twelve from Holzheim (with Ignat Daniltsev), Moscow House of Photography, Moscow, Russian Federation.
	2006	Black Towels for Karachokheli, EK Art Bureau, Moscow, Russian Federation.
	2007	54 Winters, Museum Centre of the Russian State University for Humanities, Moscow, Russian Federation.
		Screens, Shusev State Museum of Architecture, Moscow, Russian Federation.
		Silver-Gold. 33,702 Putins and Other Histories, Paperworks Gallery, Moscow, Russian Federation.
	2008	There Is There Ain't None There Is, GMG Gallery, Moscow, Russian Federation.
	2009	Views of Zarechye, National Centre for Contemporary Arts, Moscow, Russian Federation.
	2010	Much-Little-Little-Much, Stella Art Foundation, Moscow, Russian Federation.
Selected Group Exhibitions	1977	La Nuova Arte Sovietica: Una prospettiva non ufficiale, la Biennale di Venezia, Venice, Italy.
	1981	Russian New Wave, Contemporary Russian Art Center of America, New York, USA.
	1982	First AptArt Exhibition, AptArt Gallery (N Alekseev's apartment), Moscow, USSR.
	1983	Come Yesterday and You'll Be First, City Without Walls Gallery, Newark, USA.
	1984	AptArt in Tribeca, Contemporary Russian Art Center of America, New York, USA.
	1985	AptArt. Moscow Vanguard in the 80s, Washington Project for the Arts, Washington, USA.
		Russian Art Show, Danceteria, New York, USA.
	1986	Art against Commerce, Bitza Park, Moscow, USSR.
	1987	Creative Atmosphere and Art Process. First exhibition of the Avantgardists' Club, Proletarsky District Exhibition Hall at Vostochnaya Street, Moscow, USSR.
		Retrospective of the Work of Moscow Artists 1957-1987, Hermitage Amateur Society, Exhibition Room on 100 Profsoyuznaya St, Moscow, USSR.
	1988	5 Russes à Toulouse, Centre Culturel de L'Aerospatiale, Toulouse, France.
	1989	Expensive Art (Exhibition of the Avantgardists' Club), Moscow Palace of Youth, Moscow, USSR.
	1991	MANI Museum—40 Moskauer Künstler, Frankfurter Karmeliterkloster, Frankfurt am Main, Germany.

1992–1993	a Mosca... a Mosca, Villa Campoleto, Herculaneum, Italy; Galleria Comunale d'Arte Moderna, Bologna, Italy.
1993	Adresse provisoire pour l'art contemporain russe, Musée de la Poste, Paris, France.
1994	2nd Cetinjski Bijenale, Cetinje, Montenegro.
1995	Kunst im verborgenen. Nonkonformisten Russland 1957–1995, Wilhelm-Hack-Museum, Ludwigshafen am Rhein, Germany; Documenta-Halle, Kassel, Germany; Staatliches Lindenau-Museum, Altenburg, Germany; Manege Central Exhibition Hall, Moscow, Russian Federation.
1996	Fluxus: Yesterday, Today, and Tomorrow. History without Borders, Central House of Artist, Moscow, Russian Federation.
1997	Ecology of the Void (Exhibition of the Avantgardists' Club), Insitute of Contemporary Art, Moscow, Russian Federation.
1999	Artist's Book of the 1970s–1990s, Pushkin State Museum of Fine Arts, Moscow, Russian Federation.
2003	Moskauer Konzeptualismus, Kupferstichkabinett, Berlin, Germany.
2005	AptArt. 1982–1984, EK ArtBureau, Moscow, Russian Federation. Apartment Exhibitions. 1956–1979, Museum Centre of the Russian State University for Humanities, Moscow, Russian Federation. Accomplice, State Tretyakov Gallery, Moscow, Russian Federation. International Biennale of Contemporary Art 2005, Prague, Czech Republic.
2007	Woe from Wit, State Literary Museum, Moscow, Russian Federation. 1st Thessaloniki Biennale of Contemporary Art, Thessaloniki, Greece. Sots Art, State Tretyakov Gallery, Moscow, Russian Federation; La Maison Rouge, Paris, France.

Elena Elagina

	1949	Born in Moscow.
	1964–1976	Worked with Ernst Neizvestny.
	1979–present	Member of the Collective Actions group.
	1987–present	Member of the Avantgardists' Club.
	2000	Co-Founder and Chairwoman of the Board of the 'Artistic Projects' Foundation, Moscow, Russian Federation.
		Currently lives and works in Moscow, Russian Federation.
Selected Solo Exhibitions	1996	Laboratory of Great Deeds, Obscuri Viri Gallery, Moscow, Russian Federation.
	2009	In Situ. Igor Makarevich and Elena Elagina, Kunsthistorisches Museum, Vienna, Austria.
Selected Group Exhibitions	1987	Creative Atmosphere and Art Process, First exhibition of the Avantgardists' Club, Proletarsky District Exhibition Hall at Vostochnaya Street, Moscow, USSR.
		Retrospective of the Work of Moscow Artists 1957–1987, Hermitage Amateur Society, Exhibition Room on 100 Profsoyuznaya Street, Moscow, USSR.
	1988	Second Exhibition of the Avantgardists' Club, Exhibition Room of the Proletarsky District in Peresvetov Lane, Moscow, USSR.
	1989	Perspectives of Conceptualism (3rd exhibition of the Avantgardists' Club), Exhibition Room of the Proletarsky District in Peresvetov Lane, Moscow, USSR.
	1990	Towards the Object, Sadovniki Gallery, Exhibition Room of the Krasnogvardeisky District, Moscow, USSR.
		Female Worker, Exhibition Room on 26 Oktyabrskaya Street, Moscow, USSR.
		In de USSR en Erbuiten, Stedelijk Museum, Amsterdam, The Netherlands.
	1990–1991	Between Spring and Summer: Soviet Conceptual Art in the Era of Late Communism, Tacoma Art Museum, Tacoma, USA; Institute of Contemporary Art, Boston, USA; Des Moines Art Center, Des Moines, USA.
	1991	MANI Museum—40 Moskauer Künstler, Frankfurter Karmeliterkloster, Frankfurt am Main, Germany.
		Visitation (exhibition of the Avantgardists' Club), Exhibition Room of the Proletarsky District in Peresvetov Lane, Moscow, USSR.
		Private Activities, Na Solyanke Exhibition Room, Moscow, USSR.
		Novecento. An Experiment in Museifying New Art, Central House of Artist, Moscow, USSR.
		Artistos Russos Contemporaneos, Auditorio de Galicia, Santiago de Compostela, Spain.
	1991–1993	Perspectives of Conceptualism, The University of Hawaii Art Gallery, Honolulu, Hawaii, USA; Clocktower Gallery, PS1, New York, USA; North Carolina Museum of Art, Raleigh, USA.
	1992–1993	Humanitarian Aid. Parcels for Germany, Central House of the Artist, Moscow, Russian Federation; Tränenpalast, Berlin, Germany.
	1993	Monuments: Transformation for the Future, World Financial Center, New York, USA; Central House of Artist, Moscow, Russian Federation; Kunstihoone, Tallinn, Estonia.
	1993–1996	After Perestroika: Kitchenmaids or Stateswomen, Centre International d'Art Contemporain de Montreal, Montreal, Canada; Picker Art Gallery, Colgate University, Hamilton, USA; DePress Art Center and Gallery, Hope College, Holland, USA; Western Gallery, Western Washington University, Bellingham, USA; Iris and B Gerald Cantor Art Gallery, College of the Holy Cross, Worchester, USA; Art Museum, Cranbrook Academy of Art, Bloomfield Hills, USA; Art Gallery of Mount Saint Vincent's University, Halifax, Canada; Atlanta College of Art Gallery, Atlanta, USA.

1995	Female Worker 2, L-Gallery, Moscow, Russian Federation. Esotericum, XL-Gallery, Moscow, Russian Federation. Kunst im verborgenen. Nonkonformisten Russland 1957–1995, Wilhelm-Hack-Museum, Ludwigshafen am Rhein, Germany; Documenta-Halle, Kassel, Germany; Staatliches Lindenau-Museum, Altenburg, Germany; Manege Central Exhibition Hall, Moscow, Russian Federation. Zeichnungen der Moskauer Szene, Galerie Hohenthal & Littler, Munich, Germany. On Beauty, Regina Gallery, Moscow, Russian Federation.
1996	ClAva 96, Exhibition Room of the Proletarsky District in Peresvetov Lane, Moscow, Russian Federation. The Moscow Studio 1991–1996: A Five Years Retrospective of Printmaking, The Corcoran Gallery of Art, Washington, USA; Mimi Ferzt Gallery, New York, USA.
1997	Collective Actions, Exit Art, New York, USA.
1999	Gender Boundaries, Gallery of the Svobodnaya Kultura Association, St Petersburg, Russian Federation. Recollections. Memory Slips, Museum Centre of the Russian State University for Humanities, Moscow, Russian Federation.
2002	Art in the Feminine, State Tretyakov Gallery, Moscow, Russian Federation.
2003	Beware, Religion! Sakharov Museum and Public Centre, Moscow, Russian Federation.
2004	Esotericum. Tarot Cards, Moscow Museum of Modern Art, Moscow, Russian Federation. Eurografik, Moscow Museum of Modern Art, Moscow, Russian Federation.
2005	Gender Worries, Moscow Museum of Modern Art, Moscow, Russian Federation.
2005–2006	Essence of Life/Art, Ludwig Museum, Budapest, Hungary; State Tretyakov Gallery, Moscow, Russian Federation; State Russian Museum, St Petersburg, Russian Federation.
2006	Artists against the State: Perestroika Revisited, Ronald Feldman Gallery, New York, USA.
2008	Total Enlightenment. Conceptual Art in Moscow 1960–1990, Schirn Kunsthalle, Frankfurt am Main, Germany; Fundación Juan March, Madrid, Spain.

Sabine Hänsgen

	1955	Born in Dusseldorf, Germany.
		Studied Slavic literature, history and art history. Graduated from the Ruhr-Universität, Bochum, Germany; grant of the DAAD for studying at the VGIK (State Institute of Cinema), Moscow, USSR.
	1985–present	Participating in the performances of the Collective Actions group, founding the video-archives of the MANI Museum, collecting an audiovisual archive of Moscow conceptualism.
		Lives in Bochum and Berlin, Germany.
Solo Exhibition	1996	Video Collection of the MANI Museum, Galery Obscuri Viri, Moscow, Russian Federation.
Selected Group Exhibitions	1987	Creative Atmosphere and Art Process. First exhibition of the Avantgardists' Club, Proletarsky District Exhibition Hall at Vostochnaya Street, Moscow, USSR.
	1988	Second Exhibition of the Avantgardists' Club, Exhibition Room of the Proletarsky District in Peresvetov Lane, Moscow, USSR.
		Ich lebe—ich sehe, Kunstmuseum, Bern, Switzerland.
	1989	Expensive Art (Exhibition of the Avantgardists' Club), Moscow Palace of Youth, Moscow, USSR.
	1990	Catalogue, Moscow Palace of Youth, Moscow, USSR.
		Schizo-China (Exhibition of the Avantgardists' Club), Exhibition Room on Frunzenskaya, Moscow, USSR.
	1991	Visitation (exhibition of the Avantgardists' Club), Exhibition Room of the Proletarsky District in Peresvetov Lane, Moscow, USSR.
		MANI Museum—40 Moskauer Künstler, Frankfurter Karmeliterkloster, Frankfurt am Main, Germany.
	1995	Kunst im Verborgenen. Nonkonformisten Russland 1957–1995. Wilhelm-Hack-Museum, Ludwigshafen am Rhein, Germany, Documenta Halle, Kassel, Germany; Staatliches Lindenau-Museum, Altenburg, Germany; Manege Central Exhibition Hall, Moscow, Russian Federation.
	1999	Literatur und Kunst zwischen Ost und West, Klingspor-Museum, Offenbach am Main, Germany.
	2003	Literature and Art Between East and West, Kaliningrad Art Gallery, Kaliningrad, Russian Federation.
	2005	Kollektive Kreativität, Kunsthalle Fridericianum, Kassel, Germany.
	2006	Russische Souvenirs, Zentrum für interdisziplinäre Forschung, Bielefeld
	2007	History of Russian Video-Art (Volume 1), Moscow Museum of Modern Art, Moscow, Russian Federation.
		Landschaft (Entfernung), Württembergischer Kunstverein, Stuttgart, Germany.
		On Geekdom, Benaki Museum, Athens, Greece.
	2009	Subversive Praktiken. Kunst unter Bedingungen politischer Repression 60er–80er/Südamerika/Europa, Württembergischer Kunstverein, Stuttgart, Germany.
		Vadim Zakharov's Collection and the Artchives, National Centre for Contemporary Arts, Moscow, Russian Federation.
	2010	The Track: Virtuosen der Täuschung. Ein Einblick in das Universum der Gruppe Kollektive Aktionen, Steirischer Herbst, Graz, Austria.

Georgy Kizevalter

	1955	Born in Moscow.
	1977	Graduated from the Moscow State Pedagogical Institute, Moscow, USSR.
	1976–1989	Member of the Collective Actions group.
	1982–1984	Participated in the AptArt Gallery.
	1988–1996	Member of the Avangardists' Club.
	1998–2006	Lived in Canada.
		Lives and works in Moscow, Russian Federation.
Selected Solo Exhibitions	1983	Vassya's Museum, Galery AptArt, Moscow, USSR.
	1990	And Where is the National School? Galeria Fernando Duran, Madrid, Spain.
	1991	Kabakov. Kizevalter. Makarevich, Galeria PARAL.LEL 39, Valencia, Spain.
		For Official Use Only, Sadovniki Gallery, Exhibition Room of the Krasnogvardeisky District, Moscow, USSR.
	1993	Peripheral Vision, Velta Gallery, Moscow, Russian Federation.
	1998	For Official Use Only (with Francisci Infante-Arana), Bryansk Art Museum, Bryansk, Russian Federation.
	1998	Garages. Farewell (Leaving on Business to Canada), Institute of Contemporary Art, Moscow, Russian Federation.
	2011	Project of the New Hagiography, Moscow Museum of Modern Art, Moscow, Russian Federation.
Selected Group Exhibitions	1977	La Nuova Arte Sovietica: Una prospettiva non ufficiale, la Biennale di Venezia, Venice, Italy.
	1981	Russian New Wave, Contemporary Russian Art Center of America, New York, USA.
	1984	AptArt in Tribeca, Contemporary Russian Art Center of America, New York, USA.
	1985	AptArt. Moscow Vanguard in the 80s, Washington Project for the Arts, Washington, USA.
	1988	Ich lebe—Ich sehe, Kunstmuseum, Bern, Switzerland.
	1989	The Green Show, Exit Art, New York, USA; Dunlop Art Gallery, Regina, Canada; Mendel Art Gallery, Saskatoon, Canada.
	1990	Towards the Object, Sadovniki Gallery, Exhibition Room of the Krasnogvardeisky District, Moscow, USSR.
	1991–1993	Perspectives of Conceptualism, The University of Hawaii Art Gallery, Honolulu, USA; Clocktower Gallery, PS1, New York, USA; North Carolina Museum of Art, Riley, USA.
	1991	MANI Museum—40 Moskauer Künstler, Frankfurter Karmeliterkloster, Frankfurt am Main, Germany.
		Artistos Russos Contemporaneos, Auditorio de Galicia, Santiago de Compostela, Spain.
	1993	National Traditions and Post-Modernism, State Tretyakov Gallery, Moscow, Russian Federation.
		Monuments: Transformation for the Future, World Financial Center, New York, USA; Central House of the Artist, Moscow, Russian Federation; Kunstihoone, Tallinn, Estonia.
	1995	Kunst im Verborgenen. Nonkonformisten Russland 1957–1995, Wilhelm-Hack-Museum, Ludwigshafen am Rhein, Germany; Documenta-Halle, Kassel, Germany; Staatliches Lindenau-Museum, Altenburg, Germany; Manege Central Exhibition Hall, Moscow, Russian Federation.
		Double Game (with Anna Alchuk), Obscuri Viri Gallery, Moscow, Russian Federation; Gallery 21, St Petersburg, Russian Federation.
	1995–1996	Flug, Entfernung, Verschwinden. Konzeptuelle Moskauer Kunst, Galerie Hlavniho Mesta Prahy, Prague, Czech Republic; Haus am Waldsee, Berlin, Germany; Stadtgalerie im Sophienhof, Kiel, Germany.

1996	Fluxus: Yesterday, Today, and Tomorrow. History without Borders, Central House of Artist, Moscow, Russian Federation.
2005	Accomplices, State Tretyakov Gallery, Moscow, Russian Federation.
2006	Artists against the State: Perestroika Revisited, Ronald Feldman Gallery, New York, USA.
2007	Sots Art, State Tretyakov Gallery, Moscow, Russian Federation; La Maison Rouge, Paris, France.
2008	Total Enlightenment. Conceptual Art in Moscow 1960–1990, Schirn Kunsthalle, Frankfurt am Main, Germany; Fundación Juan March, Madrid, Spain.
2009	No Toys!? State Tretyakov Gallery, Moscow, Russian Federation.

Igor Makarevich

	1943	Born in the village of Trialeti, Georgia.
	1968	Graduated from the State Institute of Cinematography, Moscow, USSR.
	1970–present	Worked as a book illustrator and theatre designer.
	1979–present	Member of Collective Actions group.
	1987–present	Member of the Avantgardists' Club.
		Currently lives and works in Moscow, Russian Federation.
Selected Solo Exhibitions	1971	One-day Personal Exhibition, Central House of Art Workers, Moscow, USSR.
	1979	Abramov. Chuikov. Makarevitch, Centre Georges Pompidou, Paris, France.
	1990	Freedom—Liberty, Phyllis Kind Gallery, New York, USA.
	1991	Kabakov. Kizevalter. Makarevich, Galeria PARAL.LEL 39, Valencia, Spain.
	1993	Between Abandonment and Hope, Velta Gallery, Moscow, Russian Federation.
	1994	Die Mowe, Galerie Art III Inge Herbert, Berlin, Germany.
	1996	Lignomania, XL-Gallery, Moscow, Russian Federation.
	1997	Partial Change, Obscuri Viri Gallery, Moscow, Russian Federation.
		Homo Lignum, XL-Gallery, Moscow, Russian Federation.
	1998	In Search of Paradise, XL-Gallery, Moscow, Russian Federation.
		Selections from the Diary of Nikolai Ivanovich Borisov, Hand Print Workshop International, Aleksandria, USA.
	1999	Selections from the Diary of Nikolai Ivanovich Borisov or the Secret Life of Trees, XL-Gallery, Moscow, Russian Federation.
	2000	Drawings of Old Soviet Masters, XL-Gallery, Moscow, Russian Federation.
	2001	Zooantropomozy, Central House of Artist, Moscow, Russian Federation.
	2002	Masters of Contemporary Russian Mythology (together with L Tishkov), K Gallery, Washington, USA.
	2009	In Situ. Igor Makarevich and Elena Elagina, Kunsthistorisches Museum, Vienna, Austria.
Selected Group Exhibitions		
	1970	Soviet Russia, Manege Central Exhibition Hall, Moscow, USSR.
	1976	Glory to Labor, Manege Central Exhibition Hall, Moscow, USSR.
	1979	20 Jahre unabhängige Kunst aus der Sowjetunion, Museum Bochum, Bochum, Germany.
	1980	Nonconformists. Contemporary Commentary from the Soviet Union, Art Gallery, University of Maryland, Maryland, USA.
		New Tendencies in Russian Unofficial Art: 1970–1980, Museum of Soviet Unofficial Art, Jersey City, USA.
	1981	Nouvelles Tendences de l'Art Russe Non-Officiel 1970–1980, Centre Culturel de la Villedieu, Elancourt, France.
		25 Years of Soviet Unofficial Art 1956–1981, Museum of Soviet Unofficial Art, Jersey City, USA.
		Russian New Wave, Contemporary Russian Art Center, New York, USA.
	1982	Transplantation of Russian Spirituality, Visuals Studies Workshop, New York, USA.
		Aspekte sowjetscher Kunst der Gegenwart, Neue Galerie-Sammlung Ludwig, Aachen, Germany.
		First AptArt Exhibition, AptArt Gallery (N Alekseyev's apartment), Moscow, USSR.
	1982–1984	Russian Samizdat Art, Franklin Furnace Gallery, New York, USA; Visual Studies Workshop, Rochester, USA; Chappaqua Gallery, Westchester, USA; Washington Project for the Arts, Washington, USA; Ronald Feldman Gallery, New York, USA; Anderson Gallery, Commonwealth University, Richmond, USA; Hewlett Gallery, Carnegie-Mellon University, Pittsburgh, USA; LACE Gallery, Los Angeles, USA.
	1984	Les Russes au present, Le Centre Culturel de la Villedieu, Elancourt, France.

1987	Creative Atmosphere and Artistic Process (first exhibition of the Avantgardists' Club), Exhibition Room of the Proletarsky District on Vostochnaya Street, Moscow, USSR.
	Retrospective of the Work of Moscow Artists. 1957–1987, Hermitage Amateur Society, Exhibition Room on 100 Profsoyuznaya St, Moscow, USSR.
1988	Exhibition in a Russian Bath (exhibition of the Avantgardists' Club), Men's Section of the Sandunovsky Baths, Moscow, USSR.
	Second Exhibition of the Avantgardists' Club, Exhibition Room of the Proletarsky District in Peresvetov Lane, Moscow, USSR.
	Sowjetkunst heute, Museum Ludwig, Cologne, Germany.
	Post-Socialist Realism: The New Soviet Reality, St Mary's College of Maryland, Historic St Mary's City, Maryland, USA.
1988–1989	Smile, please! Galerie Comptoir de la Photographie, Paris, France; Porfolio Gallery, London, UK; Kinotsentr, Moscow, USSR.
1989	Expensive Art (exhibition of the Avantgardists' Club), Moscow Palace of Youth, Moscow, USSR.
	The Green Show, Exit Art, New York, USA; Dunlop Art Gallery, Regina, Canada; Mendel Art Gallery, Saskatoon, Canada.
1990	Towards the Object, Sadovniki Gallery, Exhibition Room of the Krasnogvardeisky District, Moscow, USSR.
	The Work of Art in the Age of Perestroika, Phyllis Kind Gallery, New York, USA.
	Adaptation and Negation of Socialist Realism, Aldrich Museum of Contemporary Art, Aldrich, Ridgefield, USA.
	In de USSR en Erbuiten, Stedelijk Museum, Amsterdam, The Netherlands.
1990–1991	Other Art. Moscow 1956–1976, State Tretyakov Gallery, Moscow, USSR; State Russian Museum, Leningrad, USSR.
	Between Spring and Summer: Soviet Conceptual Art in the Era of Late Communism, Tacoma Art Museum, Tacoma, USA; Institute of Contemporary Art, Boston, USA; Des Moines Art Center, Des Moines, USA.
1991	MANI Museum—40 Moskauer Künstler, Karmeliterkloster, Frankfurt, Germany.
	Private Activities, On Solyanka Exhibition Room, Moscow
	Artistos Russos Contemporaneos. Auditorio de Galicia, Santiago de Compostela, Spain
1991–1993	Perspectives of Conceptualism, The University of Hawaii Art Gallery, Honolulu, USA; Clocktower Gallery, PS1, New York, USA; North Carolina Museum of Art, Raleigh, USA.
1992	Exhibition in Butyrskaya Penitentiary, Butyrskaya Penitentiary, Moscow, Russian Federation.
1992–1993	a Mosca... a Mosca, Villa Campoleto, Herculaneum, Italy; Galleria Comunale d'Arte Moderna, Bologna, Italy.
	Humanitarian Aid. Parcels for Germany, Central House of the Artist, Moscow, Russian Federation; Tränenpalast, Berlin, Germany.
1993	National Traditions and Post-Modernism, State Tretyakov Gallery, Moscow, Russian Federation.
	Monuments: Transformation for the Future, World Financial Center, New York, USA; Central House of the Artist, Moscow, Russian Federation; Kunstihoone, Tallinn, Estonia.
1994	Fluchtpunkt Moskau, Ludwig Forum, Aachen, Germany.
	The Artist instead of the Artwork or Leap into the Void, Central House of the Artist, Moscow, Russian Federation.
	II Cetinjski Bijenale, Cetinje, Montenegro.
1995	Kunst im verborgenen. Nonkonformisten Russland 1957–1995, Wilhelm-Hack-Museum, Ludwigshafen am Rhein, Germany; Documenta-Halle, Kassel, Germany; Staatliches Lindenau-Museum, Altenburg, Germany; Manege Central Exhibition Hall, Moscow, Russian Federation.

	in Moskau... in Moskau... Badischer Kunstverein, Karlsruhe, Germany.
1995–1996	Flug, Entfernung, Verschwinden. Konzeptuelle Moskauer Kunst, Galerie Hlavniho Mesta Prahy, Prague, Czech Republic; Haus am Waldsee, Berlin, Germany; Stadtgalerie im Sophienhof, Kiel, Germany.
1996	Fluxus: Yesterday, Today, and Tomorrow. History without Boundaries, Central House of the Artist, Moscow, Russian Federation. From GULAG to Glasnost, Jane Voorhees Zimmerli Art Museum Rutgers, The State University of New Jersey, New Brunswick, USA. The Moscow Studio 1991–1996: A Five Years Retrospective of Printmaking, The Corcoran Gallery of Art, Washington, USA; Mimi Ferzt Gallery, New York, USA.
1997	Collective Actions, Exit Art, New York, USA. III Cetinjski Biennale, Cetinje, Montenegro.
1998	Body and the East. From the 1960s to the Present, Moderna Galerija Ljubljana, Ljubljana, Slovenia.
1998–1999	Fauna, New Manege State Exhibition Hall, Moscow, Russian Federation; Zacheta Narodowa Galeria Sztuki, Warsaw, Poland.
2002	40 Years of Non-Conformist Art, Manege Central Exhibition Hall, Moscow, Russian Federation.
2003–2004	Berlin—Moskau/Moskau—Berlin 1950–2000, Martin-Gropius-Bau, Berlin, Germany; State Historical Museum, Moscow, Russian Federation.
2004	Beyond Memory. Soviet Nonconformist and Photo-Related Works of Art, Jane Voorhees Zimmerli Art Museum Rutgers, The State University of New Jersey, New Brunswick, USA.
2004–2005	Warszawa—Moskwa/*Москва—Варшава*. 1900–2000, Zacheta Narodowa Galeria Sztuki, Warsaw, Poland; State Tretyakov Gallery, Moscow, Russian Federation.
2005	Accomplices, State Tretyakov Gallery, Moscow, Russian Federation. Russian Pop Art, State Tretyakov Gallery, Moscow, Russian Federation. Russia! Solomon R Guggenheim Museum, New York, USA.
2008	Total Enlightenment. Conceptual Art in Moscow 1960–1990, Schirn Kunsthalle, Frankfurt am Main, Germany; Fundación Juan March, Madrid, Spain.

Nikolai Panitkov

	1952	Born in Vienna, Austria.
		Graduated from the State Institute of Culture, Moscow, USSR.
	1976–present	Member of the Collective Actions group.
	1979–present	Co-organiser of the Moscow Archive of New Art (MANI) Museum
		Lives and works in Moscow, Russian Federation.
Selected Solo Exhibitions	2010	Non-Artistic Exhibition of Nikolai Panitkov, EK ArtBureau and New Space in Maly Kisselny, Moscow, Russian Federation.
Selected Group Exhibitions	1977	La Nuova Arte Sovietica: Una prospettiva non ufficiale, la Biennale di Venezia, Venice, Italy.
	1981	Nouvelles Tendences de l'Art Russe Non-Officiel. 1970–1980, Centre Culturel de la Villedieu, Elancourt, France.
		25 Years of Soviet Unofficial Art. 1956–1981, Museum of Soviet Unofficial Art, Jersey City, USA.
		Russian New Wave, Contemporary Russian Art Center, New York, USA.
	1982–1984	Russian Samizdat Art, Franklin Furnace Gallery, New York, USA; Visual Studies Workshop, Rochester, USA; Chappaqua Gallery, Westchester, USA; Washington Project for the Arts, Washington, USA; Ronald Feldman Gallery, New York, USA; Anderson Gallery, Commonwealth University, Richmond, USA; Hewlett Gallery, Carnegie-Mellon University, Pittsburgh, USA; LACE Gallery, Los Angeles, USA.
	1987	Creative Atmosphere and Artistic Process (first exhibition of the Avantgardists' Club), Exhibition Room of the Proletarsky District on Vostochnaya St, Moscow, USSR.
		Retrospective of the Work of Moscow Artists. 1957–1987, Hermitage Amateur Society, Exhibition Room on 100 Profsoyuznaya St, Moscow, USSR.
	1988	Exhibition in a Russian Bath (exhibition of the Avantgardists' Club), Men's Section of the Sandunovsky Baths, Moscow, USSR.
		Second Exhibition of the Avantgardists' Club, Exhibition Room of the Proletarsky District in Peresvetov Lane, Moscow, USSR.
	1989	Expensive Art (exhibition of the Avantgardists' Club), Moscow Palace of Youth, Moscow, USSR.
		The Green Show, Exit Art, New York, USA; Dunlop Art Gallery, Regina, Canada; Mendel Art Gallery, Saskatoon, Canada.
	1990	Towards the Object, Sadovniki Gallery, Exhibition Room of the Krasnogvardeisky District, Moscow, USSR.
		Schizo-China (Exhibition of the Avantgardists' Club), Exhibition Room on Frunzenskaya, Moscow, USSR.
		Artisti Russi Contemporanei, Museo d'Arte Contemporanea Luigi Pecci. Prato, Italy.
	1990–1991	Between Spring and Summer: Soviet Conceptual Art in the Era of Late Communism, Tacoma Art Museum, Tacoma, USA; Institute of Contemporary Art, Boston, USA; Des Moines Art Center, Des Moines, USA.
	1991	MANI Museum—40 Moskauer Künstler, Karmeliterkloster, Frankfurt, Germany.
	1991–1992	Sowjetische Kunst um 1990 (Binazionale), Kunsthalle, Dusseldorf, Germany; Israel Museum, Weisbord Pavilion, Jerusalem, Israel; Central House of Artist, Moscow, USSR.
	1991–1993	Perspectives of Conceptualism, The University of Hawaii Art Gallery, Honolulu, USA; Clocktower Gallery, PS1, New York, USA; North Carolina Museum of Art, Riley, USA.
	1994	II Cetinjski Bijena, Cetinje, Montenegro.

1995	Kunst im Verborgenen. Nonkonformisten Russland 1957–1995, Wilhelm-Hack-Museum, Ludwigshafen am Rhein, Germany; Documenta-Halle, Kassel, Germany; Staatliches Lindenau-Museum, Altenburg, Germany; Manege Central Exhibition Hall, Moscow, Russian Federation. in Moskau... in Moskau... Badischer Kunstverein, Karlsruhe, Germany.
1997	Collective Actions, Exit Art, New York, USA.
1998–1999	Fauna, New Manege State Exhibition Hall, Moscow; Zacheta Narodowa Galeria Sztuki, Warsaw, Poland.
1999–2000	Global Conceptualism: Points of Origins, Queens Museum of Art, New York, USA; Walker Art Center, Minneapolis, USA; Miami Art Museum, Miami, USA.
2003–2004	Berlin-Moskau/Moskau-Berlin 1950–2000, Martin-Gropius-Bau, Berlin; State Historical Museum, Moscow, Russian Federation.
2004	CA Objects (Objects in the Actions by the 'Collective Actions' Group), EK ArtBureau, Moscow, Russian Federation.
2004–2005	Warszawa-Moskwa/Moscow-Warsaw. 1900–2000, Zacheta Narodowa Galeria Sztuki, Warsaw, Poland; State Tretyakov Gallery, Moscow, Russian Federation.
2008	Total Enlightenment. Conceptual Art in Moscow 1960–1990, Schirn Kunsthalle, Frankfurt am Main, Germany; Fundación Juan March, Madrid, Spain.
2009	Interpreting Object in the Moscow Conceptual School. From the MANI Museum Collection, PROEKT_FABRIKA, Moscow, Russian Federation.
2009–2010	1st Charity Exhibition in Support of the MANI Museum. Part I, PROEKT_FABRIKA, Moscow, Russian Federation.
2010	Field of Action. Moscow Conceptual School and its Context, 1970s–1980s, Ekaterina Cultural Foundation, Moscow, Russian Federation.

Sergey Romashko

1952	Born in Moscow, USSR. Graduated from the Moscow State University, Moscow, USSR.
1976–present	Works in the field of concrete poetry and concrete art. Researches at the Academy of Sciences, Moscow, USSR/Russian Federation. Author of various publications on language theory and poetics. PhD on the language philosophy of the German Romantics.

Colophon

Designed by Alex Prior at Black Dog Publishing Limited.

Black Dog Publishing Limited
10A Acton Street
London WC1X 9NG
info@blackdogonline.com

British Library Cataloguing-in-Publication Data. A CIP record for this book is available from the British Library.

ISBN: 978 1 907317 34 7

Black Dog Publishing Limited, London, UK, is an environmentally responsible company.

Pavilion of Russia at the 54th International Art Exhibition—la Biennale di Venezia

Commissionaire: Stella Kesaeva
Editor and curator: Boris Groys
Assistant commissionaire: Nikolai Molok

Organisation: Ministry of Culture of the Russian Federation, Stella Art Foundation
Architecture: KUEHN MALVEZZI, Berlin
Production: Altofragile, Milano

With the support of: Mercury Group, JTI

Website: www.ruspavilion.ru

Artists: Andrei Monastyrski and the 'Collective Actions group (Andrei Monastyrski and Nikita Alekseev, Elena Elagina, Sabine Hänsgen, Georgy Kizevalter, Igor Makarevich, Nikolai Panitkov Sergey Romashko)

Trips out of Town Photography: A Abramov, N Alekseev, E Elagina, G Kizevalter, I Makarevich, A Urusov

Acknowledgments: Pavel Khoroshilov, Deputy Minister of Culture of the Russian Federation, Ramazan Koloev, Director of the Cultural Heritage and Fine Arts Department of the Ministry of Culture of the Russian Federation, Vassily Tsereteli, Director of the Moscow Museum of Modern Art, Leonid Ignat, Director General of the Venetian Pavilion Foundation, and also Clemente Di Tiene, Alberto Sandretti, Natalia Nikitin, Elena Kuprina-Lyakhovich, Anna Novikova, Tatiana Manina, Julia Ovchinnikova and Ekaterina Inozemtseva

Ministry of Culture
of the Russian Federation

STELLA ART FOUNDATION

With Support of:

JTI

МЕРКУРИЙ MERCURY

reuse recycle reduce

architecture art design
fashion history photography
theory and things

black dog publishing
london uk

www.blackdogonline.com